Ethan Russo, MD
Melanie Dreher,
Mary Lynn Mathre, RN, MSN
Editors

Women and Cannabis: Medicine, Science, and Sociology

Women and Cannabis: Medicine, Science, and Sociology has been co-published simultaneously as *Journal of Cannabis Therapeutics*, Volume 2, Numbers 3/4 2002.

*Pre-publication
REVIEWS,
COMMENTARIES,
EVALUATIONS . . .*

"This revolutionizes my clinical practice and answers questions my patients struggled with until now. Any medical text quoting Muddy Waters ought to be on all our shelves. As a historian and an herbalist I rely on the superior work provided here. It sparks insight!"

Amanda McQuade Crawford, BA, MNIMH
*Founder
North American College
of Botanical Medicine*

More pre-publication
REVIEWS, COMMENTARIES, EVALUATIONS . . .

"Why does the brain and uterus express receptors for THC, the primary active ingredient in marijuana? Furthermore, why do these same organs, along with many others, express endogenous compounds that mimic the effects of THC? These questions and many others are addressed in the nine articles collected in this book–articles mostly about gender-specific issues, written mostly by women.

We know the effects of THC on short-term memory consolidation. It seems our endogenously-produced compounds, such as anandamide, also expunge memory, especially painful memory. . . . Research presented in this text shows that anandamide is secreted in mother's milk and also stimulates appetite. Without anandamide in mother's milk, rat pups lose their suckling response and they fail to thrive and eventually die. But what are the effects of maternal marijuana use on fertility and the fetus? The jury is still out, although this book offers a myriad of evidence, ranging from molecular studies, animal studies, human case reports, and longitudinal cohort studies.

Marijuana and cannabis compounds have been used for dysmenorrhea, migraine, fibromyalgia, hyperemesis gravidarum, multiple sclerosis, cocaine withdrawal, Tourette syndrome, and many other maladies. The book explores these medical indications from historical records, enthnographic studies, clinical controlled trials, and personal accounts. Lastly, recreational use is addressed in this volume, from a unique viewpoint: 'Cannabis and harm reduction: a nursing perspective.'"

John M. McPartland, DO, MS
Associate Professor
UNITEC
Auckland, New Zealand

More pre-publication
REVIEWS, COMMENTARIES, EVALUATIONS . . .

"This well referenced and researched book on cannabis therapeutics contains eleven separate contributions with women either as subjects, patients or researchers. The editors have drawn papers from three continents and professions as diverse as biochemists and lobbyists. Nuances of North American drug control lie side by side with therapeutic mechanisms pertinent to women. . . .

The book begins with an excellent review of the historical background to the use of cannabis in obstetrics and gynecology. Two scientific papers follow introducing the critical role of endocannabinoids in reproductive function from conception to nursing. A discourse on the qualities of cannabis in restoring and maintaining visceral function is then extended from the reproductive to the gastrointestinal tract. Cannabinoids are licensed for medical use as antiemetics and, pertinent to the present book, visceral symptoms such as nausea and vomiting are often sex related. However, the controversial personal view of the role of cannabis in promoting appetite stimulation in hyperemesis gravidarum is unique. It describes the legal and medical stigmata imposed on women suffering from this condition with their associated fear and guilt yet who are left to cope without effective medical therapies and with fears compounded by evidence of fetal effects, based on studies of toxic rather than therapeutic doses of cannabis. In the same volume, in

contrast, the long-term effects of recreational use by women on their children, which may persist for years, is described eloquently in results from a Canadian cohort study. Further single case and personal reports are given of cannabis use in Tourette's syndrome and multiple sclerosis. The predominance of women presenting with multiple sclerosis is highlighted as a source of sex differences in therapeutics. The book would not be complete without sociological and nursing perspectives of recreational cannabis use, highlighted in papers from Jamaica and the US, both advocating a reassessment of risk-benefits.

This broad work brings views of original observation and studies from cannabis producers, health care professionals, users and scientific experimenters to a similarly critical audience. It will encourage debate on women's health disorders in the context of both manipulating the endocannabinoid system and investigating exogenous cannabinoid use. Those with an interest in sex-related disorders will be stimulated by this publication to consider the endocannabinoid system as a source of pathophysiology and to develop specific therapies."

Anita Holdcroft, MB ChB, MD, FRCA
Reader in Anaesthesia
Imperial College
Chelsea and Westminster Hospital
London

More pre-publication
REVIEWS, COMMENTARIES, EVALUATIONS . . .

" **C**hapters in the book cover the historical use for various conditions, including childbirth and infant feeding, as well as giving a modern rationale as to why this may be justified. The sociological and historical chapters are fascinating, and timely, as it is still unusual for womens' history to be documented. The scientific chapters cover the latest research explained in a coherent manner and have each been contributed by an expert in their field. Personal testimonies from patients add a poignant reminder that the ultimate aim of all drugs is to alleviate suffering, and cannabis has improved the quality of life in sufferers of multiple sclerosis, debilitating morning sickness of pregnancy and Tourette's syndrome. Ethan Russo is well-known and highly regarded in the area of Cannabis research, and he and his team have covered all aspects of this topic. Although it is difficult to produce a book of equal interest to scientists, sociologists and the intelligent lay-person– I think that 'Women and Cannabis' manages to do so admirably"

Elizabeth M. Williamson, PhD, MRPharmS, FLS
Senior Lecturer in Pharmacognosy and Physiotherapy
The School of Pharmacy
University of London
Editor-in-Chief
Physiotherapy Research

Women and Cannabis: Medicine, Science, and Sociology

Women and Cannabis: Medicine, Science, and Sociology has been co-published simultaneously as *Journal of Cannabis Therapeutics*, Volume 2, Numbers 3/4 2002.

The *Journal of Cannabis Therapeutics* Monographic "Separates"

Below is a list of "separates," which in serials librarianship means a special issue simultaneously published as a special journal issue or double-issue *and* as a "separate" hardbound monograph. (This is a format which we also call a "DocuSerial.")

"Separates" are published because specialized libraries or professionals may wish to purchase a specific thematic issue by itself in a format which can be separately cataloged and shelved, as opposed to purchasing the journal on an on-going basis. Faculty members may also more easily consider a "separate" for classroom adoption.

"Separates" are carefully classified separately with the major book jobbers so that the journal tie-in can be noted on new book order slips to avoid duplicate purchasing.

You may wish to visit Haworth's website at . . .

http://www.HaworthPress.com

. . . to search our online catalog for complete tables of contents of these separates and related publications.

You may also call 1-800-HAWORTH (outside US/Canada: 607-722-5857), or Fax 1-800-895-0582 (outside US/Canada: 607-771-0012), or e-mail at:

getinfo@haworthpressinc.com

Women and Cannabis: Medicine, Science, and Sociology, edited by Ethan Russo, MD, Melanie Dreher, PhD, and Mary Lynn Mathre, RN, MSN (Vol. 2, No. 3/4, 2002). *Examines the therapeutic role of medicinal marijuana in women's medicine and its implications for fertility and maternal/child health.*

Cannabis Therapeutics in HIV/AIDS, edited by Ethan Russo, MD (Vol. 1, No. 3/4, 2001). *Explores delivery methods, clinical studies, and the history of cannabis therapy with HIV/AIDS patients.*

Women and Cannabis: Medicine, Science, and Sociology

Ethan Russo, MD
Melanie Dreher, PhD
Mary Lynn Mathre, RN, MSN
Editors

Women and Cannabis: Medicine, Science, and Sociology has been co-published simultaneously as *Journal of Cannabis Therapeutics*, Volume 2, Numbers 3/4 2002.

The Haworth Integrative Healing Press
The Haworth Herbal Press
Imprints of
The Haworth Press, Inc.
New York • London • Oxford

Published by

The Haworth Integrative Healing Press®, 10 Alice Street, Binghamton, NY 13904-1580 USA

The Haworth Integrative Healing Press® is an imprint of The Haworth Press, Inc., 10 Alice Street, Binghamton, NY 13904-1580 USA.

Women and Cannabis: Medicine, Science, and Sociology has been co-published simultaneously as *Journal of Cannabis Therapeutics*, Volume 2, Numbers 3/4 2002.

The development, preparation, and publication of this work has been undertaken with great care. However, the publisher, employees, editors, and agents of The Haworth Press and all imprints of The Haworth Press, Inc., including The Haworth Medical Press® and Pharmaceutical Products Press®, are not responsible for any errors contained herein or for consequences that may ensue from use of materials or information contained in this work. Opinions expressed by the author(s) are not necessarily those of The Haworth Press, Inc. With regard to case studies, identities and circumstances of individuals discussed herein have been changed to protect confidentiality. Any resemblance to actual persons, living or dead, is entirely coincidental.

Cover design by Lora Wiggins

Library of Congress Cataloging-in-Publication Data

Women and cannabis : medicine, science, and sociology / Ethan Russo, Melanie Dreher, Mary Lynn Mathre, editors.
 p. ; cm. – (Journal of cannabis therapeutics; v. 2, no. 3/4 2002)
 Includes bibliographical references and index.
 ISBN 0-7890-2100-5 (hard : alk. paper) – ISBN 0-7890-2101-3 (pbk. : alk. paper)
 1. Cannabis–Therapeutic use. 2. Marijuana–Therapeutic use. 3. Cannabinoids–Therapeutic use. 4. Women–Diseases–Alternative treatment.
 [DNLM: 1. Cannabinoids–therapeutic use. 2. Cannabis. 3. Marijuana Smoking. 4. Phytotherapy. 5. Plant Preparations–therapeutic use. 6. Women's Health. QV 766 W872 2002] I. Russo, Ethan. II. Dreher, Melanie Creagan. III. Mathre, Mary Lynn. IV. Series.
 RM666.C266 W664 2002
 615′.7827–dc21
                                                                              2002013697

Indexing, Abstracting & Website/Internet Coverage

This section provides you with a list of major indexing & abstracting services. That is to say, each service began covering this periodical during the year noted in the right column. Most Websites which are listed below have indicated that they will either post, disseminate, compile, archive, cite or alert their own Website users with research-based content from this work. (This list is as current as the copyright date of this publication.)

Abstracting, Website/Indexing Coverage . . . . Year When Coverage Began

- *Analgesia File, Dannemiller Memorial Educational Foundation, Texas <www.pain.com>* 2001
- *Chemical Abstracts Services <www.cas.org>* 2001
- *CNPIEC Reference Guide: Chinese National Directory of Foreign Periodicals* 2001
- *CINAHL (Cumulative Index to Nursing & Allied Health Literature), in print, EBSCO, and SilverPlatter, Data-Star, and PaperChase. (Support materials include Subject Heading List, Database Search Guide, and instructional video). <www.cinahl.com>* 2001
- *Drug Policy Information Clearinghouse* 2001
- *e-psyche, LLC <www.e-psyche.net>* 2001
- *EMBASE/Excerpta Medica Secondary Publishing Division. Included in newsletters, review journals, major reference works, magazines & abstract journals. <www.elsevier.nl>* 2002
- *FACT, Focus on Alternative & Complementary Therapies <www.ex.ac.uk/FACT>* 2001
- *FINDEX <www.publist.com>* 2000
- *Greenfiles* 2001
- *Herb Research Foundation <www.herbs.org>* 2000

(continued)

*Special Bibliographic Notes related to special journal issues (separates)
and indexing/abstracting:*

- indexing/abstracting services in this list will also cover material in any "separate" that is co-published simultaneously with Haworth's special thematic journal issue or DocuSerial. Indexing/abstracting usually covers material at the article/chapter level.
- monographic co-editions are intended for either non-subscribers or libraries which intend to purchase a second copy for their circulating collections.
- monographic co-editions are reported to all jobbers/wholesalers/approval plans. The source journal is listed as the "series" to assist the prevention of duplicate purchasing in the same manner utilized for books-in-series.
- to facilitate user/access services all indexing/abstracting services are encouraged to utilize the co-indexing entry note indicated at the bottom of the first page of each article/chapter/contribution.
- this is intended to assist a library user of any reference tool (whether print, electronic, online, or CD-ROM) to locate the monographic version if the library has purchased this version but not a subscription to the source journal.
- individual articles/chapters in any Haworth publication are also available through the Haworth Document Delivery Service (HDDS).

Women and Cannabis:
Medicine, Science, and Sociology

CONTENTS

ABOUT THE EDITORS

Ethan Russo, MD, is a child and adult neurologist at Montana Neuro-behavioral Specialists. He has had a lifetime interest in medicinal plants. He is also Adjunct Associate Professor in the Department of Pharmaceutical Sciences at the University of Montana and Clinical Associate Professor in the Department of Medicine at the University of Washington. Dr. Russo has published numerous peer-reviewed articles on ethnobotany, herbal medicine, and cannabis, and he has lectured nationally on those subjects. He is the author of the *Handbook of Psychotropic Herbs, Cannabis and Cannabinoids: Pharmacology, Toxicology, and Therapeutic Potential*, and a novel, *The Last Sorcerer: Echoes of the Rainforest* (Haworth). He is also the founding editor of Haworth's *Journal of Cannabis Therapeutics: Studies in Endogenous, Herbal, & Synthetic Cannabinoids*.

Melanie Dreher, PhD, is Kelting Dean and Professor at The University of Iowa College of Nursing. Early in her tenure, Dr. Dreher was the host of the first clinical conference on the medical use of cannabis. She is the author of *Working Men and Ganja* and several articles and reports depicting the use of cannabis by women, children, Rastafarian communities, and working-class men in Jamaica. Dr. Dreher serves on the editorial review boards of the *Journal of Ethnicity in Substance Abuse*, the *Journal of Psychoactive Drugs*, the *Journal of Substance Abuse*, and the *Journal of Cannabis Therapeutics*. Her honors include the May A. Brunson Award for outstanding achievement for the advancement of university women, the Chancellor's Medal from The University of Massachusetts, and a citation from the U.S. Ambassador to Jamaica for her contribution to the welfare of that country. In 1999, she was selected by the Director of the National Institutes of Health to serve as a charter member of the Council of Public Representatives.

Mary Lynn Mathre, RN, MSN, is Cofounder and President of Patients Out of Time, a nonprofit organization devoted to educating health care professionals and the public about the therapeutic uses of cannabis. She works with five of the seven legal medical marijuana patients who are enrolled in the Federal Compasionate Use Investigational New Drug Program. Ms. Mathre is the editor of *Cannabis in Medical Practice* and has written resolutions for several professional organizations in support of patient access to medical marijuana, including those of the Virginia Nurses Society on Addictions, the Virginia Nurses Association, the National Nurses Society on Addictions, and the American Public Health Association. Her work has been featured in *The American Nurse*, and she serves on the editorial boards of the *Journal of Cannabis Therapeutics* and the *Journal of Addictions Nursing*. She is also a member of the International Advisory Board for *The Drug and Alcohol Professional*. Ms. Mathre was Director of NORML's Council on Marijuana and Health from 1986-1992, and was a member of NORML's Board of Directors from 1988-1994. In addition, she was the first President of the Virginia Nurses Society on Addictions and served on the Board of Directors and as Secretary for the National Nurses Society on Addictions (now the International Nurses Society on Addictions).

Introduction:
Women and Cannabis:
Medicine, Science, and Sociology

The *Journal of Cannabis Therapeutics: Studies in Endogenous, Herbal & Synthetic Cannabinoids* is pleased to present its second special issue on the subject of *Women and Cannabis: Medicine, Science, and Sociology*. This topic is particularly appropriate on a couple of levels. Firstly, medical research has been remiss in addressing women's issues on a historical basis. Secondly, many gender-specific conditions, and female-predominant medical conditions are popularly treated with cannabis (Grinspoon and Bakalar 1997). These include dysmenorrhea, migraine (Russo 2001; Russo 1998), fibromyalgia, and a wide variety of autoimmune disorders such as rheumatoid arthritis (Malfait et al. 2000), and multiple sclerosis. The latter receives particular attention in this publication.

This survey begins with a historical review of cannabis in treatment of obstetrical and gynecological conditions. A surprising volume and depth of documentation is evident, which only now is subject to scientific investigation and verification. A "fertile field" for additional research is evident.

An Italian research team, Bari et al., examine the critical role that endocannabinoids play in fertilization mechanisms. The last decade has revealed numerous physiological roles in which this system plays a key part.

Ester Fride follows with another illustration, that of endocannabinoids and neonatal feeding. It would seem that without this necessary endocannabinoid stimulus, we might all starve to death just as life was commencing. The presence of trace concentrations of endocannabinoids in breast milk underline the importance of this system in physiological maintenance of life and homeostasis.

In order to achieve successful birth, pregnancy maintenance is a critical prerequisite. Wei-Ni Lin Curry examines the controversial treatment of

[Haworth co-indexing entry note]: "Introduction: Women and Cannabis: Medicine, Science, and Sociology." Russo, Ethan. Co-published simultaneously in *Journal of Cannabis Therapeutics* (The Haworth Integrative Healing Press, an imprint of The Haworth Press, Inc.) Vol. 2, No. 3/4, 2002, pp. 1-3; and: *Women and Cannabis: Medicine, Science, and Sociology* (ed: Ethan Russo, Melanie Dreher, and Mary Lynn Mathre) The Haworth Integrative Healing Press, an imprint of The Haworth Press, Inc., 2002, pp. 1-3. Single or multiple copies of this article are available for a fee from The Haworth Document Delivery Service [1-800-HAWORTH, 9:00 a.m. - 5:00 p.m. (EST). E-mail address: getinfo@haworthpressinc.com].

1

hyperemesis gravidarum with cannabis in an "underground research study." Provocative questions and possibilities result.

What of the sequelae of maternal cannabis usage? Peter Fried reviews the large body of literature that has examined the progeny of such pregnancies and their possible effects on cognition in children.

How should we educate about clinical cannabis? Mary Lynn Mathre tells us from the perspective of an addiction treatment nurse specialist.

Melanie Dreher presents an anthropological and sociological study from Jamaica that supports the prospect that cannabis, itself labeled as a drug of abuse, might well serve to treat and prevent addiction to cocaine, an idea first proposed in the 19th century (Mattison 1891), but still causing notice in the 21st. In the lyrics to his 1981 song, "Champagne and Reefer," blues artist, Muddy Waters commented on the issue (Waters 1981):

> I'm gonna get high
> Gonna get high just as sure as you know my name.
> Y'know I'm gonna get so high this morning
> It's going to be a crying shame.
> Well you know I'm gonna stick with my reefer
> Ain't gonna be messin' round with no cocaine.

Mila Jansen, an inventor and businesswoman from Holland, and Robbie Terris present the rationale behind the clinical use of cannabis as hashish, and the modern methods she has developed for its production.

Kirsten Müller-Vahl et al. review the effects of cannabis in the movement disorder, Tourette syndrome, and present a detailed case study where it seemed to be beneficial.

Clare Hodges comments on her affliction with multiple sclerosis, a cruel disease whose victims have been at the forefront of clinical cannabis claims. She documents her experience and those of other patients.

Denis Petro follows with a seminal review of the topic and the evidence to date that supports a role for cannabis in MS treatment.

We hope that this collection will advance the topic of women's medicine and at least promote the consideration of cannabis and cannabinoid treatment of recalcitrant clinical conditions.

Ethan Russo, MD

REFERENCES

Grinspoon, L., and J.B. Bakalar. 1997. *Marihuana, the forbidden medicine.* Rev. and exp. ed. New Haven, CT: Yale University Press.

Malfait, A.M., R. Gallily, P.F. Sumariwalla, A.S. Malik, E. Andreakos, R. Mechoulam, and M. Feldmann. 2000. The nonpsychoactive cannabis constituent cannabidiol is an oral anti-arthritic therapeutic in murine collagen-induced arthritis. *Proc Natl Acad Sci USA* 97(17):9561-6.

Mattison, J.B. 1891. Cannabis indica as an anodyne and hypnotic. *St. Louis Medical and Surgical J* 61:265-71.

Russo, E. 1998. Cannabis for migraine treatment: The once and future prescription? An historical and scientific review. *Pain* 76(1-2):3-8.

Russo, E.B. 2001. Hemp for headache: An in-depth historical and scientific review of cannabis in migraine treatment. *J Cannabis Therapeutics* 1(2):21-92.

Waters, Muddy. 1981. *Champagne and Reefer*. From King Bee, ASIN: B0000025LD. Sony/Columbia.

Cannabis Treatments
in Obstetrics and Gynecology:
A Historical Review

Ethan Russo

SUMMARY. Cannabis has an ancient tradition of usage as a medicine in obstetrics and gynecology. This study presents that history in the literature to the present era, compares it to current ethnobotanical, clinical and epidemiological reports, and examines it in light of modern developments in cannabinoid research.

The author believes that cannabis extracts may represent an efficacious and safe alternative for treatment of a wide range of conditions in women including dysmenorrhea, dysuria, hyperemesis gravidarum, and menopausal symptoms. *[Article copies available for a fee from The Haworth Document Delivery Service: 1-800-HAWORTH. E-mail address: <getinfo@ haworthpressinc.com> Website: <http://www.HaworthPress.com> © 2002 by The Haworth Press, Inc. All rights reserved.]*

Ethan Russo, MD, is Clinical Assistant Professor of Medicine, University of Washington, Adjunct Associate Professor of Pharmacy, University of Montana, and Clinical Child and Adult Neurologist, Montana Neurobehavioral Specialists, 900 North Orange Street, Missoula, MT 58902 USA (E-mail: erusso@blackfoot.net).

The author would like to thank the dedicated women of the Interlibrary Loan office at the Mansfield Library of the University of Montana, whose continued assistance has helped to revitalize lost medical knowledge. Dr. John Riddle provided valuable guidance, while Drs. Indalecio Lozano, David Deakle and Daniel Westberg translated key passages.

[Haworth co-indexing entry note]: "Cannabis Treatments in Obstetrics and Gynecology: A Historical Review." Russo, Ethan. Co-published simultaneously in *Journal of Cannabis Therapeutics* (The Haworth Integrative Healing Press, an imprint of The Haworth Press, Inc.) Vol. 2, No. 3/4, 2002, pp. 5-35; and: *Women and Cannabis: Medicine, Science, and Sociology* (ed: Ethan Russo, Melanie Dreher, and Mary Lynn Mathre) The Haworth Integrative Healing Press, an imprint of The Haworth Press, Inc., 2002, pp. 5-35. Single or multiple copies of this article are available for a fee from The Haworth Document Delivery Service [1-800-HAWORTH, 9:00 a.m. - 5:00 p.m. (EST). E-mail address: getinfo@haworthpressinc.com].

KEYWORDS. Cannabis, cannabinoids, medical marijuana, THC, obstetrics, gynecology, dysmenorrhea, miscarriage, childbirth, fertility, history of medicine

INTRODUCTION

For much of history the herbal lore of women has been secret. As pointed out in John Riddle's book, *Eve's Herbs* (Riddle 1997), botanical agents for control of reproduction have been known for millennia, but have often been forgotten over time or lost utterly, as in the case of the Greek contraceptive, *sylphion*. The same is true for other agents instrumental in women's health, frequently due to religious constraints. One botanical agent that exemplifies this lost knowledge is cannabis. As will be discussed, its role as an herbal remedy in obstetric and gynecological conditions is ancient, but will surprise most by its breadth and prevalence. Cannabis appears in this role across many cultures, Old World and New, classical and modern, among young and old, in a sort of herbal vanishing act. This study will attempt to bring some of that history to light, and place it in a modern scientific context.

THE ANCIENT WORLD
AND MEDIEVAL MIDDLE AND FAR EAST

The earliest references to cannabis in female medical conditions probably originate in Ancient Mesopotamia. In the 7th century BCE, the Assyrian King Ashurbanipal assembled a library of manuscripts of vast scale, including Sumerian and Akkadian medical stone tablets dating to 2000 BCE. Specifically according to Thompson, *azallû*, as hemp seeds were mixed with other agents in beer for an unspecified female ailment (Thompson 1924). *Azallû* was also employed for difficult childbirth, and staying the menses when mixed with saffron and mint in beer (Thompson 1949). Usage of cannabis rectally and by fumigation was described for other indications.

Cannabis has remained in the Egyptian pharmacopoeia since pharaonic times (Mannische 1989), administered orally, rectally, vaginally, on the skin, in the eyes, and by fumigation. The Ebers Papyrus has been dated to the reign of Amenhotep I, circa 1534 BCE, while some hints suggest an origin closer to the 1st Dynasty in 3000 BCE (Ghalioungui 1987). One passage (Ebers Papyrus 821) describes use of cannabis as an aid to childbirth (p. 209): "Another: *smsm-t* [shemshemet]; ground in honey; introduced into her vagina (*iwf*). This is a contraction."

The *Zend-Avesta*, the holy book of Zoroastrianism, survives only in fragments dating from around 600 BCE in Persia. Some passages clearly point to psychoactive effects of *Banga,* which is identified as hempseed by the translator (Darmesteter 1895). Its possible role as an abortifacient is noted as follows (Fargard XV, IIb., 14 (43), p. 179):

> And the damsel goes to the old woman and applies to her for one of her drugs, that she may procure her miscarriage; and the old woman brings her some Banga, or Shaêta ["another sort of narcotic"], a drug that kills in womb or one that expels out of the womb, or some other of the drugs that produce miscarriage . . .

Physical evidence to support the presence of medicinal cannabis use in Israel/Palestine was found by Zias et al. (1993) in a burial tomb, where the skeleton of a 14 year-old girl was found along with 4th century bronze coins. She apparently had failed to deliver a term fetus due to cephalopelvic disproportion. Gray carbonized material was noted in the abdominal area (Figure 1). Analysis revealed phytocannabinoid metabolites. The authors stated (p. 363),

FIGURE 1. Carbonized residue from 4th century Judea, containing phytocannabinoid elements, as a presumed obstetrical aid. (Permission Courtesy of the Israel Antiquities Authority.)

"We assume that the ashes found in the tomb were cannabis, burned in a vessel and administered to the young girl as an inhalant to facilitate the birth process."

Budge (1913) noted Syriac use of cannabis to treat anal fissures, as might occur postpartum.

Dwarakanath (1965) described a series of Ayurvedic and Arabic tradition preparations containing cannabis indicated as aphrodisiacs and treatments for pain. It was noted that cannabis was employed in Indian folk medicine onwards from the 4th-3rd centuries BCE.

In the 9th century, Sabur ibn Sahl in Persia cited use of cannabis in the *Al-Aqrabadhin Al-Saghir*, the first *materia medica* in Arabic (Kahl 1994). According to the translation of Indalecio Lozano of the Universidad de Granada, Spain (personal communication, Feb. 4, 2002), an intranasal base preparation of juice from cannabis seeds was mixed with a variety of other herbs to treat migraine, calm uterine pains, prevent miscarriage, and preserve fetuses in their mothers' abdomens.

In the 11th century, the Andalusian physician, Ibn Wafid al-Lajmi indicated that drying qualities of hemp seeds would inhibit maternal milk production. Tabit ibn Qurra claimed that they would reduce female genital lubrication when mixed in a potion with lentils and vinegar (Lozano 1993).

In the 13th century, the famous Persian physician, Avicenna (ibn Sina) recommended seeds and leaves of cannabis to resolve and expel uterine gases (Lozano 1998).

According to Lozano (2001), Ibn al-Baytar prescribed hemp seed oil for treatment of hardening and contraction of the uterus (al-Baytar 1291).

In the *Makhzan-ul-Adwiya,* a 17th century Persian medical text, it was claimed that cannabis leaf juice (Dymock 1884, p. 606) "checks the discharge in diarrhoea and gonorrhoea, and is diuretic."

Farid Alakbarov has recently brought to light the amazing richness of cannabis therapeutics of medieval Azerbaijan (Alakbarov 2001). Four citations are pertinent. Muhammad Riza Shirwani employed hempseed oil in the 17th century to treat uterine tumors. Contemporaneously, another author advised likewise (Mu'min 1669). Tibbnama recommended a poultice of cannabis stems and leaves to treat hemorrhoids, and the leaves mixed with asafetida for "hysteria" (Tibbnama 1712).

In China, the *Pen T'sao Kang Mu,* or *Bencao Gang Mu* was compiled by Li Shih-Chen in 1596 based on ancient traditions. This was later translated as Chinese *Materia Medica* (Stuart 1928). In it, cannabis flowers were recommended for menstrual disorders. Seed kernels were employed for postpartum difficulties. It was also observed (p. 91), "The juice of the root is . . . thought to have a beneficial action in retained placenta and post-partum hemorrhage."

EUROPEAN AND WESTERN MEDICINE

The earliest European references to the use of cannabis in women's medicine may derive from Anglo-Saxon sources. In the 11th century *Old English Herbarium* (Vriend 1984, CXVI, p.148), *haenep*, or hemp is recommended for sore breasts. This was translated as follows (Crawford 2002, p. 74): "Rub [the herb] with fat, lay it to the breast, it will disperse the swelling; if there is a gathering of diseased matter it will purge it."

The Österreichische Nationalbibliothek in Vienna, Austria displays a manuscript of the *Codex Vindobonensis 93*, said to be a 13th century southern Italian copy of a work produced in previous centuries, or even earlier Roman sources (Zotter 1996). Plate 108 depicts a clearly recognizable cannabis plant above the figure of a bare-breasted woman (Figure 2). According to a translation of Drs. David Deakle and Daniel Westberg (personal communication 2002), the Latin inscription describes the use of cannabis mixed into an ointment and rubbed on the breasts to reduce swelling and pain.

A translation in Old Catalan of Ibn Wafid's work above, interpreted it differently, indicating that hemp seeds, when eaten in great quantity, liberate maternal milk and treat pain of amenorrhea (Lozano 1993; personal communication, 2002).

Citing the *Kräuterbuch* of Tabernaemontanus in 1564, it was noted (Kabelik, Krejei, and Santavy 1960, p. 7), "Women stooping due to a disease of the uterus were said to stand up straight again after having inhaled the smoke of burning cannabis."

In England, in the *Theatrum Botanicum (Parkinson, Bonham, and L'Obel 1640)*, John Parkinson noted (p. 598) "Hempe is cold and dry . . . the Emulsion or decoction of the seede, stayeth laskes and fluxes that are continuall, . . ."

In 1696, Georg Eberhard Rumpf (Rumphius), a German physician in the service of the Dutch crown, reported on the use of cannabis root in Indonesia to treat gonorrhea (Rumpf and Beekman 1981, p. 197): "the green leaves of the female plant, cooked in water with Nutmeg, to drink to folks who felt a great oppression in their breasts, along with stabs, as if they had Pleuritis too."

According to Hamilton (1852), Valentini recommended hemp seed emulsion in the previous century to treat *furor uterinus*, a loosely defined malady of the era, frequently associated with nymphomania, melancholia or other ills, more fully discussed by Dixon (1994).

In his book, *Medicina Britannica*, Short (1751) employed cannabis for treatment of obstruction of the menses, even of chronic duration. In one case, he stated (p. 137-138), "I once ordered only the Hemp alone, where they [menses] had been obstructed not only Months, but some Years, with Success; and, when it could not break the Uterine or Vaginal Vessels, the Woman threw up Blood from the Lungs, but had them naturally the next Time."

FIGURE 2. Plate from the *Codex Vindobonensis 93* from the 13th century or earlier, depicting use of cannabis to allay breast swelling and pain. (From Bildarchiv d., with permission of the Österreichishe Nationalbibliothek, Vienna, Austria.)

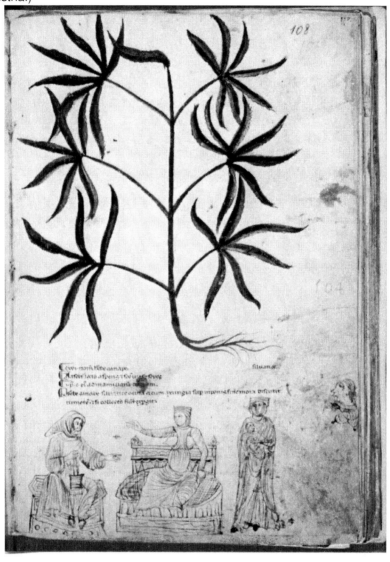

Short (1751) also described a combination of hemp in "New-wort" (steeped crushed grain used in brewing beer) with feverfew (*Tanacetum parthenium*) and pennyroyal (*Mentha pulegium*) employed on three successive nights to (p. 137) "bring down the *Menses minime fallax*." Feverfew has anti-inflammatory effects, while pennyroyal is a known abortifacient (Riddle 1997). Thus, this treatment may well have induced miscarriage.

Finally, Short (1751, p. 138) noted this of a complex herbal mixture with hemp: "Some pretend the following a great Secret against Pissing the Bed . . ."

In 1794, the *Edinburgh New Dispensatory* noted use of a hemp seed oil emulsion in milk, useful for "heat of urine," "incontinence of urine," and "restraining venereal appetites" (Lewis 1794, p. 126).

After the reintroduction of cannabis to Western medicine in the form of solid oral extracts and tinctures by O'Shaughnessy (1842), its spectrum of activity quickly extended to many conditions. The first citation of its use for uterine hemorrhage in modern medicine is probably from Churchill (1849), and its discovery for this indication was apparently serendipitous (p. 512):

> We possess two remedies for these excessive discharges, at the time of the menses going off, which were not in use in Dr. Fothergill's time [18th century]. I mean *ergot of rye*, and *tincture of Indian hemp*. . . .
>
> The property of Indian hemp, of restraining uterine hemorrhage, has only been known to the profession a year or two. It was accidentally discovered by my friend, Dr Maguire of Castleknock, and since then it has been extensively tried by different medical men in Dublin, and by myself, with considerable success. The tincture of the resin is the most efficacious preparation, and it may be given in doses of from five to fifteen or twenty drops three times a day, in water. Its effects, in many cases, are very marked, often instantaneous, but generally complete after three or four doses. In some few cases of ulceration in which I have tried it on account of the hemorrhage, it seemed to be equally beneficial.

Alexander Christison extended the work of Churchill and applied Indian hemp to the problem of childbirth (Christison 1851), offering the following (pp. 117-118):

> Indian hemp appears to possess a remarkable power of increasing the force of uterine contraction during labour . . .
>
> One woman, in her first confinement, had forty minims of the tincture of cannabis one hour before the birth of the child. The os uteri was then of the size of a shilling, the parts very tender, with induration around the os uteri. The pains quickly became very strong, so much so as to burst the membranes, and project the liquor amnii to some distance, and soon the

head was born. The uterus subsequently contracted well.

Another, in her first confinement, had one drachm of the tincture, when the os uteri was rigid, and the size of a half-crown ; from this the labour became very rapid.

Another, in her first confinement, had also one drachm of the tincture, when the os uteri was the size of a half-crown. Labour advanced very rapidly, and the child was born in an hour and a-half. There were severe after-pains.

Subsequently, Christison studied the oxytocic effects of cannabis tincture systematically in seven cases. He made several conclusions (pp. 120-121):

> Shortening of the [pain] interval was in general a more conspicuous phenomenon than prolongation of the pain.–
>
> It is worthy of remark, that in none of these cases were the ordinary physiological effects produced ; there was no excitement or intoxicating action, and there did not seem to be the least tendency to sleep in any of them.
>
> . . . While the effect of ergot does not come on for some considerable time, that of hemp, if it is to appear, is observed within two or three minutes. Secondly,-The action of ergot is of a lasting character, that of hemp is confined to a few pain shortly after its administration. Thirdly,-The action of hemp is more energetic, and perhaps more certainly induced, than that of ergot.
>
> There appears little doubt, then, that the Indian hemp may often prove of essential service in promoting uterine contraction in tedious labours.

Grigor (1852) also examined the role of tincture of *Cannabis indica* in facilitation of childbirth. In 9 cases, little was noticeable, but in 7, including 5 primiparous women (p. 125):

> I have noticed the contractions acquire great increase of strength and frequency immediately on swallowing the drug, and have seen four or five minutes ere the effect ensued ; . . . when effectual it is capable of bringing the labour to a happy conclusion considerably within a half of the time that would other have been required . . .
>
> I have not observed it to possess any anaesthetic effects . . .
>
> I consider the expulsive action of the cannabis to be stronger than that of ergot, but less certain in its effect . . .
>
> . . . nor have unpleasant consequences, so far as I have seen, appeared afterwards.

By 1854, the first uses of therapeutic cannabis were acknowledged in the *Dispensatory of the United States* (Wood and Bache 1854), and these effects of cannabis to hasten childbirth without anesthesia were noted (p. 339).

Willis (1859) reviewed past literature on therapeutic cannabis, and then described his own experience, which was frequently cited subsequently (p. 176):

> I have used the Indian hemp for some time and in many diseases, especially in those connected with the womb, in neuralgic dysmenorrhoea, in menorrhagia, in cessation of menstruation where the red discharge alternates with uterine leucorrhoea of long continuance, in repeated attacks of uterine hemorrhage, in all cases of nervous excitability, and in tedious labor, where there is restlessness of the patient, with ineffectual propulsive action of the uterus.
>
> ... I was led to the use of hemp in puerperal convulsions, having also seen its beneficial effects in convulsions in general, after all the common remedies had been tried without relief.

Willis opined that based on literature and experience (p. 178), "It is a safe conclusion, from the many facts which have been published, that Indian hemp deserves further trial; in all cases making sure that the preparation used is good."

McMeens (1860) headed an Ohio State Commission that examined medical effects of cannabis. In addition to many references cited above, he reported on a Dr. M.D. Mooney of Georgia, who noted that a mixture of milk sugar and *Cannabis indica* extract (20 mg) taken every 3-4 h to treat gonorrhea was (p. 90) "successful in every case in from five to seven days."

That same year, a popular text (Stillé 1860) cited many contemporary authorities, noted irregular effects, and opined (vol. 2, p. 88), "From some experiments, cannabis would appear to excite contractions of the uterus."

Wright (1862) specifically noted the benefit of cannabis in relieving vomiting of pregnancy. In an initial letter, he discussed the case of a woman where all other available remedies had failed (pp. 246-247): "In a patient of mine, who was suffering to an extent that threatened death, with vomiting, I found the vomiting completely arrested by cannabis indica, given in repeated doses of three grains every four hours, until several doses were taken." He later revisited the issue in a subsequent article (Wright 1863), and explained (p. 75), "*Cannabis indica* does not paralyze the nerves, but strengthens them directly. It does not *constipate* by paralysis–it *cures* by beneficent virtues."

Silver (1870) devoted an entire article to the use of cannabis to treat menorrhagia and dysmenorrhea, reporting 5 cases in detail, all relieved nicely with cannabis within a few doses. He also referred to a colleague, who had never failed in over a hundred cases to control pain and discomfort in these disorders within 3 doses. When flow was not checked after early treatment, Silver felt this diagnostic of "organic mischief" (p. 60) due to uterine fibroids, cervical carcinoma or other cause.

Grailey Hewitt authored a comprehensive textbook of obstetrics and gynecology. Cannabis was endorsed as a hemostatic treatment for menorrhagia, analgesic in dysmenorrhea and uterine cancer (Hewitt 1872). He compared it to other available remedies for the latter, including belladonna, hyoscyamus, opium and chloroform, remarking (p. 416), "The Indian hemp is, however, better entitled to consideration, and in many cases undoubtedly exercises a marked influence in allaying or preventing pain."

In another contemporary text (Scudder 1875), the author observed (p. 100), "I have employed the Cannabis specially to relieve irritation of the kidneys, bladder and urethra. It will be found especially beneficial in vesical and urethral irritation, and is an excellent remedy in the treatment of gonorrhoea."

Cannabis was also popular in France for Ob-Gyn indications. Racime (1876) described medical usage of hashish and Indian hemp (p. 443, [translation EBR]): "In women, hemp has a most manifest action on the uterus; this action translates itself into a contraction of the uterine muscular fibers."

A selection from a broad French review follows (Michel 1880, pp. 111-112 [translation EBR]):

> Illnesses of the genito-urinary organs.-Indian hemp has been employed in a large number of uterine affections, but principally in the diverse disturbances of menstruation. The tendency of authors is to administer it while the pain element predominates. . . .
>
> We have ourselves administered it often and in diverse cases of uterine hemorrhage: we have always seen success as well in postpartum hemorrhages, cases in which we employ it today in preference to the ergot of rye . . .
>
> . . . The reader would well permit us to affirm that but one first spoonful of the potion against menorrhagia (see the formula) has almost always succeeded in sufficiently diminishing the flow of blood. Rarely, the patient has had to take 4 spoonfuls. What has certainly struck us in its proper action is that its influence seems to have an effect on the following cycles; the Indian hemp acts, according to our observation and the remarks of Churchill himself, like a regulator of the catamenial function. Administered, in effect, during one sole period, sometimes two, rarely three, the menses return henceforth to just proportions and all medication becomes unnecessary. I know not of a similar effect that has been reported with ergotine or ergot of rye.

Michel also endorsed cannabis treatment for blennorrhagia, or bloody uterine mucous discharge.

In 1883, two consecutive letters to the *British Medical Journal* attested to the benefits of extract of *Cannabis indica* in menorrhagia, treating both pain and bleeding successfully with a few doses. In the first, cannabis was termed "a valuable remedy" (Brown 1883, p. 1002):

> Indian hemp has such specific use in menorrhagia–there is no medicine which has given such good results . . . A few doses {commencing with 5 minims of tincture} are sufficient . . . The failures are so few, that I venture to call it a specific in menorrhagia. The drug deserves a trial.

The second letter also extolled the benefits of cannabis (Batho 1883, p. 1002):

> . . . considerable experience of its employment in menorrhagia, more especially in India, has convinced me that it is, in that country at all events, one of the most reliable means at our disposal. I feel inclined to go further, and state that it is par excellence the remedy for that condition, which, unfortunately, is very frequent in India.
>
> I have ordered it, not once, but repeatedly, in such cases and always with satisfactory results. The form used has been the tincture, and the dose ten to twenty minims, repeated once or twice in the twenty-four hours. It is so certain in its power of controlling menorrhagia, that it is a valuable aid to diagnosis in cases where it is uncertain whether an early abortion may or may not have occurred. Over the hemorrhage attending the latter condition, it appears to exercise but little force. I can recall one case in my practice in India, where my patient had lost profusely at each period for years, until the tincture was ordered; subsequently, by commencing its use, as a matter of routine, at the commencement of each flow, the amount was reduced to the ordinary limits, with corresponding benefit to the general health. Neither I this, nor in any other instance in which I prescribed the drug, were any disagreeable physiological effects observed.

One dissenting voice of the era was that of Oliver (1883) who felt that cannabis was not useful in dysmenorrhea since (p. 905) "its action seems so variable and the preparation itself so unreliable, as to be hardly worthy of a place on our list of remedial agents at all." Quality control problems with cannabis were a frequent concern throughout its reign in Western medicine.

Sydney Ringer, the British pioneer of intravenous fluid therapy, observed the following of *Cannabis indica* extract (Ringer 1886, p. 563):

> It is said to relieve dysuria, and strangury, and to be useful in retention of urine, dependent on paralysis from spinal disease. It is used occasionally

in gonorrhoea. It is very useful in menorrhagia, or dysmenorrhoea. Half a grain to a grain thrice daily, though a grain every two hours, or hourly, is sometime required in those who can tolerate so large a dose, often relieve the pain of dysmenorrhoea. It is said to increase the energy of the internal contractions.

In India, it was reported of *Cannabis indica* (McConnell 1888, p. 95), "its powerful effect in controlling uterine hemorrhage (menorrhagia, &c.) has been repeatedly recorded by competent observers, and its employment for the relief of such affections is well understood and more or less extensively resorted to."

Farlow (1889) penned a treatise on the use of rectal preparations of cannabis describing its use in young women before marriage to alleviate premenstrual symptoms and subsequent dysmenorrhea (p. 508):

> If the excitement can be moderated, if the pelvic organs can be made less irritable, there will be less pain, less hemorrhage, less weakness, and consequently a much longer period of health between the catamenia. This, I feel sure, can often be very successfully done by the rectal use of belladonna and cannabis indica, beginning a few days before the menstrual symptoms or prodromes appear.

Farlow continued by describing another setting in sexually active, but nulliparous women (p. 508):

> After marriage and before childbirth, the uterus and pelvis, especially the left ovary, are very liable to be tender and irritable, even when there is no evident organic disease. The backache, bearing down, pain in the side, groin and legs, the frequent micturition, painful coitus, constipation and headache are often much relieved by the suppositories.

Finally, Farlow mentioned another cannabis indication (p. 580): "At the menopause the well-known symptoms, the various reflexes, the excitement, the irritability, and pain in the neck of the bladder, flashes of heat, and cold, according to my experience, can frequently be much mitigated, by the suppositories."

Farlow employed low doses of these agents, 1/4 grain each (15 mg) or extracts of belladonna and *Cannabis indica*, administered by rectal suppository at night, or bid. Apparently no intoxication was necessary for therapeutic benefit (p. 509): "I do not think there is anything to be gained by pushing the drugs to their physiological action."

Aulde (1890) recommended cannabis extract for dysmenorrhea, sometimes combined with gelsemium (pp. 525-526):

The majority of these cases uncomplicated by displacements, such as seen in young girls and married women, will be promptly benefited, and the menstrual flow appears, when there is no further trouble until the next period.

. . . Cannabis has been highly recommended for the relief of *menorrhagia*, but is not curative in the true sense of the term.

Sir John Russell Reynolds was personal physician to Queen Victoria, and it has been widely acknowledged that she received monthly doses of *Cannabis indica* for menstrual discomfort throughout her adult life. In 1890, after more than thirty years' experience with the agent, Reynolds reported (Reynolds 1890, p. 38), "Indian hemp . . . is of great service in cases of simple spasmodic dysmenorrhoea."

Another textbook of the era noted the following therapeutic indications for *Cannabis indica* (Cowperthwaite 1891, p. 188): "Said to be especially useful in gonorrhoea when the chordee is well marked. Uterine colic."

J.B. Mattison wrote extensively on therapeutic cannabis. He noted the following among several gynecological conditions reviewed (Mattison 1891, p. 268): "In genito-urinary disorders it often acts kindly-the renal pain of Bright's disease ; and it calms the pain of clap equal to sandal or copaiva, and is less unpleasant."

The Indian Hemp Drugs Commission of 1893-1894 exhaustively examined the uses and abuses of cannabis, noting its indication for prolonged labor and dysmenorrhea (Kaplan 1969; Commission 1894).

In this era, patent medicines containing cannabis were very common. One preparation, named "Dysmenine," contained cannabis with a variety of other herbal tinctures, "Indicated for Dysmenorrhea, Menstrual Colic, and Cramps" (Figure 3). Interestingly, one component was capsicum, raising the possibility of synergistic action on cannabinoid and vanilloid receptors.

An 1898 text opined of the fluidextract of cannabis (Lilly 1898, p. 32), "Its anodyne power is marked in chronic metritis and dysmenorrhea."

Shoemaker (1899) reported a case of endometritis with metrorrhagia, that required surgery, but in which (p. 481) "Marked relief of symptom was afforded, however, by the administration of Indian hemp. It relieved pain and diminished hemorrhage, and was highly valued by the patient."

Lewis (1900) observed the following (p. 251):

Dysmenorrhea, not due to anatomical of inflammatory causes, is, in my opinion, one of the principal indications for indian hemp. No other drug acts so promptly and with fewer after effects.

From my own personal observation, I am convinced that cannabis indica does exert a powerful influence on muscular contraction, particularly of the uterus. It may not, as Bartholow says, have the power of initiating uterine contraction, but I have demonstrated time and time again to my own satisfaction that the presence of the merest contractile effort is enough to permit its fullest effects. It is therefore of some service in uterine hemorrhage, but since its action is much slower than that of ergot, it is not as useful in those sudden hemorrhages great enough to require immediate check. I have noticed, however, that ergot is considerably quicker and more prolonged in its action when combined with cannabis indica.

The drug is very useful in profuse menstruation, decreasing the flow nicely without completely arresting it, as ergot very frequently and improperly does.

Felter and Lloyd (1900) described numerous Ob-Gyn indications for cannabis (pp. 426-427):

The pains of *chronic rheumatism, sciatica, spinal meningitis, dysmenorrhea, endometritis, subinvolution*, and the vague pains of *amenorrhoea*, with depression, call for cannabis. Owing to a special action upon the reproductive apparatus, it is accredited with averting *threatened abortion....*

Cannabis is said in many cases to increase the strength of the uterine contractions during parturition, in atonic conditions, without the unpleasant consequences of ergot, and for which purpose it should be used in the form of tincture (see below), 30 drops, or specific cannabis, 10 drops, in sweetened water or mucilage, as often as required. In *menorrhagia*, the tincture in doses of 5 or 10 drops, 3 or 4 times a day, has checked the discharge in 24 or 48 hours.

The greatest reputation of cannabis has been acquired from its prompt results in certain disorders of the genito-urinary tract. In fact, its second great keynote or indication is irritation of the genito-urinary tract, and the indication is even of more value when associated with general nervous depression.

It is therefore useful in *gonorrhoeas, chronic irritation of the bladder, in chronic cystitis*, with painful micturition, and in *painful urinary affections generally*. It makes no difference whether a urethritis be specific or not, or whether it is acute or chronic, the irritation is a sufficient guide to the selection of cannabis. Use it in *gonorrhoea* to relieve the *ardor urinae*, and to prevent urethral spasm and avert chordee, and in *gleet*, to relive the irritation and discharge; employ it also in *spasm of the vesical sphincter*, in *dysuria* and in *strangury*, when spasmodic. Burning and scalding in passing urine, with frequent desire to micturate, are always relieved by cannabis.

FIGURE 3. Photo of "Dysmenine" a late 19th century patent medicine for menstrual cramps, containing cannabis. (Photo by Ethan Russo, with permission of Michael Krawitz, the Cannabis Museum.)

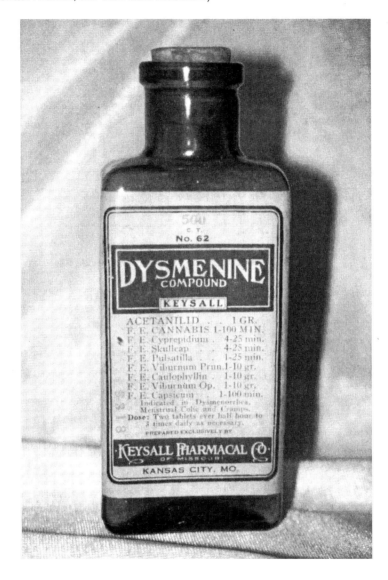

The authors clearly understood that the potency of the preparation directly affected clinical results. While both Indian hemp and American hemp were said to be effective, much higher doses of the latter were said to be required.

In a popular American text of the era, Bartholow (1903) noted (p. 557):

> It is well established that hemp has the power to promote uterine contractions. It can not initiate them, but increased their energy when action has begun. It may be given with ergot. In consequence of this power which it possesses to affect the muscular tissue of organic life, hemp is used successfully in the treatment of *menorrhagia*. It is said to be especially useful in that form of *menorrhagia* which occurs in the climacteric period (Churchill). It has, more recently, been show to possess the power to arrest *hemorrhage* from any point, but it is chiefly in menorrhagia that much good is accomplished. . . .
>
> This agent has also been used with success in the treatment of *gonorrhoea*. It diminishes the local inflammation, allays chordee, and lessens the pain and irritation, with accompanying restlessness.

In Ceylon, Ratnam (1916) defended use of therapeutic cannabis against legislative challenges (p. 37): "I and other medical practitioners have used it extensively in the treatment of tetanus, asthma and uterine disorders, especially dysmenorrhea and menorrhagia."

In a text of the era, cannabis was deemed useful in menopausal headaches (Hare 1922), as well as the following (p. 182):

> In cases of *uterine subinvolution, chronic inflammation*, and *irritation* cannabis is of great value, and it has been found of service in *metrorrhagia* and *nervous and spasmodic dysmenorrhea*. Not only does it relieve pain, but it also seems to act favorably upon the muscular fibers of the uterus.

Another popular text (Sajous and Sajous 1924) cited cannabis as an analgesic for menopause, uterine disturbances, dysmenorrhea, menorrhagia and impending abortion, and postpartum hemorrhage.

In 1928, in *Pharmacotherapeutics, materia medica and drug action*, the authors remarked on the ability of cannabis to counteract "painful cramps" and its "particular influence over visceral pain" (Solis-Cohen and Githens 1928, p. 1702). More specifically, they noted (p. 1705):

> Cannabis acts favorably upon the uterine musculature and may be used as a synergist to ergot in sluggish labor. It is useful also in relieving the pain of chronic *metritis* and *dysmenorrhea* and reduces the flow in *menorrhagia*. It is employed as a symptomatic remedy in *gonorrhea* in

doses of 1/4 grain (0.015 Gm.) of the extract four times a day, relieving the pain, dysuria, and chordee.

An anonymous editor (probably Morris Fishbein) noted the ability of cannabis to achieve a labor with pain burden substantially reduced or eliminated, followed by a tranquil sleep (Anonymous 1930, p. 1165):

> Hence a woman in labor may have a more or less painless labor. If a sufficient amount of the drug is taken, the patient may fall into a tranquil sleep form which she will awaken refreshed. . . . As far as is known, a baby born of a mother intoxicated with cannabis will not be abnormal in any way.

The *British Pharmaceutical Codex* retained an indication for cannabis in treatment of dysmenorrhea in 1934 (Pharmaceutical Society of Great Britain 1934).

Despite the fact that cannabis had been dropped from the *National Formulary* the previous year, Morris Fishbein, the editor of the *Journal of the American Medical Association*, continued to recommend cannabis in migraine associated with menstruation (Fishbein 1942, p. 326):

> In this instance the patient may be given either sodium bromide or fluidextract of cannabis three days before the onset of the menstrual period, continued daily until three days after the menstrual period. . . . The dose of fluidextract of cannabis is five drops three times daily, increased daily by one drop until eleven drops, three times daily, are taken. Then the dosage is reduced by one drop daily until 5 drops are taken three times daily and so on.

Medical investigation of cannabis persisted in Czechoslovakia. One group noted success in use of a cannabis extract in alcohol and glycerine to treat rhagades, or fissures, on the nipples of nursing women to prevent staphylococcal mastitis (Kabelik, Krejei, and Santavy 1960).

MODERN ETHNOBOTANY OF CANNABIS IN OBSTETRICS AND GYNECOLOGY

In the folk medicine of Germany, in the late 19th century (Rätsch 1998, p. 122), a cannabis preparation was "laid on the painful breasts of women who have given birth; hemp oil is also rubbed onto these areas; hempseed milk is used to treat bladder pains and dropsy."

Although the carminative properties of cannabis seeds had been noted since the time of Galen, Lozano (2001) notes that al-Mayusi (1877) claimed similar properties for the leaves, and to treat uterine gases.

In 19th century Persia, Schlimmer (1874) reported his observations on usage of *Cannabis indica* leaves as a treatment for urethritis associated with the practice of prostitution. In modern Iran, Zargari (1990) notes continued use of *Cannabis sativa* seed oil rubbed on the breasts to diminish or even completely prevent lactation.

Cannabis or *nasha* was employed medicinally despite Soviet prohibition in Tashkent in the 1930s (Benet 1975, pp. 46-47): "A mixture of lamb's fat with *nasha* is recommended for brides to use on their wedding night to reduce the pain of defloration." In the same culture (p. 47), "An ointment made by mixing hashish with tobacco is used by some women to shrink the vagina and prevent fluor alvus [leukorrhea]." More fancifully, Benet noted that in German folk medicine (p. 46), "sprigs of hemp were placed over the stomach and ankles to prevent convulsions and difficult childbirth."

Nadkarni (1976) reported the use in India of a poultice of cannabis for hemorrhoids, and (p. 263) "The concentrated resin exudate (resinous matters) extracted from the leaves and flowering tops or agglutinated spikes of C. sativa, and known as *nasha* or *charas* . . . is valuable in preventing and curing . . . dysuria and in relieving pain in dysmenorrhea and menorrhagia . . ."

In a book about medicinal plants of India (Dastur 1962), we see the following (p. 67): "Charas [hashish] . . . is of great value in-dysuria . . . it is also used as an anaesthetic in dysmenorrhea . . . . Charas is usually given in one-sixth to one-fourth grain doses." A seed infusion was also employed to treat gonorrhea.

Aldrich (1977) has extensively documented the Tantric use of cannabis in India from the 7th century onward as an aid to sexual pleasure and enlightenment (p. 229):

> The Kama Sutra and Ananga Ranga eloquently detail Hindu sexual techniques, and the Tantras transform such sexual practices into a means of meditational yoga.
> . . . In Hindu Tantrism, the female energy (shakti) is dynamic and paramount: the male is passive and takes all his vitality from the shakti. . . . In Buddhist Tantra it is just the opposite: the male is active and assumes the dynamic role of compassion, while the female is the passive embodiment of wisdom.

We have little modern research to document a biochemical basis to these claims, which persist, nonetheless. In his inimitable prose, Ott (2002, p. 29) has stated of cannabis, "many women I have known are effusively enthusiastic about its aphrodisiacal amatory tributes."

A treatise on cannabis usage in India includes the following citation (Chopra and Chopra 1957, p. 12): "It [cannabis resin] is considered a sovereign remedy for relieving pain in dysmenorrhea and menorrhagia, and against dysurea."

In Cambodia, mothers reportedly use hemp products extensively after birth (Martin 1975), making an infusion of ten flowering tops to a liter of water to provide a sense of well-being. When insufficient milk is present for nursing, female hemp flowers are combined with other herbs for ingestion. An alcoholic extract of cannabis and various barks is said to alleviate postpartum stiffness. Another hemp extract mixture is employed to cure hemorrhoids and polyps of the sex organs.

In Vietnam (Martin 1975), cannabis seed kernels in a preparation called sac thuoc are said to cure dysmenorrhea, or provide a feeling of wellness after childbirth. Citing Martin's work, Rubin noted the following usage in Vietnam (Rubin 1976, p. 3): "21 kernels boiled in water may be given to the expectant mother to reset the neonate in normal position at birth."

Hemp is of ancient use in China, but it was noted (Shou-zhong 1997, p. 148): "In modern clinical practice, Hemp Seeds are still in wide use. They are able to . . . promote lactation, hasten delivery, and disinhibit urination and defecation."

Perry and Metzger (1980) noted continued folk use of cannabis in China and Southeast Asia, where the seeds were specially prepared for treatment of uterine prolapse and as a birthing aid.

In South Africa, a Sotho herbalist used cannabis to facilitate childbirth (Hewat 1906, p. 98), and was "in the habit of getting his patient stupified by much smoking of dagga."

In modern times, urban Africans have also employed cannabis medicinally for a number of purposes (Du Toit 1980), as one informant related (p. 209):

"... pregnant women should always have some burnt for her so as to have a completely healthy child." But is particularly during childbirth that "pregnant women were given dagga to make them brave," and "so that they wouldn't feel pain."

In Brazil, it was observed (Hutchinson 1975, p. 180), "Such an infusion [of marijuana leaves] is taken to relieve rheumatism, 'female troubles,' colic and other common complaints."

In a 20th century English herbal, Grieve (1971) noted the following uses of hemp (p. 397): "The tincture helps parturition, and is used in senile catarrh, gonorrhoea, menorrhagia, chronic cystitis and all painful urinary affections. An infusion of the seed is useful in after pains and prolapsus uteri." Dosages were provided (p. 397): "Of tincture for menorrhagia, 5 to 10 minims. Three to four times a day (i.e., 24 grains of resinous extract in a fluid ounce of rectified spirit)."

Finally, this passage was offered (p. 397): "The following is stated to be a certain cure for gonorrhoea. Take equal parts of tops of male and female hemp in blossom. Bruise in a mortar, express the juice, and add an equal portion of alcohol. Take 1 to 3 drops every two to three hours."

Merzouki et al. (Merzouki, Ed-derfoufi, and Molero Mesa 2000) have examined the usage of cannabis as part of herbal mixtures employed by Moroccan herbalists to induce therapeutic abortion, concluding that the cannabis component did not produce this effect, but rather other clearly toxic components were responsible. The herbal mixture is applied per vaginam, or alternatively, its smoke is fumigated in close proximity to the genitals (Merzouki 2001).

By the late 1960s, cannabis cures entered the scene in modern America. A popular treatise on marijuana noted medicinal effects (Margolis and Clorfene 1969, p. 26):

> You'll also discover that grass is an analgesic, and will reduce pain considerably. As a matter of fact, many women use it for dysmenorrhea or menorrhagia when they're out of Pamprin or Midol. So if you have an upset stomach, or suffer from pain of neuritis or neuralgia, smoke grass. If pains persist, smoke more grass.

Popular cannabis folklore, thus, did not escape American consciousness. Another example was noted by Thompson (1972, p. 3): "In the Jack's Creek area of Fayette County, Kentucky, poultices with hemp leaves are supposed to relieve hemorrhoidal pains and bleeding when applied in the appropriate area of the human body."

RECENT THEORY AND CLINICAL DATA

Solomon Snyder, the discoverer of opiate receptors, examined cannabis' pros and cons as an analgesic (Snyder 1971, p. 14):

> For there are many conditions, such as migraine headaches or menstrual cramps, where something as mild as aspirin gives insufficient relief and opiates are too powerful, not to mention their potential for addiction. Cannabis might conceivably fulfill a useful role in such conditions.

In the mid-1970s, Noyes et al. wrote several articles on analgesic effects of cannabis. In case reports (Noyes and Baram 1974), one young woman successfully employed cannabis to treat the pain and anxiety after a tubal ligation, and another in dysmenorrhea (p. 533): "The relief she got from smoking was prompt, complete, and consistently superior to that from aspirin."

In 1993, Grinspoon and Bakalar published *Marihuana, the forbidden medicine*, and subsequently revised it (Grinspoon and Bakalar 1997). The book contains numerous "anecdotal" testimonials from patients and doctors documenting clinical efficacy of cannabis where other drugs were ineffective. An entire section with case studies was included on premenstrual syndrome (PMS), menstrual cramps, and labor pains, supporting excellent symptomatic relief at low doses without cognitive impairment.

Numerous surveys cite cannabis usage for obstetric and gynecological complaints, but in one Australian example, 51% of the women indicated indications for PMS or dysmenorrhea (Helliwell 1999).

Rätsch (1998) has observed (p. 162), "Several women who delivered their babies at home have told me that they smoked or ate hemp products to ease the painful contractions and the birth process in general."

Beyond direct effects mediated by the cannabinoid receptors, McPartland has proposed that therapeutic effects of cannabis in dysmenorrhea involve anti-inflammatory mechanisms (McPartland 1999, 2001).

It has been observed that women with PMS exhibit a fault in fatty acid metabolism that impedes the conversion of linoleic acid (LA) to gamma-linolenic acid (GLA) and prostaglandins. A daily dose of 150-200 milligrams of GLA over a twelve-week period significantly improved PMS-related symptoms (Horrobin and Manku 1989). As pointed out by Leson and Pless (2002), this amount of GLA can be supplied by only 5 ml of hemp seed oil daily.

Experimentally, Δ^9-THC inhibited herpes virus replication (HSV-1 and HSV-2) *in vitro*, even at low concentrations (Blevins and Dumic 1980), and was suggested for trials of topical usage.

An Italian group recently demonstrated the inhibition of proliferation of human breast cancer cells by anandamide *in vitro* (De Petrocellis et al. 1998); 2-arachidonylglycerol and the synthetic cannabinoid HU-210 acted similarly, while this activity was blocked by the CB_1 antagonist, SR 141716A. It was felt that these effects were mediated through inhibition of endogenous prolactin activity at its receptor. It is likely that THC acts similarly. Palmitylethanolamide has subsequently been demonstrated to inhibit expression of fatty acid amidohydrolase, thereby enhancing the antiproliferative effects of anandamide on human breast cancer cells (Di Marzo et al. 2001).

Recent animal work has elucidated the role of endocannabinoids in mammalian fertility. Recently Das et al. (1995) detected CB_1 receptor mRNA in mouse uterus, thus suggesting that this organ is capable of anandamide production. Anandamide (arachidonylethanolamide, AEA) and Δ^9-THC inhibited forskolin-stimulated cyclic AMP production in mouse uterus, whereas cannabidiol did not, suggesting that the uterine site is active in endocannabinoid production.

Schmid et al. (1997) demonstrated very high levels of anandamide in the peri-implantation mouse uterus. Data suggest that down-regulation of AEA levels promote uterine receptivity, while up-regulation may inhibit implantation. It was surmised that aberrant AEA synthesis or expression may be etiological in early pregnancy failure or infertility. The corresponding role that THC or cannabis may have in human females at the time of fertilization and implantation is open to conjecture, but deserves further investigation.

Wenger et al. (1997) claimed similarity in effects of injected THC and AEA in pregnant rats, prolonging length of gestation, and increasing stillbirths, perhaps due to inhibition of prostaglandin synthesis. The same lead author posited cannabinoid influences on hypothalamic and pituitary endocrine functions in a subsequent paper (Wenger et al. 1999).

Paria et al. (2001) suggested the need for tight regulation of endocannabinoid signaling during synchronization of embryonic development and uterine receptivity. They demonstrated inhibition of implantation in wild-type mice with sustained high-level exposure to "natural cannabinoid" while not in CB_1 $(-/-)/CB_2$ $(-/-)$ double knockout mutant mice.

Issues of cannabis use in human pregnancy remain a great concern. The topic is reviewed in (Fried 2002; Murphy 2001; Zimmer and Morgan 1997). A variety of studies have demonstrated transient effects of cannabis on endocrine hormone levels, but no consistent effects seem to occur in chronic settings (Russo et al. 2002). Certainly subtle changes at critical times of fertilization or implantation may be significant. A valid assessment was provided (Murphy 1999, p. 379): "the hormone milieu at the time of exposure may dictate a woman's hormonal response to marijuana smoking."

Studies are hampered by the obvious fact that laboratory animals are not human in their responses. Estrous cycles and behaviors in animals are not always analogous to menstrual cycles and other physiological effects in women. Nevertheless, animal data suggest that in female rats, at least, THC acts on the CB_1 receptor to initiate signal transduction with membrane dopamine and intracellular progesterone receptors to initiate sexual responses (Mani, Mitchell, and O'Malley 2001).

One available approach to the issues is provided by examining factors in spontaneous abortions. In a study of 171 women, 25% of pregnancies ended spontaneously within 6 weeks of the last menses. Cannabis exposure seemed to have no observable effect in these cases (Wilcox, Weinberg, and Baird 1990).

The population of Ottawa, Ontario, Canada has been extensively examined over the last two decades with respect to cannabis effects in pregnancy. In a small study of cannabis using mothers vs. abstainers (O'Connell and Fried

1984), ocular hypertelorism and "severe epicanthus" were only noted in children born to users.

In 1987, the Ottawa group compared effects of cannabis, tobacco, alcohol and caffeine during gestation (Fried ct al. 1987). Whereas tobacco negatively affected neonatal birth weight and head circumference, and alcohol was associated with lower birth weight and length, no effects on any growth parameters were ascribable to maternal cannabis usage.

In a subsequent study (Witter and Niebyl 1990), examination of 8350 birth records revealed that 417 mothers (5%) claimed cannabis-only usage in pregnancy, but no association was noted with prematurity or congenital anomalies. The authors suggested that previously ascribed links to cannabis were likely confounded by concomitant alcohol and tobacco abuse.

A group in Boston noted a decrease in birth weight of 79 g in infants born to 331 of 1226 surveyed mothers with positive using drug screen for cannabis (p = 0.04) (Parker and Zuckerman 1999), but no changes in gestation, head circumference or congenital abnormalities were noted.

The largest study of the issue to date evaluated 12,424 pregnancies (Linn et al. 1983). Although low birth weight, shortened gestation and malformations seemed to be associated with maternal cannabis usage, when logistic regression analysis was employed to control for other demographic and exposure factors, this association fell out of statistical significance.

Dreher has extensively examined prenatal cannabis usage in Jamaica (Dreher 1997; Dreher, Nugent, and Hudgins 1994), wherein the population observations were not compounded by concomitant alcohol, tobacco, or polydrug abuse. This study is unique in that regard, no less due to the heavy intake of cannabis ("ganja"), often daily, in this cohort of Rastafarian women. No differences were seen between groups of cannabis-using and non-cannabis-using mothers in the weight, length, gestational age or Apgar scores of their infants (Dreher, Nugent, and Hudgins 1994). Deleterious effects on progeny of cannabis smokers were not apparent; in fact, developmental precocity was observed in some measures in infants born to women who smoked ganja daily. The author noted (Dreher 1997, p. 168):

> The findings from Jamaica, however, suggest that prenatal cannabis exposure is considerably more complex than we might first have thought. Loss of appetite, nausea and fatigue compound the "bad feeling" that women in this study commonly reported. For many women, ganja was seen as an option that provided a solution to these problems, i.e., to increase their appetites, control and prevent the nausea of pregnancy, assist them to sleep, and give them the energy they needed to work. . . . The women with several pregnancies, in particular, reported that the feelings of depression and desperation attending motherhood in their impover-

ished communities were alleviated by both social and private smoking. In this respect, the role of cannabis in providing both physical comfort and a more optimistic outlook may need to be reconceptualized, not as a recreational vehicle of escapism, but as a serious attempt to deal with difficult physical, emotional, and financial circumstances.

DISCUSSION AND CONCLUSIONS

This presentation supports the proposition that cannabis has been employed historically for legion complaints in obstetrics and gynecology. To list briefly, these include treatment of: menstrual irregularity, menorrhagia, dysmenorrhea, threatened abortion, hyperemesis gravidarum, childbirth, postpartum hemorrhage, toxemic seizures, dysuria, urinary frequency, urinary retention, gonorrhea, menopausal symptoms, decreased libido, and as a possible abortifacient.

It is only recently that a physiological basis for these claims has been available with the discovery of the endocannabinoid system. Limited research to date supports these claims in terms of cannabinoid analgesia, antispasmodic and anti-inflammatory activities, but requires additional study to ascertain mechanisms and confounding variables.

Recommendations for cannabis therapeutics have often supported only utilization for terminal, intractable, or chronic disorders (Joy, Watson, and Benson 1999). However, simple logic would indicate that side effects of any medicine would be less evident when the agent is employed sporadically. Generally, that situation prevails for many of the listed Ob-Gyn indications for cannabis. Available historical and epidemiological data supports very low toxicity, even in pregnancy, to mother or child. Professor Philip Robson of Oxford has summarized the situation with cannabis in obstetrics nicely (Lords 1998, p. 123):

> If you could have an agent which both speeded labour up, prevented hemorrhage after labour and reduced pain, this would be very desirable. Cannabis is so disreputable that nobody would begin to think of that and yet that is really an obvious application that we should seriously consider with perhaps some basic research and pursue it.

A few intriguing issues remain. Is cannabis truly an abortifacient? Our four specific references are equivocal, one ancient (Darmesteter 1895), one old (Short 1751), and two modern (Merzouki, Ed-derfoufi, and Molero Mesa 2000; Merzouki 2001), but these and current epidemiological data would seem to indicate that cannabis does not produce this effect *sui generis*. Perhaps its actual role is one to *mitigate side effects* of the active components.

Numerous citations historically support the notion that cannabis is quite potent in its obstetric and gynecological actions, with specific attestation that medical benefits are frequently obtained at doses that are sub-psychoactive. The therapeutic ratio of cannabis with respect to cognitive impairment seems generous.

Another mystery worthy of additional study surrounds the very rapid activity claimed for cannabis extracts in promotion of labor (Grigor 1852; Christison 1851). Certainly modern anecdotal claims of a similar nature are legion when cannabis is smoked. Pharmacodynamically, oral administration of extracts would be unlikely to provide benefits within minutes. Perhaps these tinctures were demonstrating a sublingual or mucosal absorption akin to those in modern trials of cannabis-based medical extracts (Whittle, Guy, and Robson 2001).

In summary, the long history of cannabis in women's medicine supports further therapeutic investigation and application to a large variety of difficult clinical conditions. Cannabis as a logical medical alternative in obstetrics and gynecology may yet prove to be, in the words of Robson (1998), a phoenix whose time it is to rise once more.

REFERENCES

Alakbarov, F.U. 2001. Medicinal properties of cannabis according to medieval manuscripts of Azerbaijan. *J Cannabis Therapeutics* 1(2):3-14.

al-Baytar, ibn. 1291. *Kitab al-Yami' li-mufradat al-adwiya wa-l-agdiya.* Bulaq.

Aldrich, M.R. 1977. Tantric cannabis use in India. *J Psychedelic Drugs* 9(3):227-33.

Anonymous. 1930. Effects of alcohol and cannabis during labor. *J Amer Med Assoc* 94(15):1165.

Aulde, J. 1890. Studies in therapeutics-Cannabis indica. *Therapeutic Gazette* 14:523-6.

Bartholow, R. 1903. *A practical treatise on materia medica and therapeutics.* 11th ed. New York: D. Appleton.

Batho, R. 1883. Cannabis indica. *Brit Med J* (May 26):1002.

Benet, S. 1975. Early Diffusion and Folk Uses of Hemp. In *Cannabis and Culture*, edited by V. Rubin. The Hague, Paris: Mouton.

Blevins, R.D., and M.P. Dumic. 1980. The effect of delta-9-tetrahydrocannabinol on herpes simplex virus replication. *J Gen Virol* 49(2):427-31.

Brown, J. 1883. Cannabis indica; A valuable remedy in menorrhagia. *Brit Med J* 1(May 26):1002.

Budge, E.A.W. 1913. *The Syriac Book of Medicines.* London: Oxford University.

Chopra, I.C., and R.W. Chopra. 1957. The use of cannabis drugs in India. *Bull Narc* 9:4-29.

Christison, A. 1851. On the natural history, action, and uses of Indian hemp. *Monthly J of Medical Science of Edinburgh, Scotland* 13:26-45, 117-21.

Churchill, F. 1849. *Essays on the puerperal fever and other diseases peculiar to women.* London: Sydenham Society.

Commission, Indian Hemp Drugs. 1894. *Report of the Indian Hemp Drugs Commission, 1893-94.* Simla: Govt. Central Print. Office.

Cowperthwaite, A.C. 1891. *A text-book of materia medica and therapeutics.* 6th ed. Chicago: Gross & Delbridge.

Crawford, V. 2002. A homelie herbe: Medicinal cannabis in early England. *J Cannabis Therapeutics* 2(2):71-9.

Darmesteter, J. 1895. *Zend-Avesta, Part I, The Vendidad.* London: Oxford University.

Das, S.K., B.C. Paria, I. Chakraborty, and S.K. Dey. 1995. Cannabinoid ligand-receptor signaling in the mouse uterus. *Proc Natl Acad Sci USA* 92(10):4332-6.

Dastur, J.F. 1962. *Medicinal plants of India and Pakistan.* Bombay: D.B. Taraporevala Sons.

De Petrocellis, L., D. Melck, T. Bisogno, and V. Di Marzo. 2000. Endocannabinoids and fatty acid amides in cancer, inflammation and related disorders. *Chem Phys Lipids* 108 (1-2):191-209.

De Petrocellis, L., D. Melck, A. Palmisano, T. Bisogno, C. Laezza, M. Bifulco, and V. Di Marzo. 1998. The endogenous cannabinoid anandamide inhibits human breast cancer cell proliferation. *Proc Natl Acad Sci USA* 95(14):8375-80.

Di Marzo, V., D. Melck, P. Orlando, T. Bisogno, O. Zagoory, M. Bifulco, Z. Vogel, and L. De Petrocellis. 2001. Palmitoylethanolamide inhibits the expression of fatty acid amide hydrolase and enhances the anti-proliferative effect of anandamide in human breast cancer cells. *Biochem J* 358(Pt 1):249-55.

Dixon, L.S. 1994. Beware the wandering womb–painterly reflections of early gynecological theory. *Cancer Invest* 12(1):66-73.

Dreher, M.C., K. Nugent, and R. Hudgins. 1994. Prenatal marijuana exposure and neonatal outcomes in Jamaica: an ethnographic study. *Pediatrics* 93(2):254-60.

Dreher, M.C. 1997. Cannabis and pregnancy. In *Cannabis in medical practice.* Edited by M.L. Mathre. Jefferson, NC: McFarland.

Du Toit, B.M. 1980. *Cannabis in Africa: A survey of its distribution in Africa, and a study of cannabis use and users in multi-et[h]nic South Africa.* Rotterdam: A.A. Balkema.

Dwarakanath, C. 1965. Use of opium and cannabis in the traditional systems of medicine in India. *Bull Narc* 17:15-9.

Dymock, W. 1884. *The vegetable materia medica of Western India.* Bombay: Education Society's Press.

Farlow, J.W. 1889. On the use of belladonna and Cannabis indica by the rectum in gynecological practice. *Boston Med Surg J* 120:507-9.

Felter, H.W., and J.U. Lloyd. 1900. *King's American Dispensatory.* Cincinnati, OH: Ohio Valley Co.

Fishbein, M. 1942. Migraine Associated with Menstruation. *J Amer Med Assoc* 237:326.

Fried, P.A., B. Watkinson, R.F. Dillon, and C.S. Dulberg. 1987. Neonatal neurological status in a low-risk population after prenatal exposure to cigarettes, marijuana, and alcohol. *J Dev Behav Pediatr* 8(6):318-26.

Fried, P.A. 2002. Pregnancy. In *Cannabis and cannabinoids: Pharmacology, toxicology and therapeutic potential*. Edited by F. Grotenhermen and E.B. Russo. Binghamton, NY: The Haworth Press, Inc.

Ghalioungui, P. 1987. *The Ebers papyrus: A new English translation, commentaries and glossaries*. Cairo: Academy of Scientific Research and Technology.

Grieve, M. 1971. *A modern herbal*. New York: Dover Publications.

Grigor, J. 1852. Indian hemp as an oxytocic. *Monthly J of Medical Sciences* 14:124.

Grinspoon, L. and J.B. Bakalar. 1997. *Marihuana, the forbidden medicine*. Rev. and exp. ed. New Haven: Yale University Press.

Hamilton, E. 1852. *The Flora Homoeopathica; or the medicinal plants used as homoeopathic remedies*. London: H. Bailliere.

Hare, H.A. 1922. *A text-book of practical therapeutics*. 18th ed. Philadelphia, New York: Lea & Febiger.

Helliwell, D. 1999. GPs are key informants in medicinal cannabis survey. *GP Speak, Newsletter of the Northern Rivers Division of General Practice*. (April):4.

Hewat, M.L. 1906. *Bantu folk lore*. Capetown, South Africa: Maskew Miller.

Hewitt, G. 1872. *The pathology, diagnosis and treatment of diseases of women, including the diagnosis of pregnancy*. 2nd American ed. Philadelphia: Lindsay & Blakiston.

Horrobin, D.F., and M.S. Manku. 1989. Premenstrual syndrome and premenstrual breast pain (cyclical mastalgia): Disorders of essential fatty acid (EFA) metabolism. *Prostaglandins Leukot Essent Fatty Acids* 37(4):255-61.

Hutchinson, H.W. 1975. Patterns of marihuana use in Brazil. In *Cannabis and culture*, edited by V. Rubin. The Hague: Mouton.

ibn Sina. 1294. *Al-Qanun fi l-tibb*. Bulaq.

Irawani, H.S. bin S.K. 17th century. *Fawa'id al-Hikmat* (Benefits of Wisdom). The manuscript of the Institute of Manuscripts (Baku). Code: B 39/19955, (medieval Azerbaijani/Persian).

Joy, J.E., S.J. Watson, and J.A. Benson, Jr. 1999. Marijuana and medicine: Assessing the science base. Washington, DC: Institute of Medicine.

Kabelik, J., Z. Krejei, and F. Santavy. 1960. Cannabis as a medicament. *Bull Narc* 12:5-23.

Kahl, O. 1994. *Sabur ibn Sahl: Dispensatorium parvum (al-Aqrabadhin al-Saghir)*. Leiden: E.J. Brill.

Kaplan, J. 1969. *Marijuana. Report of the Indian Hemp Drugs Commission, 1893-1894*. Silver Spring, MD: Thos. Jefferson.

Leson, G., and P. Pless. 2002. Hemp seed and hemp oil. In *Cannabis and cannabinoids: Pharmacology, toxicology and therapeutic potential*. Edited by F. Grotenhermen and E.B. Russo. Binghamton, NY: The Haworth Press, Inc.

Lewis, H.E. 1900. *Cannabis indica*: A study of its physiologic action, toxic effects and therapeutic indications. *Merck's Archives of Materia Medica and its Uses* 2:247-51.

Lewis, W. 1794. *The Edinburgh new dispensatory*. 4th ed. ed. Edinburgh: M. Lavoisier.

Lilly. 1898. *Lilly's Handbook of Pharmacy and Therapeutics*. Indianapolis: Lilly and Company.

Linn, S., S.C. Schoenbaum, R.R. Monson, R. Rosner, P.C. Stubblefield, and K.J. Ryan. 1983. The association of marijuana use with outcome of pregnancy. *Am J Public Health* 73(10):1161-4.

Lords, House of. 1998. *Cannabis: the scientific and medical evidence: Evidence.* London: House of Lords Select Committee on Science and Technology, Stationery Office.

Lozano, I. 1993. Estudios y documentos sobre la historia del cáñamo y del hachís en el islam medieval. Doctoral dissertation, Departamento de Estudios Semíticos, Universidad de Granada, Spain.

Lozano, I. 1998. *Solaz del espíritu en el hachís y el vino y otros textos árabes sobre drogas.* Granada, Spain: Universidad de Granada.

Lozano, I. 2001. The therapeutic use of *Cannabis sativa* L. in Arabic medicine. *J Cannabis Therapeutics* 1(1):63-70.

Mani, S.K., A. Mitchell, and B.W. O'Malley. 2001. Progesterone receptor and dopamine receptors are required in Delta 9-tetrahydrocannabinol modulation of sexual receptivity in female rats. *Proc Natl Acad Sci USA* 98(3):1249-54.

Mannische, L. 1989. *An ancient Egyptian herbal.* Austin: University of Texas.

Margolis, J.S., and R. Clorfene. 1969. *A child's garden of grass (The official handbook for marijuana users).* North Hollywood, CA: Contact Books.

Martin, M.A. 1975. Ethnobotanical aspects of cannabis in Southeast Asia. In *Cannabis and Culture.* Edited by V. Rubin. The Hague, Paris: Mouton Publishers.

Mattison, J.B. 1891. Cannabis indica as an anodyne and hypnotic. *St. Louis Med Surg J* 61:265-71.

McConnell, J.F.P. 1888. Uses of Cannabis indica. *Practitioner* 40:95-8.

McMeens, R.R. 1860. Report of the Ohio State Medical Committee on *Cannabis indica.* White Sulphur Springs, OH: Ohio State Medical Society.

McPartland, J.M. 1999. Marijuana and medicine: The endocrine effects of cannabis. *Altern Ther Women's Health* 1(6):41-4.

McPartland, J.M. 2001. Cannabis and eicosanoids: A review of molecular pharmacology. *J Cannabis Therapeutics* 1(1):71-83.

Merzouki, A. 2001. El cultivo del cáñamo (*Cannabis sativa* L.) en el Rif, Norte de Marruecos, taxonomía, biología y etnobotánica. doctoral dissertation, Departamento de biología vegetal, Universidad de Granada, Spain.

Merzouki, A., F. Ed-derfoufi, and J. Molero Mesa. 2000. Hemp (*Cannabis sativa* L.) and abortion. J Ethnopharmacol 73(3):501-3.

Michel. 1880. Propriétés médicinales de l'Indian hemp ou du Cannabis indica. *Montpellier Medical* 45:103-16.

Mu'min, S.M. 1669. *Tuhfat al-Mu'minin* (Gift of Religious Believers). The manuscript of the Institute of Manuscripts (Baku). Code: M 243/3747 (in Persian).

Murphy, L. 1999. Cannabis effects on endocrine and reproductive function. In *The health effects of cannabis.* Edited by H. Kalant, W.A. Corrigall, W. Hall and R.G. Smart. Toronto, Canada: Centre for Addiction and Mental Health.

Murphy, L. 2001. Hormonal system and reproduction. In *Cannabis and cannabinoids: Pharmacology, toxicology and therapeutic potential.* Edited by F. Grotenhermen and E.B. Russo. Binghamton, NY: The Haworth Press, Inc.

al-Mayusi. 1877. *Kamil al-sina'a al-tibbiya.* Bulaq.

Nadkarni, K.M. 1976. *Indian materia medica.* 3rd ed. 2 vols. Vol. 1. Bombay: Popular Prakashan.

Noyes, R., Jr., and D.A. Baram. 1974. Cannabis analgesia. *Compr Psychiatry* 15(6): 531-5.

O'Connell, C.M., and P.A. Fried. 1984. An investigation of prenatal cannabis exposure and minor physical anomalies in a low risk population. *Neurobehav Toxicol Teratol* 6(5):345-50.

Oliver, J. 1883. On the action of Cannabis indica. *Brit Med J* 1:905-6.

O'Shaughnessy, W.B. 1842. *Bengal dispensatory and companion to the pharmacopoeia*. London: Allen.

Ott, J. 2002. Pharmaka, philtres, and pheromones. Getting high and getting off. *Bull Multidisciplin Assoc Psychedelic Stud* 12(1):26-32.

Paria, B.C., H. Song, X. Wang, P.C. Schmid, R.J. Krebsbach, H.H. Schmid, T.I. Bonner, A. Zimmer, and S.K. Dey. 2001. Dysregulated cannabinoid signaling disrupts uterine receptivity for embryo implantation. *J Biol Chem* 276(23):20523-8.

Parker, S.J., and B.S. Zuckerman. 1999. The effects of maternal marihuana use during pregnancy on fetal growth. In *Marihuana for medicine*. Edited by G.G. Nahas. Totowa, NJ: Humana Press.

Parkinson, J., T. Bonham, and M. de L'Obel. 1640. *Theatrum botanicum: The theater of plants*. London: Tho. Cotes.

Perry, L.M., and J. Metzger. 1980. *Medicinal plants of East and Southeast Asia: Attributed properties and uses*. Cambridge: MIT Press.

Pharmaceutical Society of Great Britain. 1934. *The British pharmaceutical codex*. London: Pharmaceutical Press.

Racime, H. 1876. Le Haschisch ou chanvre indien. *Montpelier Medical* 36:432-49.

Ratnam, E.V. 1916. *Cannabis indica. J Brit Med Assoc, Ceylon Branch* 13:30-4.

Rätsch, C. 1998. *Marijuana medicine: A world tour of the healing and visionary powers of cannabis*. Rochester, VT: Healing Arts Press.

Reynolds, J.R. 1890. Therapeutical uses and toxic effects of *Cannabis indica. Lancet* 1:637-8.

Riddle, J.M. 1997. *Eve's herbs: A history of contraception and abortion in the West*. Cambridge, MA: Harvard University.

Ringer, S. 1886. *A handbook of therapeutics*. 11th ed. New York: W. Wood.

Robson, P. 1998. Cannabis as medicine: time for the phoenix to rise? *Brit Med J* 316(7137):1034-5.

Rubin, V. 1976. Cross-cultural perspectives on therapeutic uses of cannabis. In *The therapeutic potential of marihuana*. Edited by S. Cohen and R.C. Stillman. New York: Plenum Medical.

Rumpf, G.E., and E.M. Beekman. 1981. *The poison tree: Selected writings of Rumphius on the natural history of the Indies, Library of the Indies*. Amherst: University of Massachusetts.

Russo, E.B., M.L. Mathre, A. Byrne, R. Velin, P.J. Bach, J. Sanchez-Ramos, and K.A. Kirlin. 2002. Chronic cannabis use in the Compassionate Investigational New Drug Program: An examination of benefits and adverse effects of legal clinical cannabis. *J Cannabis Therapeutics* 2(1):3-57.

Sajous, C., and M. Sajous. 1924. Cannabis indica (Indian hemp: hashish). In *Sajous's analytic cyclopedia of practical medicine*. Philadelphia: Davis.

Schlimmer, J.L. 1874. *Terminologie medico-pharmaceutique et anthropologique francaise-persane.* Teheran: Lithographie d'Ali Goulikhan.

Schmid, P.C., B.C. Paria, R.J. Krebsbach, H.H. Schmid, and S.K. Dey. 1997. Changes in anandamide levels in mouse uterus are associated with uterine receptivity for embryo implantation. *Proc Natl Acad Sci USA* 94(8):4188-92.

Scudder, J.M. 1875. *Specific medication and specific medicines.* Cincinnati, OH: Wilstach, Baldwin and Co.

Shoemaker, J.V. 1899. The therapeutic value of *Cannabis indica. Texas Medical News* 8(10):477-88.

Short, T. 1751. *Medicina Britannica: Or a treatise on such physical plants, as are generally to be found in the fields or gardens in Great-Britain.* 3rd ed. Philadelphia: B. Franklin and D. Hall.

Shou-zhong, Y. 1997. *The divine farmer's materia medica: A translation of the Shen Nong Ben Cao Jing.* Boulder, CO: Blue Poppy Press.

Silver, A. 1870. On the value of Indian hemp in menorrhagia and dysmenorrhoea. *Medical Times and Gazette* 2:59-61.

Snyder, S.H. 1971. *Uses of marijuana.* New York: Oxford University.

Solis-Cohen, S., and T.S. Githens. 1928. *Pharmacotherapeutics, materia medica and drug action.* New York: D. Appleton.

Stillé, A. 1860. *Therapeutics and materia medica: A systematic treatise on the action and uses of medicinal agents, including their description and history.* Philadelphia: Blanchard and Lea.

Stuart, G.A. 1928. *Chinese Materia Medica.* Shanghai: Presbyterian Mission.

Tibbnama. 1712. (The Book of Medicine). The manuscript of the Institute of Manuscripts (Baku). Code: C 331/1894, (medieval Azerbaijani).

Thompson, L.S. 1972. *Cannabis sativa* and traditions associated with it. *Kentucky Folklore Record* 18:1-4.

Thompson, R.C. 1924. *The Assyrian herbal.* London: Luzac and Co.

Thompson, R.C. 1949. *A dictionary of Assyrian botany.* London: British Academy.

Vriend, H.J. de. 1984. *The Old English Herbarium and, Medicina de quadrupedibus, Early English Text Society.* London: Oxford University.

Wenger, T., G. Fragkakis, P. Giannikou, K. Probonas, and N. Yiannikakis. 1997. Effects of anandamide on gestation in pregnant rats. *Life Sci* 60(26):2361-71.

Wenger, T., B.E. Toth, C. Juaneda, J. Leonardelli, and G. Tramu. 1999. The effects of cannabinoids on the regulation of reproduction. *Life Sci* 65(6-7):695-701.

Whittle, B.A., G.W. Guy, and P. Robson. 2001. Prospects for new cannabis-based prescription medicines. *J Cannabis Therapeutics* 1(3-4):183-205.

Wilcox, A.J., C.R. Weinberg, and D.D. Baird. 1990. Risk factors for early pregnancy loss. *Epidemiology* 1(5):382-5.

Willis, I.P. 1859. *Cannabis indica.* Boston Med Surg J 61:173-8.

Witter, F.R., and J.R. Niebyl. 1990. Marijuana use in pregnancy and pregnancy outcome. *Am J Perinatol* 7(1):36-8.

Wood, G.B., and F. Bache. 1854. *The dispensatory of the United States.* Philadelphia: Lippincott, Brambo & Co.

Wright, T.L. 1862. Correspondence. *Cincinnati Lancet and Observer* 5(4):246-7.

Wright, T.L. 1863. Some therapeutic effects of *Cannabis indica. Cincinnati Lancet and Observer* 6(2):73-5.

Zargari, A. 1990. *Medicinal plants*. 4th ed. Vol. 4. Teheran: Teheran University Publications.

Zias, J., H. Stark, J. Sellgman, R. Levy, E. Werker, A. Breuer, and R. Mechoulam. 1993. Early medical use of cannabis. *Nature* 363(6426):215.

Zimmer, L.E., and J.P. Morgan. 1997. *Marijuana myths, marijuana facts: A review of the scientific evidence*. New York: Lindesmith Center.

Zotter, H. 1996. *Medicina antiqua: Codex Vindobonensis 93 der Österreichischen Nationalbibliothek: Kommentar, Glanzlichter der Buchkunst; Bd. 6*. Graz: Akademische Druck-u. Verlagsanstalt.

Endocannabinoid Degradation
and Human Fertility

M. Bari
N. Battista
A. Cartoni
G. D'Arcangelo
M. Maccarrone

SUMMARY. Anandamide (AEA) impairs mouse pregnancy and embryo development. Here, we overview the role of AEA in sexual function, focusing on AEA degradation during human pregnancy. Human peripheral lymphocytes express the AEA-hydrolyzing enzyme fatty acid amide hydrolase (FAAH), which decreases in miscarrying women. FAAH is regulated by progesterone and Th1/Th2 cytokines, whereas the AEA transporter and the AEA binding cannabinoid receptors are not affected. Taken together, our results appear to add the endocannabinoids to the

M. Bari, BS, and N. Battista, BS, are Research Assistants, and M. Maccarrone, PhD (E-mail: Maccarrone@med.uniroma2.it), is Assistant Professor at the Department of Experimental Medicine and Biochemical Sciences, University of Rome "Tor Vergata," Via Montpellier 1, I-00133 Rome, Italy.

A. Cartoni, PhD, is Research Assistant and G. D'Arcangelo is Technical Assistant at the Department of Chemical Sciences and Technologies, University of Rome "Tor Vergata," Italy.

The authors contributed equally to this work. They wish to thank Prof. A. Finazzi Agrò for continuing support and helpful discussions, and Drs. Katia Falciglia, Marianna Di Rienzo and Riccardo Pauselli for skillful assistance.

The authors gratefully acknowledge financial support from the Ministero dell'Università e della Ricerca Scientifica e Tecnologica-Consiglio Nazionale delle Ricerche (MURST-CNR Biotechnology Program L. 95/95), Rome.

[Haworth co-indexing entry note]: "Endocannabinoid Degradation and Human Fertility." Bari, M. et al. Co-published simultaneously in *Journal of Cannabis Therapeutics* (The Haworth Integrative Healing Press, an imprint of The Haworth Press, Inc.) Vol. 2, No. 3/4, 2002, pp. 37-49; and: *Women and Cannabis: Medicine, Science, and Sociology* (ed: Ethan Russo, Melanie Dreher, and Mary Lynn Mathre) The Haworth Integrative Healing Press, an imprint of The Haworth Press, Inc., 2002, pp. 37-49. Single or multiple copies of this article are available for a fee from The Haworth Document Delivery Service [1-800-HAWORTH, 9:00 a.m. - 5:00 p.m. (EST). E-mail address: getinfo@haworthpressinc.com].

37

hormone-cytokine array involved in the control of human pregnancy, and suggest that FAAH might be a useful diagnostic marker for large scale, routine monitoring of gestation in humans. *[Article copies available for a fee from The Haworth Document Delivery Service: 1-800-HAWORTH. E-mail address: <getinfo@haworthpressinc.com> Website: <http://www. HaworthPress.com>* © *2002 by The Haworth Press, Inc. All rights reserved.]*

KEYWORDS. Anandamide, cytokines, endocannabinoids, human fertility, sex hormones

INTRODUCTION

Endocannabinoids are an emerging class of lipid mediators, isolated from brain and peripheral tissues (Devane et al. 1992; Mechoulam et al. 1998), which mimic some of the psychotropic, hypnotic and analgesic effects of cannabinoids (Calignano et al. 1998; Meng et al. 1998). The latter compounds, and in particular Δ^9-tetrahydrocannabinol, were reported to have adverse effects on reproductive functions, including retarded embryo development, fetal loss and pregnancy failure (Das et al. 1995; Ness et al. 1999). A major endocannabinoid, anandamide (*N*-arachidonoylethanolamine, AEA), has been shown to impair pregnancy and embryo development in mice (Paria et al. 1996). Down-regulation of anandamide levels in mouse uterus has been associated with increased uterine receptivity, which instead decreased when AEA was up-regulated (Schmid et al. 1997). AEA is an endogenous ligand for both the brain-type (CB_1R) and the spleen-type (CB_2R) cannabinoid receptors, mimicking several actions of cannabinoids on the central nervous system and in peripheral tissues (Di Marzo 1998). CB_1R activation is detrimental for mouse preimplantation and development (Yang et al. 1996; Wang et al. 1999), but appears to accelerate trophoblast differentiation (Paria et al. 2000). A recent study has shown that sex steroids control the expression of the CB_1R gene in the anterior pituitary gland of both male and female rats, leading to the speculation that such a regulatory mechanism might be operational also in the reproductive organs (Gonzales et al. 2000). Moreover, the role of progesterone receptor in Δ^9-tetrahydrocannabinol modulation of sexual receptivity in female rats has been also demonstrated (Mani et al. 2001) and dysregulation of cannabinoid signalling has been shown to disrupt uterine receptivity for embryo implantation in mice (Paria et al. 2001). The effect of AEA via CB_1R and CB_2R depends on its concentration in the extracellular space, which is controlled by a two-step process: (i) cellular uptake by a specific AEA membrane transporter (AMT), and (ii) intracellular degradation by the AEA-hydrolyzing enzyme fatty acid amide hydrolase (FAAH). Since the first report showing an

AEA-degrading enzyme (Deutsch and Chin 1993), AMT and FAAH have been characterized in several mammalian cell lines (Di Marzo et al. 1999; Beltramo et al. 1997; Hillard et al. 1997) and more recently in human cells in culture, in brain (Maccarrone et al. 1998), in platelets (Maccarrone et al. 1999) and in mastocytes (Maccarrone et al. 2000a).

Despite the growing evidence that AEA adversely affects uterine receptivity and embryo implantation in mice (reviewed by Paria and Dey, 2000) and that AEA degradation by FAAH may have physiological significance in these processes (Paria et al. 1996; Paria et al. 1999; Maccarrone et al. 2000b), the regulation of FAAH during early pregnancy is still obscure. Recently, we observed down-regulation of FAAH expression in pseudopregnant mice, suggesting that FAAH modulation was independent of the presence of embryos in the uterus, and found that sex hormones like progesterone and estrogen down-regulate FAAH activity by reducing gene expression (Maccarrone et al. 2000b).

DISTRIBUTION OF FAAH AND AMT

FAAH was localized in the luminal and glandular epithelia of non pregnant mouse uterus (Maccarrone et al. 2000b). *In situ* hybridization consistently detected FAAH mRNA primarily in uterine luminal and glandular epithelial cells (Paria et al. 1999). Also human uterine epithelial cells had a remarkable FAAH activity, which increased more than five times in human adenocarcinoma cells (Maccarrone et al. 2000b). These findings, summarized in Figure 1, are consistent with an epithelial localization of FAAH also in the human endometrium. In this context, it is noteworthy that the Km values of FAAH from mouse or human uterus (approximately 7 µM) were comparable to those recently reported for human brain and for human neuroblastoma and lymphoma cell lines, whereas apparent Vmax values varied (Maccarrone et al. 1998; Maccarrone et al. 2000b). Therefore, it can be proposed that the same enzyme is differently expressed in various species or in different tissues of the same species. Sequence homology between rat, mouse and human FAAH genes (Giang et al. 1997) suggests that indeed FAAH gene is highly conserved. Therefore, the hormonal regulation of FAAH observed in mouse uterus might hold true also for the human counterpart.

FAAH activity was also demonstrated and characterized in mouse blastocysts (Maccarrone et al. 2000b). In order to be hydrolyzed by FAAH, AEA must be transported into the cell. Recent experiments performed on rat neuronal and leukemia cells (Bisogno et al. 1997), on human neuronal and immune cells (Maccarrone et al. 1998) and on human endothelial cells (Maccarrone et al. 2000c), clearly showed the presence of a high-affinity AEA

FIGURE 1. *FAAH activity and expression in human uterus.* FAAH activity (white bars) and content (hatched bars) were significantly increased in human adenocarcinoma cells compared to healthy epithelial cells. Antigen competition ELISA (black bars) validated the specificity of FAAH quantitation. 100% = 600 ± 50 pmol.min^{-1}.mg protein^{-1} (activity) or 0.500 ± 0.050 A_{405} units (content).

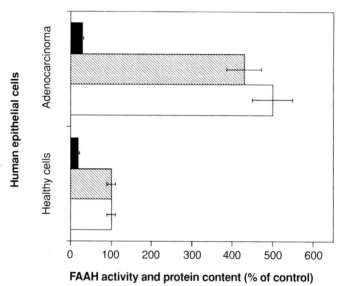

membrane transporter (AMT) in the cell outer membranes. A similar AMT was found in mouse blastocysts (Maccarrone et al. 2000b). The affinity of this transporter was comparable to that of AMT in rat astrocytes (Km = 320 nM) (Beltramo et al. 1997) and human cells (Km = 130-200 nM) (Maccarrone et al. 1998). The blastocyst's AMT and FAAH might play a critical role in implantation, because nanomolar concentrations of AEA were found to inhibit embryo development and blastocysts hatching *in vitro* (Schmid et al. 1997; Paria et al. 1998; Maccarrone et al. 2000b). Both detrimental effects of AEA were inhibited by a CB_1R antagonist, in line with the hypothesis that they were mediated by this receptor (Yang et al. 1996).

AEA AND THE INDUCTION OF APOPTOSIS

Interestingly, AEA was found to induce apoptosis in blastocysts, and this effect was not prevented by CB_1R or CB_2R antagonists (Maccarrone et al. 2000b). This rules out the involvement of either cannabinoid receptor in the induction of programmed cell death by the endocannabinoids, and suggests that the arrest of embryo development and blastocyst hatching by AEA did not involve the deployment of apoptotic programmes (Afford et al. 1996; Tonnetti et al. 1999). Consistently, AEA has been shown to inhibit cancer cell proliferation (De Petrocellis et al. 1998), and to induce apoptosis in lymphocytes (Schwarz et al. 1994), neuronal cells (Maccarrone et al. 2000d), and brain tumors (Galve-Roperh et al. 2000). These findings are in keeping with the notion that Δ^9-tetrahydrocannabinol promotes apoptosis in glioma cells, through a CB_1R independent mechanism (Sànchez et al. 1998).

Collectively, our findings lead to a general picture suggesting that a decreased FAAH activity in mouse uterus during early pregnancy might allow higher levels of AEA, which can be instrumental in modifying endometrium during pregnancy. However, the toxic effects of AEA to the blastocysts are prevented by the activity of AMT and FAAH in these cells, which rapidly scavenge the endocannabinoid. These events are under hormonal control, showing an interplay between endocannabinoids and sex hormones in regulating fertility in mammals. In this line, a recent report has demonstrated that FAAH promoter has a putative estrogen receptor binding site (Puffenbarger et al. 2001), further strengthening the concept of a common hormone-endocannabinoid network. From this stand-point, we sought to ascertain the role of endocannabinoid degradation in human fertility.

ENDOCANNABINOID DEGRADATION AND HUMAN FERTILITY

Spontaneous abortion is the most common adverse outcome of pregnancy, associated with considerable pain, suffering and medical costs (Kline et al. 1989; Sozio and Ness 1998). Early markers of miscarriage have long been sought for their clinical relevance, though they have not yet been identified (Goldstein et al. 1994; Redline et al. 1994). Little is known about the influence of lifestyle on spontaneous abortion, although cigarette smoking and the use of illicit drugs have been implicated as adverse factors (Walsh 1994; Ness et al. 1999).

Peripheral lymphocytes play a critical role in embryo implantation and successful pregnancy in humans (Piccinni et al. 1998). These cells produce leukemia inhibitory factor (LIF) and immunomodulatory proteins, which favor fetal implantation and survival (Szekenes-Bartho and Wegmann 1996; Stewart and Cullinan 1997; Duval et al. 2000). More generally, lymphocytes regulate a hormonal-cytokine network at the fetal-maternal interface, and a defect in the integrity of this network may result in fetal loss (Szekenes-Bartho and Wegmann 1996; Stewart and Cullinan 1997; Piccinni et al. 1998; Duval et al.

2000). Progesterone (P), a hormone essential for the maintenance of pregnancy, is also known to modulate immune function (Correale et al. 1998) and to elicit an immunological response critical for normal gestation (Szekenes-Bartho and Wegmann 1996; Szekenes-Bartho et al. 1996). Indeed, P has been shown to favor the development of human T lymphocytes producing type 2 T-helper (Th2) cytokines (interleukins 3, 4 and 10, and transforming growth factor β2), which inhibit the anti-fertility Th1-type cytokines (tumor necrosis factor α, interleukin-2 and interferon-γ), thus allowing the survival of fetal allograft and successful pregnancy (Piccinni et al. 1995; Piccinni et al. 1996). The interactions between this cytokine network and the trophoblast are depicted in Figure 2. More recently, the P-induced Th2 bias has been found to stimulate the release of leukemia inhibitory factor (LIF) from T lymphocytes, mediated by IL-4 (Piccinni et al. 1998). Clinical data, showing that women with unexplained recurrent abortions have a reduced LIF production, suggest that the latter is indeed critical for implantation and maintenance of fetus in humans (Piccinni et al. 1998; Sharkey 1998; Taupin et al. 1999). FAAH might limit the pathophysiological effects of AEA and the other congeners by hydro-

FIGURE 2. *Interaction between Th1/Th2 cytokines and trophoblast.* Type 2 T-helper (Th2) cytokines (interleukin (IL)-3, IL-4, IL-10 and transforming growth factor β2, TGF-β2) favor blastocyst implantation and successful pregnancy, by promoting, either directly or indirectly: (i) trophoblast growth, (ii) inhibition of natural killer (NK) cell activity, and (iii) stimulation of natural suppressor cells. Conversely, type 1 T-helper (Th1) cytokines (tumor necrosis factor α (TNF-α), IL-2, IL-12 and interferon (INF)-γ) impair gestation, by causing direct damage to the trophoblast, by stimulating NK cells and by enhancing TNF-α secretion by macrophages.

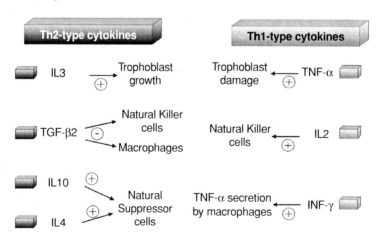

lyzing them (Giang et al. 1997; Goparaju et al. 1998). Therefore, FAAH activity in lymphocytes might be involved in controlling pregnancy failure by regulating the level of AEA in uterus. In particular, it can be proposed that endocannabinoids may interfere with the lymphocyte-dependent cytokine network which regulates the development and maintenance of successful pregnancy in humans (Piccinni et al. 1998).

FAAH IN MATERNAL LYMPHOCYTES
AND HUMAN GESTATION

In this line, we have recently demonstrated that decreased activity and expression of FAAH in peripheral lymphocytes is an early (< 8 weeks of gestation) marker of human spontaneous abortion (Maccarrone et al. 2000e). Indeed, in a clinical study, we measured FAAH activity, [^{3}H]AEA uptake by AMT and [^{3}H]CP55.940 binding to CBR in lymphocytes isolated from 100 healthy women at 7-8 weeks of gestation (Maccarrone et al. 2001). This is the earliest time in gestation where the difference between FAAH content in women who miscarried and those who did not was found to be significant (Maccarrone et al. 2000e). The *a posteriori* association between the gestation outcome and the FAAH activity and expression, AMT activity or CBR binding, showed that FAAH activity and protein were lower in all the 15 women who miscarried than in the 85 who did not, whereas AMT activity and CBR binding were similar in both groups (Table 1). These observations point towards a key-role for FAAH, but not for AMT or CBR, in lymphocyte-mediated control of the hormone-cytokine network at the fetal-maternal interface. Since FAAH might indirectly control AMT, by maintaining the concentration gradient which drives AEA facilitated diffusion through AMT itself (Deutsch et al. 2001), it can be speculated that by controlling FAAH the cell controls also the transport of AEA, and hence its activity in the extracellular space. In this frame, we further investigated how FAAH might be regulated by fertility-related signal molecules.

We found that *in vitro* treatment of human lymphocytes with P, at the concentrations found in serum during pregnancy (from 0.02 to 0.30 µg/ml) (Piccinni et al. 1995), enhanced FAAH activity and gene expression in a dose-dependent manner, as did treatment of human lymphocytes with Th2-type cytokines IL-4 or IL-10. Conversely, treatment with Th1-type cytokines IL-12 or IFN-γ reduced FAAH activity and expression (Maccarrone et al. 2001). We also found that treatment of lymphocytes with P, IL-4, IL-10, IL-12, or IFN-γ did not quite affect AMT activity, neither did it affect [^{3}H]CP55.940 binding to CBR (Maccarrone et al. 2001).

TABLE 1. CBR Binding, AMT Activity, and FAAH Activity and Content in Women Who Miscarried and Those Who Did Not

Parameter	Women with normal gestation	Women who miscarried
CBR binding	20380 ± 1930	20400 ± 1795
(cpm·mg protein^{-1})	(100%)	(100%)
AMT activity	50 ± 4	49 ± 4
(pmol·min^{-1}·mg protein^{-1})	(100%)	(100%)
FAAH activity	133 ± 9	48 ± 5
(pmol·min^{-1}·mg protein^{-1})	(100%)	(36%)
FAAH content	0.250 ± 0.030	0.130 ± 0.020
(A$_{405}$ units)	(100%)	(52%)

High FAAH activity should lower the level of its substrate, and indeed in a following study we have shown that healthy women (with higher lymphocyte FAAH) have lower blood AEA compared to aborting patients (Maccarrone et al. 2002). As noted above, peripheral lymphocytes play a critical role in human pregnancy by producing LIF (Sharkey 1998). Therefore, we tested whether the endocannabinoids would affect LIF release from peripheral T cells. We found that treatment of human lymphocytes with AEA reduced the production of LIF, an effect counteracted by SR141716, but not by SR144528 nor by capsazepine, a selective antagonist of vanilloid receptors (Zygmunt et al. 1999). Therefore, inhibition of LIF release by AEA was mediated by CB$_1$ receptors only.

Altogether, these data suggest that a low FAAH activity, and hence higher AEA levels, can lead to spontaneous abortion by reducing LIF production. This unprecedented effect of AEA is consistent with its adverse effects on embryo implantation and development in mouse (Paria et al. 1996; Schmid et al. 1997; Yang et al. 1996; Di Marzo 1998; Wang et al. 1999; Maccarrone et al., 2000b). Moreover, keeping in mind the role of LIF in regulating growth and differentiation of neurons and endothelial cells (Taupin et al. 1999), a wider implication of the present findings can be anticipated. The interplay among P, cytokines, FAAH, endocannabinoids and LIF is depicted in Figure 3. It is shown that P, by interacting with its receptor, increases the synthesis of FAAH, which in turn reduces the extracellular concentration of AEA by driving its import through the AMT transporter. In this way the effect of AEA on LIF release by binding to type 1 cannabinoid receptors is reduced. FAAH activation by P is further enhanced by interleukin-4. This cytokine can also directly activate FAAH, as does interleukin-10, whereas interleukin-12 or interferon-γ inhibit FAAH activity. The scheme also shows that nitric oxide

FIGURE 3. *AEA, progesterone and leukemia inhibitory factor in human lymphocytes.* Progesterone (P), by interacting with its intracellular receptor, increases the synthesis of FAAH, which in turn reduces the extracellular concentration of AEA by driving its import through the AEA membrane transporter (AMT). In this way the effect of AEA on leukemia inhibitory factor (LIF) release by binding to type 1 cannabinoid receptors (CBR) is reduced. FAAH activation by P is further enhanced by interleukin-4 or interleukin-10 (omitted for the sake of clarity), whereas it is partly prevented by interleukin-12 or interferon-γ (omitted for the sake of clarity). Also nitric oxide (NO), produced from L-arginine (L-Arg) by CBR-activated nitric oxide synthase (NOS), stimulates AEA degradation, by enhancing AMT and preventing the inhibition of FAAH by lipoxygenase (LOX) activity.

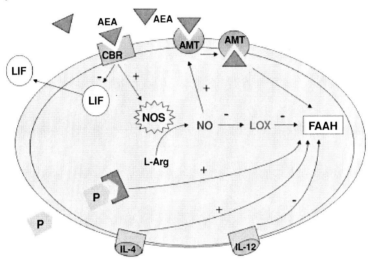

(NO), produced from L-arginine by CBR-activated nitric oxide synthase, stimulates AEA degradation, by (i) enhancing AMT activity (Maccarone et al. 2000c), and (ii) preventing the inhibition of FAAH by lipoxygenase (Maccarrone et al. 1998; Maccarrone et al. 2000a). This is noteworthy, because of the manifold roles of NO in male and female fertility (Chwalisz and Garfield 2000; Kuo et al. 2000; Sikka et al. 2001; Herrero et al. 2001), thus adding a further player in the endocannabinoids/hormone/cytokine network regulating the reproductive function.

CONCLUSIONS

The reported findings give a biochemical ground to the previous observation that low FAAH activity correlates with spontaneous abortion in humans

(Maccarrone et al. 2000e). They represent the first evidence of a link between the hormone-cytokine network responsible for successful pregnancy and the peripheral endocannabinoid system, and suggest that FAAH, but not anandamide transporter or CB receptors, might be critical for this link. These results might represent also a useful framework for the interpretation of a novel interaction between P and exogenous cannabinoids, recently shown to regulate female sexual receptivity (Mani et al. 2001). They also suggest that quantitation of FAAH protein in lymphocytes might be an accurate marker of spontaneous abortion in humans, easy to measure in routine analyses.

REFERENCES

Afford, S.C., S. Randhawa, A.G. Eliopoulos, S.G. Hubscher, L.S. Young and D.H. Adams. 1999. CD40 activation induces apoptosis in cultured human hepatocytes via induction of cell surface fas ligand expression and amplifies fas-mediated hepatocyte death during allograft rejection. *J Exp Med* 189:441-446.

Beltramo, M., N. Stella, A. Calignano, S.Y. Lin, A. Makriyannis and D. Piomelli. 1997. Functional role of high-affinity anandamide transport, as revealed by selective inhibition. *Science* 277:1094-1097.

Calignano, A., G. La Rana, A. Giuffrida and D. Piomelli. 1998. Control of pain initiation by endogenous cannabinoids. *Nature* 394:277-281.

Chwalisz, K. and R.E. Garfield. 2000. Role of nitric oxide in implantation and menstruation. *Human Reproduction* 15:96-111.

Correale, J., M. Arias and W. Gilmore. 1998. Steroid hormone regulation of cytokine secretion by proteolipid protein-specific CD+ T cell clones isolated from multiple sclerosis patients and normal control subjects. *J Immunol* 161:3365-3374.

Das, S.K., B.C. Paria, I. Chakraborty, S.K. Dey. 1995. Cannabinoid ligand-receptor signaling in the mouse uterus. *Proc Natl Acad Sci USA* 92:4332-4336.

De Petrocellis, L., D. Melck and A. Palmisano. 1998. The endogenous cannabinoid anandamide inhibits human breast cancer cell proliferation. *Proc Natl Acad Sci USA* 95:8375-8380.

Deutsch, D.G. and S.A. Chin. 1993. Enzymatic synthesis and degradation of anandamide, a cannabinoid receptor agonist. *Biochem Pharmacol* 46:791-796.

Deutsch, D.G., S.T. Glaser, J.M. Howell, J.S. Kuntz, R.A. Puffenbarger, C.J. Hillard and N. Abumrad. 2001. The cellular uptake of anandamide is coupled to its breakdown by fatty acid amide hydrolase (FAAH). *J Biol Chem* 276:6967-6973.

Devane, W.A., L. Hannus, A. Breuer et al. 1992. Isolation and structure of a brain constituent that binds to the cannabinoid receptor. *Science* 258:1946-1949.

Di Marzo, V. 1998. "Endocannabinoids" and other fatty acid derivatives with cannabimimetic properties: biochemistry and possible physiopathological relevance. *Biochim Biophys Acta* 1392:153-175.

Di Marzo, V., T. Bisogno, L. De Petrocellis, D. Melck, P. Orlando, J.A. Wagner and G. Kunos. 1999. Biosynthesis and inactivation of the endocannabinoid 2-arachidonoylglycerol in circulating and tumoral macrophages. *Eur J Biochem* 264:258-267.

Duval, D., B. Reinhardt, C. Kedinger and H. Boeuf. 2000. Role of suppressors of cytokine signaling (Socs) in leukemia inhibitory factor (LIF)-dependent embryonic stem cell survival. *FASEB J* 14:1577-1584.

Galve-Roperh, I., C. Sànchez, M.L. Cortes, T.G. del Pulgar, M. Izquierdo and M. Guzman. 2000. Anti-tumoral action of cannabinoids: involvement of sustained ceramide accumulation and extracellular signal-regulated kinase activation. *Nature Med* 6:313-316.

Giang, D.K. and B.F. Cravatt. 1997. Molecular characterization of human and mouse fatty acid amide hydrolase. *Proc Natl Acad Sci USA* 94:2238-2242.

Goldstein, S.R. 1994. Sonography in early pregnancy failure. *Clin Obstet Gynecol* 37:681-692.

Gonzalez, S., T. Bisogno and T. Wenger. 2000. Sex steroid influence on cannabinoid CB1 receptor mRNA and endocannabinoid levels in the anterior pituitary gland. *Biochem Biophys Res Commun* 270:260-266.

Goparaju, S.K., N. Ueda, H. Yamaguchi and S. Yamamoto. 1998. Anandamide amidohydrolase reacting with 2-arachidonoylglycerol, another cannabinoid receptor ligand. *FEBS Lett* 422: 69-73.

Herrero, M.B., E. de Lamirande and C. Gagnon. 2001. Tyrosine nitration in human spermatozoa: a physiological function of peroxynitrite, the reaction product of nitric oxide and superoxide. *Mol Hum Reprod* 7:913-921.

Hillard, C.J., W.S. Edgemond, A. Jarrahian and W.B. Campbell. 1997. Accumulation of *N*-arachidonoylethanolamine (anandamide) into cerebellar granule cells occurs via facilitated diffusion. *J Neurochem* 69:631-638.

Kline, J., Z. Stein and M. Susser. 1989. *Conception to birth: Epidemiology of prenatal development.* eds. New York: Oxford University Press.

Kuo, R.C., G.T. Baxter, S.H. Thompson, S.A. Stricker, C. Patton, J. Bonaventura and D. Epel. 2000. NO is necessary and sufficient for egg activation at fertilization. *Nature* 406:633-636.

Maccarrone, M., M. Bari, T. Lorenzon, T. Bisogno, V. Di Marzo and A. Finazzi-Agrò. 2000c. Anandamide uptake by human endothelial cells and its regulation by nitric oxide. *J Biol Chem* 275:13484-13492.

Maccarrone, M., T. Lorenzon, M. Bari, G. Melino and A. Finazzi-Agrò. 2000d. Anandamide induces apoptosis in human cells via vanilloid receptors. Evidence for a protective role of cannabinoid receptors. *J Biol Chem* 275:31938-31945.

Maccarrone, M., H. Valensise, M. Bari, N. Lazzarin, C. Romanini and A. Finazzi-Agrò. 2000e. Relation between decreased anandamide hydrolase concentrations in human lymphocytes and miscarriage. *Lancet* 355:1326-1329.

Maccarrone, M., H. Valensise, M. Bari, N. Lazzarin, C. Romanini and A. Finazzi-Agrò. 2001. Progesterone up-regulates anandamide hydrolase in human lymphocytes. Role of cytokines and implications for fertility. *J Immunol* 166:7183-7189.

Maccarrone, M., L. Fiorucci, F. Erba, M. Bari, A. Finazzi-Agrò and F. Ascoli. 2000a. Human mast cells take up and hydrolyze anandamide under the control of 5-lipoxygenase, and do not express cannabinoid receptors. *FEBS Lett* 468:176-180.

Maccarrone, M., M. Bari, A. Menichelli, D. Del Principe, A. Finazzi-Agrò. 1999. Anandamide activates human platelets through a pathway independent of the arachidonate cascade. *FEBS Lett* 447:277-282.

Maccarrone, M., M. De Felici, M. Bari, F. Klinger, G. Siracusa and A. Finazzi-Agrò. 2000b. Down-regulation of anandamide hydrolase in mouse uterus by sex hormones. *Eur J Biochem* 267:2991-2997.

Maccarrone, M., M. Van der Stelt, A. Rossi, G.A.Veldink, J.F.G. Vliegenthart and A. Finazzi-Agrò. 1998. Anandamide hydrolysis by human cells in culture and brain. *J Biol Chem* 273: 32332-32339.

Maccarrone, M., T. Bisogno, H. Valensise, N. Lazzarin, F. Fezza, C. Manna, V. Di Marzo and A. Finazzi Agrò. 2002. Low fatty acid amide hydrolase and high anandamide levels are associated with spontaneous abortions in women receiving IVF-derived embryos. *Mol Hum Reprod* (in press).

Mani, S.K., A. Mitchell and B.W. O'Malley. 2001. Progesterone receptor and dopamine receptors are required in Δ^9-tetrahydrocannabinol modulation of sexual receptivity in female rats. *Proc Natl Acad Sci USA* 98:1249-1254.

Mechoulam, R., E. Fride and V. Di Marzo. 1998. Endocannabinoids. *Eur J Pharmacol* 359:1-18.

Meng, I.D., B.H. Manning, W.J. Martin, H.L. Fields. 1998. An analgesia circuit activated by cannabinoids. *Nature* 395:381-383.

Ness, R.B., J.A. Grisso, N. Hirschinger, N. Markovic, L.M. Shaw, N.L. Day and J. Kline. 1999. Cocaine and tobacco use and the risk of spontaneous abortion. *N Engl J Med* 340:333-339.

Paria, B.C., D.D. Deutsch and S.K. Dey. 1996. The uterus is a potential site for anandamide synthesis and hydrolysis: differential profiles of anandamide synthase and hydrolase activities in the mouse uterus during the periimplantation period. *Mol Rep Dev* 45:183-192.

Paria, B.C. and S.K. Dey. 2000. Ligand-receptor signaling with endocannabinoids in preimplantation embryo development and implantation. *Chem Phys Lipids* 108: 211-220.

Paria, B.C., W. Ma, D.M. Andrenyak, P.C. Schmid, H.H. Schmid, D.E. Moody, H. Deng, A. Makriyannis and S.K. Dey. 1998. Effects of cannabinoids on preimplantation mouse embryo development and implantation are mediated by brain-type cannabinoid receptors. *Biol Reprod* 58:1490-1495.

Paria, B.C., H. Song, X. Wang, P.C. Schmid, R.J. Krebsbach, H.H. Schmid, T.I. Bonner, A. Zimmer and S.K. Dey. 2001. Dysregulated cannabinoid signaling disrupts uterine receptivity for embryo implantation. *J Biol Chem* 276:20523-20528.

Paria, B.C., X. Zhao, J. Wang, S.K. Das and S.K. Dey. 1999. Fatty-acid amide hydrolase is expressed in the mouse uterus and embryo during the periimplantation period. *Biol Reprod* 60:1151-1157.

Piccinni, M.P. and S. Romagnani. 1996. Regulation of fetal allograft survival by hormone-controlled Th1-and Th2-type cytokines. *Immunol Res* 15:141-150.

Piccinni, M.P., L. Beloni, C. Livi, E. Maggi, G. Scarselli and S. Romagnani. 1998. Defective production of both leukemia inhibitory factor and type 2 T-helper cytokines by decidual T cells in unexplained recurrent abortions. *Nature Med* 4:1020-1024.

Piccinni, M.P., M.G. Giudizi, R. Biagiotti, L. Beloni, L. Giannarini, S. Sampognaro, P. Parronchi, R. Manetti, F. Annunziato and C. Livi. 1995. Progesterone favors the development of human T helper cells producing Th2-type cytokines and promotes both IL-4 production and membrane CD30 expression in established Th1 cell clones. *J Immunol* 155:128-133.

Puffenbarger, R.A., O. Kapulina, J.M. Howell and D.G. Deutsch. 2001. Characterization of the 5′-sequence of the mouse fatty acid amide hydrolase. *Neurosci Lett* 314:21-24.

Redline, R.W., M. Zaragoza and T. Hassold. 1999. Prevalence of developmental and inflammatory lesions in nonmolar first-trimester spontaneous abortions. *Hum Pathol* 30:93-100.

Sànchez, C., I. Galve-Roperh, C. Canova, P. Brachet and M. Guzman. 1998. Δ^9-Tetrahydrocannabinol induces apoptosis in C6 glioma cells. *FEBS Lett* 436:6-10.

Schmid, P.C., B.C. Paria, R.J. Krebsbach, H.H.O. Schmid and S.K. Dey. 1997. Changes in anandamide levels in mouse uterus are associated with uterine receptivity for embryo implantation. *Proc Natl Acad Sci USA* 94:4188-4192.

Schwarz, H., F.J. Blanco and M. Lotz. 1994. Anandamide, an endogenous cannabinoid receptor agonist, inhibits lymphocyte proliferation and induces apoptosis. *J Neuroimmunol* 55:107-115.

Sharkey, A. 1998. Cytokines and implantation. *Rev Reprod* 3:52-61.

Sikka, S.C. 2001. Relative impact of oxidative stress on male reproductive function. *Curr Med Chem* 8:851-862.

Sozio, J. and R.B. Ness. 1998. Chlamydial lower genital tract infection and spontaneous abortion. *Infect Dis Obstet Gynecol* 6:8-12.

Stewart, C.L. and E.B. Cullinan. 1997. Preimplantation development of the mammalian embryo and its regulation by growth factors. *Dev Genet* 21:91-101.

Szekenes-Bartho J. and T.G. Wegmann. 1996. A progesterone-dependent immunomodulatory protein alters the Th1/Th2 balance. *J Reprod Immunol* 1:81-95.

Szekeres-Bartho, J., Z. Faust, P. Varga, L. Szereday and K. Kelemen. 1996. The immunological pregnancy protective effect of progesterone is manifested via controlling cytokine production. *Am J Reprod Immunol* 35:348-351.

Taupin, J.-L., S. Minvielle, J. Thèze, Y. Jacques Y. and J.F. Moreau. 1999. *The interleukin-6 family of cytokines and their receptors*. In Thèze, J., ed. The cytokine network and immune functions. New York: Oxford University Press.

Tonnetti, L., M.C. Veri, E. Bonvini and L. D'Adamio. 1999. A role for neutral sphingomyelinase-mediated ceramide production in T cell receptor-induced apoptosis and mitogen-activated protein kinase-mediated signal transduction. *J Exp Med* 189:1581-1589.

Walsh, R.A. 1994. Effects of maternal smoking on adverse pregnancy outcomes: Examination of the criteria of causation. *Hum Biol* 66:1059-92.

Wang, J., B.C. Paria, S.K. Dey and D.R. Armant. 1999. Stage-specific excitation of cannabinoid receptor exhibits differential effects on mouse embryonic development. *Biol Reprod* 60:839-844.

Yang, Z.-M., B.C. Paria and S.K. Dey. 1996. Activation of brain-type cannabinoid receptors interferes with preimplantation mouse embryo development. *Biol Reprod* 55:756-761.

Zygmunt, P.M., J. Petersson, D.A. Andersson, H. Chuang, M. Sorgard, V. Di Marzo, D. Julius and E.D. Högestätt. 1999. Vanilloid receptors on sensory nerves mediate the vasodilator action of anandamide. *Nature* 400:452-457.

Cannabinoids and Feeding: The Role of the Endogenous Cannabinoid System as a Trigger for Newborn Suckling

Ester Fride

SUMMARY. Cannabinoids are known to enhance appetite by activating cannabinoid (CB_1) receptors. This phenomenon is exploited to combat cachexia and loss of appetite in cancer and AIDS patients. The endocannabinoid 2-arachidonylglycerol (2-AG) is present in milk. Evidence is presented supporting a critical role for CB_1 receptors in survival of mouse pups. Thus neonates do not gain weight and die within the first week of life when their receptors are blocked. This is due apparently, to an inability to ingest maternal milk. This suggests that the endocannabinoid-CB_1 receptor system is unique in its absolute control over the initiation of the neonatal milk suckling response. It is further proposed that cannabis-based medicines should be developed to benefit infant failure to thrive. *[Article copies available for a fee from The Haworth Document Delivery Service: 1-800-HAWORTH. E-mail address: <getinfo@haworthpressinc. com> Website: <http://www.HaworthPress.com> © 2002 by The Haworth Press, Inc. All rights reserved.]*

Ester Fride, PhD, is Associate Professor, Department of Behavioral Sciences, and Head, Laboratory of Behavioral Biology, College of Judea and Samaria, Ariel, Israel 44837.

This work was supported in part by a grant from the Danone Research Institute in Israel.

[Haworth co-indexing entry note]: "Cannabinoids and Feeding: The Role of the Endogenous Cannabinoid System as a Trigger for Newborn Suckling." Fride, Ester. Co-published simultaneously in *Journal of Cannabis Therapeutics* (The Haworth Integrative Healing Press, an imprint of The Haworth Press, Inc.) Vol. 2, No. 3/4, 2002, pp. 51-62; and: *Women and Cannabis: Medicine, Science, and Sociology* (ed: Ethan Russo, Melanie Dreher, and Mary Lynn Mathre) The Haworth Integrative Healing Press, an imprint of The Haworth Press, Inc., 2002, pp. 51-62. Single or multiple copies of this article are available for a fee from The Haworth Document Delivery Service [1-800-HAWORTH, 9:00 a.m. - 5:00 p.m. (EST). E-mail address: getinfo@ haworthpressinc.com].

KEYWORDS. Cannabinoids, endocannabinoids, feeding, appetite, nursing, suckling, neonatal

ABBREVIATIONS. CB_1, cannabinoid 1, 2-AG, 2-arachidonylglycerol, CBD, cannabidiol

Cannabis is well known appetite stimulant (Abel 1971; Mattes et al. 1994; Fride 2002a). It is possible that the enhancement of appetite is selective for snack foods (Foltin, Brady, and Fischman 1986; Mattes, Shaw, and Engelman 1994). A role of the endocannabinoid system in the primitive invertebrate, *Hydra vulgaris*, has been demonstrated (De Petrocellis et al. 1999), thus pointing at a very widespread stimulatory role for cannabinoids in feeding. This, for most cannabis users, undesirable "side effect," has been clinically utilized for a number of years to combat a reduction in appetite and consequent weight reduction and wasting, as seen in conditions including AIDS and cancer (Mechoulam, Hanus, and Fride 1998). However, few controlled clinical studies have been performed (Bennett and Bennett 1999). In open pilot studies, dronabinol (Δ^9-THC) caused weight gain in the majority of subjects (Plasse et al. 1991). A relatively low dose of dronabinol, 2.5 mg twice daily, enhanced appetite and stabilized body weight in AIDS patients suffering from anorexia (Beal et al. 1997) for at least 7 months. In another study on AIDS patients, no weight gain was reported over the course of 12 weeks of dronabinol administration (2.5 mg twice a day), whereas a dose of 750 mg/day of megestrol acetate (a synthetic progestational drug), effected significant weight gain (Timpone et al. 1999). In that study, a high dose of megestrol (with potential adverse effects including dyspnea and hypertension), and a low dose of dronabinol were used. Higher doses of dronabinol may be more effective, although side effects such as weakness, confusion, memory impairment and anxiety, are a concern.

When dronabinol was administered to healthy volunteers, an increase in caloric intake was recorded after twice daily administrations for 3 days, when rectal suppositories were used, rather than the oral route (Mattes et al. 1994). When the effects of cannabis smoking by healthy volunteers on the intake of various types of food were compared, a selective increase in snack foods was observed (Foltin, Brady, and Fischman 1986). Thus the use of higher doses of cannabinoids as well as different routes of administration including the rectal (Bennett and Bennett 1999) or the sublingual (Whittle, Guy, and Robson 2001) route, should be further investigated.

Studies in laboratory animals have confirmed the human data, and unequivocally shown that cannabinoid 1 (CB_1) receptors mediate cannabinoid-induced increase in food ingestion (Williams and Kirkham 2002), especially of palatable foods (Koch and Matthews 2001). Thus both exogenous canna-binoids (Δ^9-THC) and the endocannabinoid anandamide-induced enhancement of appetite were reversed by the specific CB_1 antagonist SR141716A (Williams, Rogers, and Kirkham 1998; Williams and Kirkham 2002). SR141716A injected by itself reduced appetite and body weight. Whether palatability is required for the antagonist's anorectic effect is controversial (Colombo et al. 1998; Freedland, Poston, and Porrino 2000; Arnone et al. 1997). In a chronic study in mice, very low doses of anandamide (0.001 mg/kg) were effective in enhancing food intake (Hao et al. 2000), in according with a stimulatory effect of very low doses of anandamide in a series of cannabimimetic assays (Sulcova, Mechoulam, and Fride 1998).

INTERACTIONS OF THE ENDOCANNABINOID SYSTEM WITH HORMONES REGULATING FOOD INTAKE

CB_1 receptors have been located in the hypothalamus (Herkenham et al. 1991; Mailleux and Vanderhaeghen 1992), a brain structure which is important in weight regulation. Although the precise mechanism by which cannabinoid receptors enhance appetite and food intake is not known, progress has been made in recent years to uncover such mechanisms (Mechoulam and Fride 2001). Thus Arnone et al. (1997) showed that the neuropeptide Y (NPY)-induced increase in sucrose drinking was inhibited by SR141716A, possibly linking this hormone, which is known to enhance food intake (Mechoulam and Fride 2001), to cannabinoid-stimulated appetite.

The hormone leptin is produced by fat tissue and is considered to be a key signal through which the hypothalamus senses the nutritional state of the body and helps maintain weight within a narrow range (Friedman 2000; Schwartz et al. 2000).

Within the hypothalamus, the arcuate nucleus contains neurons with receptors for two appetite-stimulating peptides (neuropeptide Y and agouti-related protein), as well as receptors for two peptides that reduce appetite (α-melanocyte-stimulating hormone and cocaine-and-amphetamine-regulated transcript). Leptin directly suppresses the activity of the two appetite-stimulating peptides, and stimulates the activity of the appetite-reducing ones, thereby decreasing appetite. Other molecules indirectly affected by leptin include melanin-concentrating hormone and a family of neuropeptides called orexins, which enhance appetite, as well as corticotropin-releasing hormone and oxytocin, which cause mice to eat less and to lose weight.

Di Marzo et al. (2001) have demonstrated that the endocannabinoid receptor system is an additional factor in this already complex weight-regulating system. Thus, when they administered leptin, the levels of the endocannabinoids anandamide and 2-arachidonylglycerol in the hypothalamus of normal rats were reduced. Further evidence strengthens the idea that leptin down-regulates endocannabinoids. In a strain of obese rats in which leptin activity is impaired, the levels of endocannabinoids are higher than normal (Di Marzo et al. 2001). The same is true of obese *ob/ob* mice, which have an inherited lack of leptin, and of obese *db/db* mice, which have defective leptin receptors. Endocannabinoid levels are not affected in the cerebellum (which is commonly associated with motor coordination, but not with feeding) in these mice.

Taking together the human and animal studies, the effects of the cannabinoid system on food intake and appetite are significant, representing one of a multitude of players involved in this vital function.

ENDOCANNABINOIDS IN FOOD SUBSTANCES

The discovery of anandamide in chocolate (di Tomaso, Beltramo, and Piomelli 1996) raised the possibility that endocannabinoids contribute to the attractiveness of, and perhaps the intense craving for, this desirable food. Indeed, orally administered endocannabinoids (anandamide and 2-AG), albeit in very high doses, induced cannabimimetic effects in mice (Di Marzo et al. 1998). The very low amounts of anandamide found in cocoa powder and even lower concentrations in unfermented cocoa beans, would suggest the possibility that the anandamide in chocolate may be an artifact of processing (Di Marzo et al. 1998). Anandamide congeners that do not bind CB_1 receptors, including linoleoyl ethanolamide, oleoyl ethanolamide and oleamide ("sleep factor," Cravatt et al. 1995), all display cannabiminetic effects when applied *in vivo* (Fride at al. 1997), probably by inhibiting the fatty acid amide hydrolase (FAAH) enzyme which breaks down anandamide (see Fride 2002a). Oleamide, when given orally, displayed cannabimimetic effects in mice at doses several magnitudes higher than those present in chocolate, similar to orally administered anandamide (Di Marzo et al. 1998). Taken together, these results suggest that anandamide in chocolate, whether present in cocoa beans, or as an artifact of processing, could be responsible for any cannabinoid contribution to "chocolate craving." Future studies, testing anandamide and its congeners in more subtle behavioral assays such as "drug discrimination" or "place preference" designs may shed further light on the putative role for endocannabinoids in the rewarding effects of chocolate.

Interestingly, in the same study, and in a more recent one, relatively high concentrations of the endocannabinoid 2-AG but very low quantities of anandamide were detected in various types of milk (for instance, 8.7 ± 2.8 µg 2-AG/g extracted lipids from "mature" human milk). These concentrations of 2-AG were much higher than those found in other foods such as soybeans, hazelnuts and oatmeal (Di Marzo et al. 1998; Fride et al. 2001a).

DEVELOPMENTAL ASPECTS
OF THE ENDOCANNABINOID-CB$_1$ RECEPTOR SYSTEM

Based on the findings described above, it is suggested that, as 2-AG is found in milk in significant amounts, this endocannabinoid must be of importance for the development of the newborn mammal. Several observations on developmental aspects of the endocannabinoid system in the central nervous system support such a hypothesis.

First, "atypical distribution patterns" of CB$_1$ receptors (i.e., a transient presence during development in regions where none are found at adulthood) were detected in white matter regions including the corpus callosum and anterior commissure (connecting neuronal pathways between the left and right hemispheres) between gestational day 21 and postnatal day 5, suggesting a role for endocannabinoids in brain development (Romero et al. 1997).

Further, although initial reports studying the development of the cannabinoid receptor system during the first weeks of postnatal life in the rat described a gradual increase in brain CB$_1$ receptor mRNA (McLaughlin and Abood 1993) and in the density of CB$_1$ receptors (Belue et al. 1995; Rodriguez de Fonseca et al. 1993), in later studies CB$_1$ receptor mRNA was also detected from gestational day 11 in the rat (Buckley et al. 1998). Additional studies have uncovered more complex developmental patterns. Thus, whereas the highest levels of mRNA expression of the CB$_1$ receptor are seen at adulthood in regions such as the caudate-putamen and the cerebellum, other areas such as the cerebral cortex, the hippocampus and the ventromedial hypothalamus display the highest mRNA CB$_1$ receptor levels on the first postnatal day (Berrendero et al. 1999; Fernandez-Ruiz et al. 2000). Finally, endocannabinoids were also detected from the gestational period in rodents, 2-AG at 1000 fold higher concentrations than anandamide. Interestingly, while anandamide displayed a gradual increase, constant levels of 2-AG were measured throughout development except for a single a peak on the first postnatal day (Berrendero et al. 1999).

Is it possible therefore, that the high levels of CB$_1$ receptor mRNA and 2-AG which have been observed on the first day of life in structures including the hypothalamic ventromedial nucleus (which is associated with feeding behavior) comprise a major stimulus for the first episode of milk suckling in the newborn?

BLOCKADE OF CB₁ RECEPTORS IN NEWBORN MICE

Over the last few years, our group has investigated a role for the endocannabinoid system immediately after birth in mice. Administration of the specific CB_1 receptor antagonist SR141716A to the nursing mother had no effect on maternal weight, pup growth and development, or on maternal behavior (Fride, Ginzburg and Mechoulam, unpublished observations). However, when CB_1 receptors were blocked by SR141716A in one day old pups by a single sc injection of SR141716A, a complete growth arrest and death within the first week of life was observed in virtually all SR141716A-treated pups (Fride et al. 2001a; Figure 1).

This devastating effect of SR141716A on the pups was dose-dependent (between 5-20 mg/kg). Furthermore, for the complete (almost 100% mortality) effect to take place, the antagonist had to be injected within the first 24 hours of life. Co-administration of Δ^9-THC almost completely reversed the effect, thus strongly suggesting that the SR141716A-induced effects were CB_1 receptor mediated. Co-administration of the endocannabinoid 2-AG did not reverse the SR141716A-induced mortality, presumably due to its rapid breakdown. However, 2-AG injected together with its "entourage" (fatty acid-esters which are

FIGURE 1. Five day old vehicle-injected (left) and SR141716A-injected (right) mouse pups. Pups, from the same litter, were injected sc (10 µl/g) within 24 hr after birth with vehicle (ethanol:emulphor:saline = 1:1:18), or SR141716A (20 mg/kg).

always co-released with 2-AG, but which do not bind CB_1 receptors, and which counteract the breakdown and reuptake of 2-AG; see Ben-Shabat et al. 1998), significantly antagonized the growth-arresting effects of SR141716A on the pups (Figure 2). Subsequent experiments designed to further support the specificity of the CB_1 receptor in the mediation of the antagonist-induced pup mortality indicated that cannabidiol (CBD), the non-psychoactive, non-CB_1 receptor binding cannabinoid, did not reverse the effects of SR141716A (Fride et al. 2001a; Figure 2), while the CB_2 receptor antagonist, SR144528, did not affect pup growth (unpublished observations).

MECHANISMS OF THE CB_1 RECEPTOR BLOCKADE-INDUCED GROWTH STUNTING EFFECTS

An initial investigation of possible mechanisms involved in sequelae of CB_1 receptor blockade in pups suggested that maternal behavior toward SR141716A-injected pups was not adversely affected. On the contrary, the

FIGURE 2. Summary of survival rates in pups one week after birth after various treatments on day 1 of life. SR1 = SR141716A (20 mg/kg), SR2 = SR144528 (20 mg/kg), CBD = cannabidiol (20 mg/kg), Entourage = palmityl glycerol (5 mg/ kg) and lineoyl glycerol (10 mg/kg); these were added to the injection of 2-AG (1 mg/kg). LPA = lysophosphatidic acid (18:1, n-9, 20 mg/kg). All compounds were injected sc in the neck or flank in volumes of 10 µl/g.

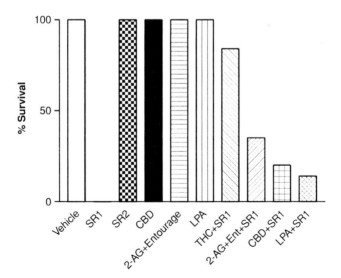

dams spent significantly more time "licking" and nursing the antagonist-treated pups (Fride et al. 2001a). Rather, the CB_1 receptor blockade on day 1 of life disables the ability of the newborns to initiate milk suckling, as their stomachs were empty of milk (Fride et al. 2001a).

More recent evidence for the role of CB_1 receptors in milk suckling is derived from CB_1 receptor-deficient ($CB_1^{-/-}$ knockout) mice, where it was observed that the CB_1 receptor antagonist had significantly less severe effects on the $CB_1^{-/-}$ pups, as compared to the effects on wild type mice (Fride et al., in preparation).

Lysophosphatidic acid (LPA) is a multifunctional lipid mediator with growth factor-like properties. LPA occurs in brain in considerable concentrations and is structurally similar to the endocannabinoid 2-AG. The LPA and CB_1 receptors display substantial (30%) homology. LPA, with 2-arachidonic acid as the acyl moiety, differs only by the absence of a phosphate group from 2-AG while a related lysophosphatidic acid (with 1-arachidonic acid as the acyl moiety) has been detected in rat brain (Sugiura et al. 1999). A defective suckling response was reported in neonatal mice that have a targeted deletion of the gene for the LPA receptor (lp_{A1}) (Contos et al. 2000). Our group therefore investigated the possibility that LPA and 2-AG may interact at their receptors. If the inhibition of milk ingestion in our experiments were due to an interaction of the CB_1 antagonist at the LPA receptor, or alternatively, if LPA interacts with the CB_1 receptor, then co-application of LPA with SR141716A on newborn pups should reverse the antagonist inhibition of pup development. This was not the case in our experiments. Thus, when LPA was co-injected with SR141716A, only a temporary delay in mortality, with borderline significance ($p = 0.09$), was observed (Fride, Rosenberg, and Mechoulam 2001b). Moreover, LPA did not bind to CB_1 receptors (Hanus and Fride, unpublished observations). Since the LPA employed contained oleic acid as the acyl moiety, and not arachidonic acid (which can not be obtained commercially), further investigation of the interaction between the LPA and CB_1 receptor systems is warranted.

Several neuroactive substances have been implicated in milk suckling. For example, Smotherman and colleagues (Petrov, Varlinskaya, and Smotherman 1998) have demonstrated an inhibition of several components of the suckling response after injection of naloxone into the cerebral ventricles of rat pups. When effects of intracisternal injections of a specific μ opiate receptor antagonist on weight gain were recorded, only a slight, transient reduction was seen; similar injections into the cerebral ventricles did not have any effect on body weight (Petrov et al. 1998).

Taken together, our studies argue for a critical role for CB_1 receptor activation in milk suckling in the newborn, presumably by 2-AG produced by the neonatal brain. As far as is known, the endocannabinoid-CB_1 receptor system is the first neural system discovered thus far that seems to display complete control over milk ingestion and neonatal survival.

CONCLUSIONS

Our data have indicated that the CB_1 receptor antagonist had to be injected within 24 hr after birth of mouse pups in order to produce a virtual 100% mortality effect (injection on day 2 resulted in less than 50% mortality). It is proposed that without CB_1 receptor activation by 2-AG (or another as yet undefined endocannabinoid) within the first 24 hr of life, the first suckling episode is not initiated. As the pups have not suckled yet, the source of this 2-AG must be the pup's brain, and not maternal milk. This is compatible with the surge of 2-AG and CB_1 receptor mRNA in the 1-day old rat brain (Berrendero et al. 1999; Fernandez-Ruiz et al. 2000). The lower levels of 2-AG and CB_1 receptors present from day 2 onward are apparently too low, or too late, to allow the suckling response to be initiated on subsequent days.

These observations further suggest that the enhancement in appetite and food intake induced by cannabinoids in the adult organism may only be the tip of the iceberg of the vital role for the cannabinoid system in milk suckling immediately after birth (Fride et al. 2001a). The comparatively more partial control of the endocannabinoid system of appetite and food intake by the mature organism should not diminish our efforts to develop cannabis-based medicines for appetite stimulation in conditions involving cachexia. Rather, it does suggest that treatment of children suffering such conditions may benefit at least as much as adults from cannabinoids to combat anorexia (Fride 2002b). Further, treating infants suffering from a failure to thrive with cannabinoid-derived medicines deserves future research.

REFERENCES

Abel, E.L. 1971. Effects of marihuana on the solution of anagrams, memory and appetite. *Nature* 231(5300):260-1.

Arnone, M., J. Maruani, F. Chaperon, M.H. Thiebot, M. Poncelet, P. Soubrie, and G. Le Fur. 1997. Selective inhibition of sucrose and ethanol intake by SR 141716, an antagonist of central cannabinoid (CB_1) receptors. *Psychopharmacology (Berl)* 132(1):104-6.

Beal, J.E., R. Olson, L. Lefkowitz, L. Laubenstein, P. Bellman, B. Yangco, J.O. Morales, R. Murphy, W. Powderly, T.F. Plasse, K.W. Mosdell, and K.V. Shepard. 1997. Long-term efficacy and safety of dronabinol for acquired immunodeficiency syndrome-associated anorexia. *J Pain Symptom Manage* 14(1):7-14.

Belue, R.C., A.C. Howlett, T.M. Westlake, and D.E. Hutchings. 1995. The ontogeny of cannabinoid receptors in the brain of postnatal and aging rats. *Neurotoxicol Teratol* 17(1):25-30.

Bennett, W.A., and S.S. Bennett. 1999. Marihuana for AIDS wasting. In *Marihuana and Medicine*, edited by G.G. Nahas, K.M. Sutin, D. Harvey, and S. Agurell. Totowa, NJ: Humana Press.

Ben-Shabat, S., E. Fride, T. Sheskin, T. Tamiri, M.H. Rhee, Z. Vogel, T. Bisogno, L. De Petrocellis, V. Di Marzo, and R. Mechoulam. 1998. An entourage effect: Inactive endogenous fatty acid glycerol esters enhance 2-arachidonoyl-glycerol cannabinoid activity. *Eur J Pharmacol* 353(1):23-31.

Berrendero, F., N. Sepe, J.A. Ramos, V. Di Marzo, and J.J. Fernandez-Ruiz. 1999. Analysis of cannabinoid receptor binding and mRNA expression and endogenous cannabinoid contents in the developing rat brain during late gestation and early postnatal period. *Synapse* 33(3):181-91.

Buckley, N.E., S. Hansson, G. Harta, and E. Mezey. 1998. Expression of the CB_1 and CB_2 receptor messenger RNAs during embryonic development in the rat. *Neuroscience* 82(4):1131-49.

Colombo, G., R. Agabio, G. Diaz, C. Lobina, R. Reali, and G. L. Gessa. 1998. Appetite suppression and weight loss after the cannabinoid antagonist SR 141716. *Life Sci* 63(8):L113-7.

Contos, J.J., N. Fukushima, J.A. Weiner, D. Kaushal, and J. Chun. 2000. Requirement for the lpA1 lysophosphatidic acid receptor gene in normal suckling behavior. *Proc Natl Acad Sci USA* 97(24):13384-9.

De Petrocellis, L., D. Melck, T. Bisogno, A. Milone, and V. Di Marzo. 1999. Finding of the endocannabinoid signalling system in Hydra, a very primitive organism: possible role in the feeding response. *Neuroscience* 92(1):377-87.

Di Marzo, V., S.K. Goparaju, L. Wang, J. Liu, S. Batkai, Z. Jarai, F. Fezza, G.I. Miura, R.D. Palmiter, T. Sugiura, and G. Kunos. 2001. Leptin-regulated endocannabinoids are involved in maintaining food intake. *Nature* 410(6830):822-5.

Di Marzo, V., N. Sepe, L. De Petrocellis, A. Berger, G. Crozier, E. Fride, and R. Mechoulam. 1998. Trick or treat from food endocannabinoids? *Nature* 396(6712): 636-7.

di Tomaso, E., M. Beltramo, and D. Piomelli. 1996. Brain cannabinoids in chocolate. *Nature* 382(6593):677-8.

Fernandez-Ruiz, J., F. Berrendero, M.L. Hernandez, and J.A. Ramos. 2000. The endogenous cannabinoid system and brain development. *Trends Neurosci* 23(1):14-20.

Foltin, R.W., J.V. Brady, and M.W. Fischman. 1986. Behavioral analysis of marijuana effects on food intake in humans. *Pharmacol Biochem Behav* 25(3):577-82.

Freedland, C.S., J.S. Poston, and L.J. Porrino. 2000. Effects of SR141716A, a central cannabinoid receptor antagonist, on food-maintained responding. *Pharmacol Biochem Behav* 67(2):265-70.

Fride, E. 2002a. Endocannabinoids in the central nervous system–an overview. *Prostaglandins, Leukotrienes and Essential Fatty Acids* in press.

Fride, E. 2002b. Cannabinoids and cystic fibrosis: A novel approach to etiology and therapy. *J Cannabis Therapeutics* 2(1): 59-71

Fride, E., Y. Ginzburg, A. Breuer, T. Bisogno, V. Di Marzo, and R. Mechoulam. 2001a. Critical role of the endogenous cannabinoid system in mouse pup suckling and growth. *Eur J Pharmacol* 419(2-3):207-14.

Fride, E., E. Rosenberg, and R. Mechoulam. 2001b. Role of endocannabinoids in newborn food intake and development: interaction with lysophopspatidic acid? *2001 Symposium on the Cannabinoids, Burlington, Vermont, International Cannabinoid Research Society 2001*:100.

Friedman, J.M. 2000. Obesity in the new millennium. *Nature* 404(6778):632-4.

Hao, S., Y. Avraham, R. Mechoulam, and E.M. Berry. 2000. Low dose anandamide affects food intake, cognitive function, neurotransmitter and corticosterone levels in diet-restricted mice. *Eur J Pharmacol* 392(3):147-56.

Herkenham, M., A.B. Lynn, M.R. Johnson, L.S. Melvin, B.R. de Costa, and K.C. Rice. 1991. Characterization and localization of cannabinoid receptors in rat brain: a quantitative in vitro autoradiographic study. *J Neurosci* 11(2):563-83.

Koch, J.E., and S.M. Matthews. 2001. Delta9-tetrahydrocannabinol stimulates palatable food intake in Lewis rats: effects of peripheral and central administration. *Nutr Neurosci* 4(3):179-87.

Mailleux, P., and J.J. Vanderhaeghen. 1992. Distribution of neuronal cannabinoid receptor in the adult rat brain: a comparative receptor binding radioautography and in situ hybridization histochemistry. *Neuroscience* 48(3):655-68.

Mattes, R.D., K. Engelman, L.M. Shaw, and M.A. Elsohly. 1994. Cannabinoids and appetite stimulation. *Pharmacol Biochem Behav* 49(1):187-95.

Mattes, R.D., L.M. Shaw, and K. Engelman. 1994. Effects of cannabinoids (marijuana) on taste intensity and hedonic ratings and salivary flow of adults. *Chem Senses* 19(2):125-40.

McLaughlin, C.R., and M.E. Abood. 1993. Developmental expression of cannabinoid receptor mRNA. *Brain Res Dev Brain Res* 76(1):75-8.

Mechoulam, R., and E. Fride. 2001. Physiology. A hunger for cannabinoids. *Nature* 410(6830):763, 765.

Mechoulam, R., L. Hanus, and E. Fride. 1998. Towards cannabinoid drugs–revisited. *Prog Med Chem* 35:199-243.

Petrov, E.S., E.I. Varlinskaya, L.A. Becker, and W.P. Smotherman. 1998. Endogenous mu opioid systems and suckling in the neonatal rat. *Physiol Behav* 65(3):591-9.

Petrov, E.S., E.I. Varlinskaya, and W.P. Smotherman. 1998. Endogenous opioids and the first suckling episode in the rat. *Dev Psychobiol* 33(2):175-83.

Plasse, T.F., R.W. Gorter, S.H. Krasnow, M. Lane, K.V. Shepard, and R.G. Wadleigh. 1991. Recent clinical experience with dronabinol. *Pharmacol Biochem Behav* 40(3):695-700.

Rodriguez de Fonseca, F., J.A. Ramos, A. Bonnin, and J.J. Fernandez-Ruiz. 1993. Presence of cannabinoid binding sites in the brain from early postnatal ages. *Neuroreport* 4(2):135-8.

Romero, J., E. Garcia-Palomero, F. Berrendero, L. Garcia-Gil, M.L. Hernandez, J.A. Ramos, and J.J. Fernandez-Ruiz. 1997. Atypical location of cannabinoid receptors in white matter areas during rat brain development. *Synapse* 26(3):317-23.

Schwartz, M.W., S.C. Woods, D. Porte, Jr., R.J. Seeley, and D.G. Baskin. 2000. Central nervous system control of food intake. *Nature* 404(6778):661-71.

Sugiura, T., S. Nakane, S. Kishimoto, K. Waku, Y. Yoshioka, A. Tokumura, and D.J. Hanahan. 1999. Occurrence of lysophosphatidic acid and its alkyl ether-linked analog in rat brain and comparison of their biological activities toward cultured neural cells. *Biochim Biophys Acta* 1440(2-3):194-204.

Sulcova, E., R. Mechoulam, and E. Fride. 1998. Biphasic effects of anandamide. *Pharmacol Biochem Behav* 59(2):347-52.

Timpone, J.G., D.J. Wright, N. Li, M.J. Egorin, M.E. Enama, J. Mayers, and G. Galetto. 1999. The safety and pharmacokinetics of single-agent and combination therapy with megestrol acetate and dronabinol for the treatment of HIV wasting syndrome. In *Marihuana and Medicine*, edited by G.G. Nahas, K.M. Sutin, D. Harvey, and S. Agurell. Totowa, NJ: Humana Press.

Whittle, B.A., G.W. Guy, and P. Robson. 2001. Prospects for new cannabis-based prescription medicines. *J Cannabis Therapeutics* 1(3-4): 183-205.

Williams, C.M., and T.C. Kirkham. 2002. Reversal of delta 9-THC hyperphagia by SR141716 and naloxone but not dexfenfluramine. *Pharmacol Biochem Behav* 71(1-2):333-40.

Williams, C.M., P.J. Rogers, and T.C. Kirkham. 1998. Hyperphagia in pre-fed rats following oral delta9-THC. *Physiol Behav* 65(2):343-6.

Hyperemesis Gravidarum
and Clinical Cannabis:
To Eat or Not to Eat?

Wei-Ni Lin Curry

SUMMARY. Hyperemesis gravidarum (HG), a debilitating ailment characterized by severe nausea and vomiting, malnutrition, and weight loss during pregnancy, occurs to 1-2% of pregnant women globally. Although the medical community offers clinical and pharmaceutical intervention, the procedures are: (1) partially effective, if at all, (2) costly and unaffordable without health insurance, (3) questionable in their long-term safety for the fetus, as most have not been scientifically tested, and (4) in more severe cases, physically painful and psychologically disempowering for the pregnant woman. This study unveils the deep suffering endured by women undergoing HG from a folkloristic perspective and proposes the use of medical cannabis as an effective natural remedy for the symptoms of HG. Due to the criminalization of cannabis and the stigma of its use during pregnancy, no formalized testing has been conducted, thus far, to investigate such a claim. While a small, underground, pilot study of cannabis treatment for HG has proven relatively promising, clinical trials are necessary for a more conclusive answer. *[Article copies available for a fee from The Haworth Document Delivery Service: 1-800-HAWORTH. E-mail address: <getinfo@haworthpressinc.com> Website: <http://www.HaworthPress.com> © 2002 by The Haworth Press, Inc. All rights reserved.]*

Wei-Ni Lin Curry, MA, is a PhD student at UCLA and is affiliated with the UCLA/Folklore Program and Archives, 1075 Public Policy Building, Box 951459, Los Angeles, CA 90095-1459 (E-mail: wcurry@ucla.edu).

[Haworth co-indexing entry note]: "Hyperemesis Gravidarum and Clinical Cannabis: To Eat or Not to Eat?" Curry, Wei-Ni Lin. Co-published simultaneously in *Journal of Cannabis Therapeutics* (The Haworth Integrative Healing Press, an imprint of The Haworth Press, Inc.) Vol. 2, No. 3/4, 2002, pp. 63-83; and: *Women and Cannabis: Medicine, Science, and Sociology* (ed: Ethan Russo, Melanie Dreher, and Mary Lynn Mathre) The Haworth Integrative Healing Press, an imprint of The Haworth Press, Inc., 2002, pp. 63-83. Single or multiple copies of this article are available for a fee from The Haworth Document Delivery Service [1-800-HAWORTH, 9:00 a.m. - 5:00 p.m. (EST). E-mail address: getinfo@haworthpressinc.com].

KEYWORDS. Hyperemesis gravidarum, HG, nausea and vomiting during pregnancy, morning sickness, cannabis, marijuana, medical marijuana, malnutrition and weight loss, anorexia, herbal treatment, antiemetics, pregnancy and health, women's health, self-help, holistic health, natural childbirth, midwifery, fetal health, fetal rights

The ideal pregnant woman radiates the image of a full-fleshed, well-nourished femininity whose presence glows of maternal well-being and ripeness. She is commonly encouraged by her family and friends to eat in increased proportions because the accepted consensus is that she is "eating for two." Her circle of loved ones will often assist her in fulfilling her food cravings. It matters not that she fancies strange foods, demands unappealing concoctions, or eats during the most unpredictable and indiscriminate times of the day (Murcott 1988). What matters is that she eats well. However, what happens when she is *unable* to eat for two? What happens when she *cannot eat for even one?*

While such a debilitating illness does not often occur, it happens to pregnant women who suffer from a disease known as *hyperemesis gravidarum* (HG) (Erick 1997; Van de Ven 1997). HG to a pregnant woman is similar to the wasting syndrome of an AIDS sufferer or a cancer chemotherapy patient whose body becomes severely emaciated, dehydrated, and malnourished due to persistent, uncontrollable vomiting and the inability to eat and drink (Grinspoon 1997). A striking difference, however, is that the survivor of HG carries the added responsibility of sustaining another life within her womb. While she perishes from hunger, her baby *in utero* continues to absorb any remains of stored fat, muscle tissue and nutrients from her body in order to survive. Compared to the weight loss endured by those undergoing AIDS or cancer chemotherapy, the HG woman's shedding of pounds is deceptively unsparing as her baby's continual growth and weight-gain disguises the actual body mass she is really losing. In essence, a pregnant woman with hyperemesis does not come anywhere near *eating for two*; she is more accurately *starving for two.*

HG, ITS MEDICALIZATION, AND THE SURVIVORS

Hyperemesis gravidarum is conservatively defined in *The Harvard Guide to Women's Health* (1996) as a debilitating condition of severe nausea and vomiting during pregnancy, resulting in malnutrition, dehydration, and weight loss. While women experience various degrees of HG, the prolonged retching and starvation often trigger the onset of other physically disabling ailments such as, but not limited to, partial paralysis, failed muscle coordination, ruptured esophagus, bloody emesis and/or stool, hemorrhage of the retina, inflamed pancreas, and/or wasting of muscle tissue. In rare cases, HG has also been associated with coma, temporary blindness, and even death (Hillborn et al. 1999; Tesfaye et al. 1998).

The following personal anecdotes of real women bring into perspective the devastation and symptoms of starvation caused by HG: "Sarah" stated, ". . . I lost a total of 30 pounds and I was skinny to begin with. I was a walking skeletal with a belly. I looked like death and smelled like poison." "Sofia" said, "With my son [first pregnancy], I just got very ill from the point the sperm met the egg. I lost 30 pounds within the first 2 months, and I stayed in bed the whole 9 months, only getting up to use the restroom." She also observed, "[second pregnancy] I was throwing up first the acid in my stomach, which is yellow, then it's orange because it's the outer layer, and then you get to the green bile which is [from] your intestines. Then once you're past that, you go straight blood."

With her first pregnancy, Sofia was at least able to swallow and digest one burrito as her entire weekly sustenance. By her second pregnancy, however, food was definitely not an option. Sofia explains:

> I knew within one week of the conception that I was pregnant. Immediately vomiting and loss of appetite. *I couldn't swallow my own spit* for the first five months of my pregnancy . . . Within the first two weeks of my pregnancy, [I was hospitalized] twice. I would have five days that I could survive at home, then I would get so dehydrated that I'd have to go to the hospital to the ER so that I could get hydrated. I'd stay in the hospital one to two days. They'd get me fully hydrated, and then they'd send me home.

Also, Sofia's attempt at the traditional folk-remedy of soda and crackers resulted in vomiting: "The doctors thought that it was all in my head–thought that I was *bulimic*." The doctors intravenously injected units of fluid into her body in an attempt to increase her caloric intake. She grimaces: "They were feeding me lard. It *smelled* like lard. It *smelled* like grease."

One who physically experiences the starvation and nausea of hyperemesis gravidarum will often encounter psychological and emotional distress. The hormonal changes and mood fluctuations that are often associated with a normal pregnancy inevitably become more severe with the onset of HG (Simpson et al. 2001). In struggling to bear her child, the HG mother must also brace herself through such symptoms as depression, unnatural fatigue, amnesia, apathy, distorted body image, fear, and/or guilt (Erick 1997; Hillborn et al. 1999; Tesfaye et al. 1998). Some even contemplate suicide, as each living moment is excruciatingly taxing and painful:

> *I wanted to die every waking hour.* I thought I was in hell. Doctors told me that I was trying to orally vomit my baby out, that the pregnancy was

not wanted. They sent me to psychiatrists claiming that all this was "in my head." Nobody understood me. My husband even left me. I was all alone with my tortured body, praying to God to give me strength to go on. (Sarah)

I . . . just wanted to die every minute that I was awake. I still consider it a miracle that I and (more importantly) my two healthy children survived. I was *depressed* throughout the pregnancies as well as from not being able to take care of my two-and-a-half year old when I was pregnant with the second. I shudder when I think about it . . . (Julia)

I'd cry every night . . . I feel that I'm a very strong individual, but this was no time to be strong. I'd cry every night, telling my husband how it hurt so bad. (Sofia)

A substantial number of HG survivors are also left with no choice but to cease employment and, if needed, temporarily relinquish the custody of their children to a more capable caregiver, such as a relative or a friend. Sofia solemnly recalls that when she was pregnant with her second child, she had to drop out of college where she was a student; she also had to give her mother legal guardianship of her seven-year-old son for the entire pregnancy, "Because I couldn't even cook or clean my own body, I couldn't do it to my own child. *And I wouldn't want him to be subjected to see me the way that I was.*"

Sadly enough, physical disability and the continual and frequent visits to the hospital for vital replenishment often isolate the HG woman from the warmth and comfort of her family and home during a time when she needs support the most.

While general nausea and vomiting, better known as morning sickness, is experienced by 70% to 80% of all pregnancies, only 1-2% is affected by the pernicious emesis and distress associated with hyperemesis gravidarum. Of this HG populace, 5% endure the debilitating symptoms for the entire nine-month period of their infant's gestation (Van de Ven 1997). Statistics taken in 1993 reveal that within one year, 42,000 women in the United States sought the help of a health care professional in an effort to counteract their symptoms of HG. In Britain, a study also shows that two of every one hundred HG mothers will opt for abortion, most likely, as a last resort to terminate their unbearable suffering and not the lives of their often much wanted unborn babies (Erick 1997). Sarah, who aborted against her will, grieves:

Two weeks ago, I terminated my very much wanted pregnancy because of hyperemesis gravidarum. This disease is so disgusting and nightmarish, I don't know how I was able to do it the first time around. *I regret the abortion* but I just have to think about HG and remember the ordeal I went through and don't want to go through again . . . Before my abortion, I was prescribed Diclectin® [a Canadian combination of vitamin B_6 and the antihistamine, doxylamine], four doses a day. It didn't help. I just wish there was a cure for this disease because *I want my baby back!*

Sofia chose not to abort, even at the strong recommendation of medical professionals and loved ones:

[When] I was five months three weeks pregnant sitting in the UCSD Medical Center for the umpteenth time, I had the chief of staff, my personal ob/gyn was a chief resident, and three other specialists–whether they be the gastro-intestinal specialist and a couple of other ones–there'd be around six or seven other specialists standing around my bed. They all came to the conclusion that I needed to abort . . . I just told them I've survived five months and three weeks, why couldn't I survive two more months?

Other women adamantly refuse to consider abortion on grounds of their moral paradigm.

While many women and infants throughout history have died due to HG, prenatal mothers in industrialized, metropolitan areas are usually spared such a fatal outcome with the assistance of approved medical modalities. Western physicians prescribe anti-emetic pharmaceutical drugs, such as metaclopramide (Reglan®), prochlorperazine (Compazine®), promethazine (Phenergan®), and ondansetron (Zofran®), to help mothers keep their nausea at bay and nourish themselves and their fetuses. The drugs, which are also commonly given to AIDS and cancer chemotherapy patients, are taken orally, intravenously, or as rectal suppositories. While the long-term risks to the human child *in utero* remains unknown, the general consensus from the medical establishment is that the risks to the mother and fetus of severe morning sickness warrant possible risks of using these drugs during pregnancy (Carlson et al. 1996). At the very least, the babies who have ingested these medications via the placenta have been born comparatively healthy; none have emerged from the womb with birth defects, as did the infant casualties of thalidomide, the pharmaceutical drug given to mothers in the 1950s to alleviate indications of morning sickness and HG.

Nevertheless, the drugs are not fail proof. According to the Summary of Data on Hyperemesis Gravidarum (Schoenberg 2000), some of the most common antiemetic medications and the safety ratings that were assigned to them by the Food and Drug Administration (FDA) are listed as follows: ten drugs (scopolamine, promethazine, prochlorperazine, chlorpromazine, trimethobenzamide, cisapride, droperidol, coricosteroids, ondansetron, and hydoxyzine) received the rating of C, six drugs (doxylamine, diphenhydramine, cyclizine, meclizine, dimenhydrinate, and metaclopramide) received the rating of B, and one drug (pyridoxine, vitamin B6) received the rating of A. A C-rating means "animal studies show risk but human studies are lacking, or there are no studies in humans or animals." A B-rating means "animal studies show no risk but human studies are inadequate, or animal studies show some risk but the risk is not supported by human studies." An A-rating signifies "no fetal risk" (Schoenberg 2000). Apparently, all the drugs listed, with the exception of one, a vitamin, are questionable in their safety, posing a potential threat to the fetus. Unsurprisingly, these pharmaceutical drugs threaten the mother, if not the baby, with many side effects and harmful allergic reactions. Sofia recounts her experience with the anti-emetic drugs–prochloperazine, metaclopramide, and promethazine, before she had to suspend her student status at her university due to HG:

> Well, the second week [of pregnancy] I was taking all three [medications]. I was sitting in lecture hall, and my body began to convulse. And literally, like an *epileptic seizure*, my tongue was upside down, my back was out of whack, [and I] couldn't control my legs or my arms. My husband conveniently was visiting me that day, and was in lecture hall with me. He had to pick me up and take me to the ER.

From that point onward, Sofia was unable to take any medications for her nausea and vomiting. It was not until she was in her sixth month of pregnancy that she was given another, ondansetron. She was discouraged from taking the drug any earlier because the doctors were uncertain of the possible side effects. Another fellow-student and HG survivor, Nora, has also professed to me that if she ever became pregnant again, she would not want to take any medications because they made her feel "drugged out" and "like a zombie" all day.

Because the modern anti-emetic medications have not succeeded in eliminating all symptoms of vomiting and nausea, and fail to stimulate the woman's appetite, mothers with hyperemesis continue to struggle with eating and maintaining (if not gaining) weight. Hence, within the framework of modern medicine, a crucial part of the women's survival relies on intake of liquid nutrition through tubes: intravenously, nasogastrically, or enterally, and often without the use of anesthesia. In certain situations, a gastrostomy tube is required for the purpose of drainage and decompression. Some may suffer from what Sofia calls a "collapsed digestive system." She noted, "[The doctors] were worried that all my organs were going to shut down, because I wasn't using them. I . . . [was having] *bowel movements maybe once every two months . . . I had no food. I had no intake.* I just didn't need to go."

To this day, six years after the birth of her daughter, Sofia is unable to digest a regular meal; unless she divides a single portion into two or three smaller servings, and unless she avoids anything too meaty, greasy, or rich, she will vomit shortly after consuming the food.

Sofia also braved the tortures of having intravenous tubes continually inserted and re-inserted into her body due to life-threatening blood clots that periodically developed as a result of being fed liquid nutrition. Sofia said that even though the nurses were administering heparin through her IV to achieve anticoagulation, the blood clots continued to recur. She recounts:

> I was around seven months pregnant when that one [about the eighth tube inserted] went bad with a blood clot close to my neck. [The doctors] immediately said, *"We need to take it out."* But they didn't know what they had done inside. There were *roots* growing all along, all around the tubes inside of my chest because all the scar tissue that had formed. And the doctor, when he was taking it out, was literally *pulling* it–mind you, I had NO ANESTHESIA, and I was in PAIN!

At this point, I could not resist interrupting her to make sure I was hearing correctly, asking: "So he basically *tore your flesh?*"

> *YES.* And when it didn't come out, he had to stick scalpels in through these bottom holes, and try to tear away the scar tissue underneath. Yeah. And my husband had to sit there and tell me everything is *"okay–don't worry, it doesn't look that bad."* But after the fact, he was like, *"I was just trying to give you moral support. That ASSHOLE was tearing you apart and I was watching every minute of it."*

Sofia emphasizes that throughout her pregnancy she had "really bad scabs everywhere." She said she looked like a *"druggy."* Just the one surgical procedure left an open, gaping wound "about the size of a quarter" above her chest for nearly a month. Unfortunately, these scars will remain with her for the rest of her life, physically and emotionally.

Sofia is one of many women whose flesh and blood are sacrificed at the price of HG medical treatments. Another hyperemesis sufferer ("Mary") is highlighted in a dietician's case study that explains the woman's struggles with receiving liquid nutrition throughout her pregnancy (Erick 1997). I have paraphrased the case. When Mary was first admitted to the hospital, she was severely malnourished and dehydrated due to HG. The hospital began medical treatments by administering an IV feeding tube for her, but it was unsuccessful due to continued malnutrition. A nasogastric tube followed. Mary vomited three of the tubes in a two-day period, so she refused further replacements. The doctors then tried a different route via a jejunostomy and gastrostomy tube, one for feeding and the other for drainage. This method remained until the time of her delivery. However, for the entire pregnancy, Mary continued to vomit in spite of anti-emesis medications. The smell of the liquid formula used for her enteral feedings also increased her nausea. Mary also continued suffering from insomnia, pancreatitis, increased bloating, abdominal pain, chest pain, thick phlegm, depression, and a distorted body image. Her partner was said to have shown disgust with the presence of the tubes sticking out of her body. Finally, she *threatened suicide* if she was not delivered immediately. A cesarean operation was performed before the expected date of delivery, as well as a permanent sterilization, done at her request. The baby was born relatively healthy at 6.45 pounds.

The story of Mary's struggles to feed herself and her baby through the devastating symptoms of HG cries for empathy and compassion. Though her doctors were most likely sincere in their intentions to keep her sickness under control, and though they succeeded in saving the life of the infant, I wonder if they realize how truly horrific their treatments really were? To what extent did they help Mary and to what extent did they hurt her, physically and psychologically? How much did they contribute to her experience of a healthy and dignified pregnancy, one that every woman deserves? Alternatives are in dire need.

Because many HG patients have shown that their nausea and vomiting are "linked to the consumption of food," the administration of liquid nutrition via feeding tubes is justified by doctors; it is argued that in sparing HG women from the physical act of smelling, masticating, and swallowing their meals, their nausea and vomiting will decrease (Van de Ven 1997). Unfortunately, in the case of both Sofia and Mary, their vomiting was triggered by the smell of the liquid formula.

The causes of hyperemesis have provoked heated speculation, but no substantial evidence has been discovered or acknowledged within the Western medical hegemony. Some scientists hypothesize the following as factors that often lead to and/or are connected to HG: hormones, increased estrogen level, nutrition, thiamine deficiency, psychological factors (Simpson et al. 2001) and the sex of the child, higher concentration of human chorionic gonadotropin level associated with a female fetus (Askling 1999; Panesar et al. 2001). As none of the factors offer a satisfactory answer, HG remains a perplexing female mystery for the present-day medical establishment. The frustration is mostly felt by women who are survivors of HG, desperately searching for a cure and increased understanding of this harrowing disease:

> I have suffered through two pregnancies with this debilitating condition . . . In both pregnancies, it started at six weeks and continued until the baby was born. I was induced early both times because I was so sick. I

tried everything: hypnosis, homeopathic treatment, acupuncture, sea sick bands, IVs, smelling ginger and lemons, Compazine®, Reglan®, Phenergan®, Atavan®, Unisom®, Zofran® (to name a few). Nothing worked. I threw up constantly, including a lot of bile and dry heaving, could barely walk and just *wanted to die every minute* . . . It is extremely frustrating how little research and ideas exist on the topic, and I feel quite confident that if men could experience the condition, there would be a remedy for it. (Julia)

The medical establishment must begin to realize that even though the HG woman is unable to eat, the only thing she really wants *is* to eat.

The HG sufferer is not simply a lifeless, unfeeling, docile body (Foucault 1995) that robotically pumps vitamins and minerals into her growing child. She is a human being who needs to eat to live. Her ability to savor her meal, to salivate, to masticate, to swallow, to digest, is a primal and essential part of her existence. The woman with hyperemesis needs more than feeding tubes and synthetic liquid nutrition. She craves and requires real food, just like her baby needs a mother, and not a machine.

CANNABIS, PREGNANCY, AND HG

I, too, am a survivor of hyperemesis gravidarum. While I suffered through severe morning sickness my first pregnancy, it was not until my second pregnancy that I experienced the merciless symptoms of life-threatening HG. Within two weeks of my daughter's conception, I became desperately nauseated and vomited throughout the day and night. Every time I attempted to eat or drink *anything*, even water, I would immediately throw it up. Because nothing would stay in my stomach, I lost twenty-one pounds within the first two weeks of hyperemesis, which was over 20% of my normal body weight at the time (105 pounds). I vomited bile of every shade, and soon began retching up blood. I was also bleeding out of my vagina due to the pressures from vomiting, and owing to the fact that my vulva was still weak from two surgeries to remove cervical cancer after my first pregnancy.

I felt so helpless and distraught that I went to the abortion clinic twice, but both times I left without going through with the procedure. My partner and my three-year-old son feared for my life. My son would often ask me, with tears streaming down his face: "Mommy, are you going to die?" Each time, I reassured him that mommy would be okay soon, but he was not convinced. Could I blame him? I felt as if my whole world was falling apart, and that the ones I loved most were being dragged down with me. I tried desperately to function as usual, to work, cook, clean, care for my son, but all of my usual duties had to be sacrificed as I spent my entire day retching into the toilet, where I would often pass out because I had no energy to walk to and from the bathroom.

When I went to an obstetrician in search of help, the options he gave me were the usual: hospitalization, intravenous feedings, and anti-emesis pharmaceutical drugs that had unknown long-term side effects with the potential of affecting my child negatively. Instead, I tried ginger, raspberry tea, soda and crackers, acupressure, meditation, all the recommended home remedies, but nothing worked. Finally, I decided to try medical cannabis. The medical cannabis initiative, The Compassionate Use Act of 1996, which had been passed by the voters of California, permits the legal use of cannabis for the severely ill. If cannabis had been so effective in alleviating the nausea and vomiting for AIDS and cancer chemotherapy patients, then why would it not work for pregnant HG patients? I asked a Harvard physician, Lester Grinspoon, who had been studying the therapeutic properties of cannabis for the past thirty-some years. He said that other women throughout history and in modern times have used cannabis for HG and experienced positive results. With his reassurance, I felt more confident in attempting to remedy my sickness with the herb.

Because I had never smoked before, I first had to learn to take the medicine, but that was a welcome task, seeing that the herb worked wonders. Just one to two little puffs at night, and if needed in the morning, resulted in an entire day of wellness. I went from not eating, not drinking, not functioning, and continually vomiting and bleeding from two orifices to being completely cured. The only HG symptom that persisted was my acute sense of smell, which in the absence of nausea and vomiting was tolerable. Not only did I eat and drink, I consumed food with a hearty and open appetite.

The cannabis worked so miraculously that at first I thought my mind was playing tricks on me, as if I was being deceived by some placebo effect. In order to test, I stopped taking the cannabis three times, and each time the uncontrollable and violent retching returned. Finally, my son, who was three years old at the time, begged me: "Mommy, *please* go take your medicine!" That was when I knew that cannabis is truly an efficacious medicine, and that yes, I could look forward to enjoying a well-nourished and dignified pregnancy.

Not only did the cannabis save my son from not having a mother during the duration of my hyperemesis, it saved the life of my child within my womb. Every day, I am grateful for her bright and vivacious existence. Developmentally, she has proven to be very advanced for her age. She began walking at eight-and-a-half months (norm eleven to thirteen months), and she began expressing herself quite articulately at a year-and-a-half. Her teachers at her children center frequently comment on her maturity and the advancement of her motor, social, and cognitive abilities. I was told by one of her teachers that the university pediatricians who frequent the school to conduct research in child development were also highly impressed by her accelerated abilities. So for my situation, it is safe for me to conclude that my choice to use cannabis as a therapeutic "folk" remedy for my HG symptoms was a positive and beneficial decision with healthful and quite amazing results for my daughter.

And no, I am *not* a "drug addict" as the stigma dictates. As soon as my symptoms of HG passed, I no longer needed to use the cannabis. My Taiwanese medical obstetrician who helped deliver my daughter informed me that since ancient times the Chinese have used cannabis to treat HG, and the smoke that is inhaled does not go to the fetus, but rather directly to the brain of the mother to help counteract her nausea and stimulate her appetite. Studies also confirm that "only relatively small amounts" of the psychoactive cannabinoid ingredient-delta-9-THC "actually cross the placenta barrier to the fetus" (Dreher 1997, p. 160). While medication in the form of pills is easily vomited by one who is susceptible to nausea, smoking/inhaling in this situation is actually a preferred route of administration. The HG mom more accurately and readily gauges the dosage of each treatment according to how she feels each time, unlike pills and suppositories that often leave one feeling "knocked-out" all day. As a result, I am in disbelief at how our government has kept such a valuable medicine from so many ailing women. If I had not experienced the cannabis myself, I would not have believed its truly effective and gentle therapeutic powers.

While I am not one to condone the use of illicit drugs during pregnancy, I strongly believe that in the case of women suffering from HG, an exception must be made in regards to the use of cannabis. In *Mothers and Illicit Drug Use: Transcending the Myths,* Susan Boyd (1999, p. 4) states:

> Critical researchers acknowledge that "crime" is a political construct . . . where selective criminalization takes place. In North America the most dangerous drugs are legal. Tobacco and alcohol are more lethal than the more benign drugs, such as marijuana, and both heroin and cocaine. The so-called dangers of illicit drugs are widely depicted by both government and the media. But the real dangers of legal drugs, including alcohol, tobacco, and pharmaceutical, are viewed differently.

She also emphasizes that of all the illicit drugs, cannabis is the most benign (Boyd 1999).

Personally, I did not appreciate my ability to use this herb until I learned of the extreme suffering experienced by other women with HG while at the hands of the well-intentioned medical community. How can one justify the extreme methods discussed previously as being less criminal than condoning women to use an herb that does not harm the fetus but simply offers the HG mother the chance to eat, drink, function normally, and experience the positive pregnancy she deserves?

Do I dare suggest that the medical hegemony and the pharmaceutical companies are suspect for not prioritizing the best interest of the mothers, but rather, their immense profit margins? For instance, while the cost for cannabis treatment, even at expensive street prices, might not exceed $400 for the entire duration of one's HG pregnancy, the medical cost of ondansetron, the anti-emetic pharmaceutical drug commonly used by HG women, is sometimes charged at $600 for each intravenous dose. Hypothetically, even if an HG sufferer took only three doses a day for sixteen weeks (the usual duration of HG, though some experience HG their entire pregnancy), the cost would be more than $200,000 (Grinspoon 1997, p. 42).

When I share my story with others, the reaction is either one of sincere enthusiasm and curiosity or apprehensive disapproval and skepticism. One HG woman, upon hearing of my self-remedy, instantly said, "*No, no, no . . . I wouldn't trust it.* What about the *side effects?* And besides, maybe your symptoms of HG were not as severe, and that's why you were okay without getting hospital treatment."

It is not surprising that my suffering was belittled and my cure denounced. Most view the use of illicit drugs, especially during pregnancy, to be deviant, threatening, and something to avoid at all costs (Boyd 1999). Murphy and Rosenbaum (1999, p. 1) state, "In modern society the use of illegal drugs during pregnancy is commonly defined as the antithesis of responsible behavior and good health. The two statuses, pregnant woman and drug user, simply do not go together."

This stigma, while serving its purposes to discourage careless behavior during pregnancy, is counterproductive in isolated situations that permit the medical use of cannabis by HG sufferers. In the United States and Canada, medical research on cannabis in relation to mothers and their offspring has produced reports that are fear-inducing and negative, often because the pregnant subjects involved use multiple drugs, come from low-income and disadvantaged situations, endure domestic violence, suffer from poor nutrition, and/or have pre-existing psychological disorders (Dreher 1997). However, propaganda and the media often conveniently exclude the latter details, misinforming the public into believing inaccurate and sensationalized perinatal risk factors caused by the side effects of the stigmatized "killer weed." These studies more accurately reveal the results of a dysfunctional lifestyle, and not the actual side effects of cannabis use. They marginalize the herb as a psychoactive, recreational drug rather than a therapeutic agent.

In the book chapter "Cannabis and Pregnancy," Melanie Dreher (1997) writes that much historical and cross-cultural evidence has been uncovered on the therapeutic uses of cannabis during pregnancy, labor, delivery, and nursing. In fact, archeological and written records substantiate that the plant was often used to treat female ailments, such as dysmenorrhea, ease labor, alleviate morning sickness/hyperemesis gravidarum, and/or facilitate childbirth in places such as: Ancient Egypt, Judea, and Assyria (Mathre 1997), ancient China (Grinspoon 1997; Mathre 1997, p. 36), historical Europe (Benet 1975), rural Southeast Asia, specifically Cambodia, Thailand, Laos, and Vietnam (Martin 1975), Jamaica (Dreher 1975), Africa (Du Toit 1980), and colonial and contemporary America (Grinspoon 1997; Mathre 1997; Wright 1862; www. folkmed.ucla.edu). Dreher's anthropological study reconfirms many of the historical and contemporary findings. Conducted in Jamaica amongst Rastafarians who highly esteem cannabis as a sacred herb and therapeutic agent for a wide spectrum of ailments, the researchers in the study were stunned to discover that babies whose mothers used cannabis throughout their pregnancy (whether or not they had the symptoms of nausea and vomiting) were healthier, more advanced, more alert, and less irritable than infants whose mothers did not use cannabis. What the team revealed through time-consuming, labor-intensive research and observation, Jamaican women knew all along, claiming that (Dreher 1997, p. 164):

> smoking and drinking *ganja* [cannabis] was good for the mother and the baby because it relieved the nausea of pregnancy, increased appetite, gave them strength to work, helped them relax and sleep at night, and in general, relieved the "bad feeling" associated with pregnancy.

From personal experience with my own "cannabis baby," I can attest to the validity of these conclusions. Similar to the results of the study, my daughter is "healthier, more advanced, more alert, and less irritable" than other infants her age.

TWO WOMEN'S STORIES
OF USING FOLK, ALTERNATIVE MEDICINE

In Winter 2000, when I discovered through various parenting and childbirth websites the pervasiveness of HG, I decided to post a short message in a midwifery Internet site, sharing with others that I had discovered a non-pharmaceutical, natural cure and that anyone interested could contact me at my E-mail address. I felt that unless I shared my experiential knowledge, I would be withholding valuable information from women who could otherwise benefit from this re-discovered ancient folk remedy. Due to its controversial and illicit nature, I purposely posted a message that was vague, suppressing the fact that I was referring to cannabis. Only when I received an electronic-mail query did I reveal to the person the actual name of the herb, along with an option to request more detailed information if they were still interested. Of over fifty people who wrote to me in the following months to learn more about the herbal medicine, two women followed through, deciding to use cannabis medicinally for their hyperemesis. They both had negative experiences with mainstream medical procedures and pharmaceutical drugs during their previous pregnancies and were determined to find alternatives. When they first corresponded with me they were not pregnant, but after months of researching further into the prospect of using cannabis they eventually felt secure enough to conceive, hoping that the herb would work as efficaciously for them as it did for me. Although I did not interview them in the traditional sense, insights into their personal lives and profiles slowly emerged through correspondence.

The first woman, "Gina," is an elementary school teacher living in Southern California. When Gina first E-mailed me, she wrote:

> I had HG with my sons, now aged 19 and 17, and I had my most severe HG with my last pregnancy, which ended in a fetal demise at 14 weeks. I want to try again very much for another child (this is my second marriage, and my husband has no children). But I am deathly afraid of the HG . . . I am so glad you are researching this disease. It is a crime that so many women have to suffer.

The second woman, "Didi," shared similar feelings. In her first correspondence, she wrote:

> I would love to hear about a natural cure [other] than [pharmaceutical] medicine. I just lost a baby at 5 months [when] I was on Reglan pump and IV Picc line. I started to feel better, then the baby just died with no reason. I lost another baby two years ago at 13 weeks. Any advice is welcomed . . . My husband does not want to try again because of my condition. I should tell you I do have a 7-year-old son. I was sick with him but not as sick as I get now. I think it is because I am older now too (32-years-old).

The challenges that Gina and Didi faced in considering cannabis as a therapeutic option were similar. The first obstacle was the lack of social and medical support that they felt in considering the use of a stigmatized therapy. Although open-minded, they still experienced feelings of fear and guilt, especially while using cannabis. For instance, although Gina repeatedly stated in many of her correspondences to me that she felt "very comfortable" with the thought of treating her HG with cannabis, her confidence level was soon undermined by others: women on the internet chastised her, her husband discouraged her from relying upon it as the sole medicine, and her obstetrician was "very curt and uninterested" even before she could share with him her newly discovered medical choice. Although Gina lives in California and could logistically use medical cannabis under the protection of the Compassionate Use Act of 1996, she decided that it was best that she kept her "secret remedy" to herself, stating that she was "afraid to say anything," but was "not afraid to do it" in the privacy of her own home.

Didi also had fears in contemplating the use of the herb. When she asked her obstetrician if he could help her research the medicinal benefits of cannabis for pregnant women, he told his nurse to tell Didi that he was "too busy" and that she should do the research on her own. She followed his instruction, investigated the topic, and sent him her findings on the use of cannabis as a viable treatment for HG; in response, he refused further discussion, and sent her "pamphlets on the dangers of drugs" without additional comment. The doctor's callousness and lack of understanding and support deeply angered Didi. She later confided her feelings: "You would think that after everything I went through [losing two children due to HG], he would look into it harder with an open mind. This leads me to question . . . When I do find my next doctor [whether] to say nothing at all." Didi became more discouraged when she heard through her "sister's friend's aunt who is a nurse" that "doctors still check for drugs without your consent." In one of her E-mails, she asked me, "This is Michigan–is that possible? Will they send the social workers after me? Or is this a scare tactic?" Although I replied to her that by law, a woman has the right to not sign the consent form, she replied through E-mail with the proof of her findings:

> There was this one [woman's story posted on cannabisculture.com] that scared the SHIT out of me–by a woman named Aislinn who used cannabis throughout her pregnancy (recreationally) and they tested her baby for drugs [cannabis only]. Now they are taking her newborn away. What they said was she signed a consent form for treatment. They can test her for whatever they want. But who would think drugs? I am really scared now. I don't want to take any chances of losing my son and my new baby (whenever that happens).

A few weeks after this correspondence, Didi ceased relying on the internet as a source of communicating, opting to use the telephone for the purpose of privacy and legal safety. She reasoned that the few sites that discussed cannabis usage during pregnancy were "shut down" simultaneously and all too "coincidentally," as if the government was censoring data being exchanged over the internet and "making it harder for women" to openly exchange information. Whether this was a valid conclusion or an unfounded hypothesis I am not sure, but of certainty is the element of fear that continued to linger in Didi's consciousness.

According to researchers who have studied the properties of cannabinoids, two factors that are crucial to consider when a person uses a "psychoactive drug" such as cannabis are the "set and setting." Mathre explains in *Cannabis in Medical Practice* that "*set* refers to the mood and expectations of the user and *setting* refers to the environment in which the drug is used" (Mathre 1997, p. 175). Hence, if a person is already sensing "fear, guilt, and paranoia," these same feelings will become more exaggerated after the intake of cannabis, which can prevent the therapeutic properties from taking effect. Possibly, Gina and Didi's fear-laden set and setting took away from the women's abilities to allow the medicine to completely alleviate their symptoms. Gina stated in one of her correspondences:

> I started using [the herb] between weeks 5 and 6, when the symptoms started. It helps enormously! I still don't feel wonderful–I still don't have an appetite for food, I have to make myself eat, but at least it stays down, and I can keep my liquids up . . . I know the nutrition part is really gonna bring this thing together.

Although the cannabis actually helped her achieve the relief that no other pharmaceutical drug had offered, she confessed that she continued to feel "nervous" and "guilty." In order to hide the fact that she was using cannabis for her nausea, she also took Diclectin to explain her relief without exposing her "secret remedy" to her obstetrician. She explained: "Still taking the Diclectin. Doctor said he'll order as much as I need. But it is really the cannabis that is saving me, because some days I am too sick to swallow the pills, so I smoke about two hits, wait a while, then I am able to eat and drink a little." Therefore, even though cannabis provided the true relief, she took the Diclectin to prevent suspicion from her obstetrician. The cannabis she obtained simply did not do much for her. It made her sleep a lot, counteracted her nausea and vomiting only slightly, and made her feel "paranoid and afraid." Its unsatisfactory effects could be traced to a number of possibilities: (1) the particular strain of the cannabis, (2) her psychological and physiological state, the "set," and (3) her environmental situation, the "setting." For the first point, both Gina and I have concluded through sharing our experiences that strains of *Cannabis indica*, while more potent, were less effective for us than *Cannabis sativa* strains in counteracting the nausea and vomiting of HG. Indica seemed to render the patient more vulnerable to paranoia, while sativa alleviated nausea/vomiting without the residual feelings of "getting high." In response to the second and third points: the controversial and illicit nature of the drug, along with the government's unwillingness to conduct further research, make situations even more difficult for women who could truly benefit from comprehensive guidelines and medical endorsement.

Procuring the illicit herb proved to be a challenge for both women. Gina had an easier time in Southern California. Didi had more difficulty acquiring good product in Michigan. It was no surprise to me when she later told me that she was not getting much, if any, relief from her cannabis. By the time I committed the risky and illicit act of sending some higher quality sativa via the mail, it was already too late and she had turned to the hospitalized treatment of HG, where her doctor started her on an intravenous line to receive liquid nutrition and ondansetron to curb her nausea and vomiting.

For Gina, cannabis was effective enough to keep her out of the hospital. Through experimentation, she found she was able to "autotitrate" (Mathre 1997, p. 146) according to what her body demanded:

> I haven't been getting sick in the middle of the night, which is great, because I can get some sleep. The times I have felt sick, I just get up and take a hit, then I'm fine. Sometimes I have to take up to 6 hits a day, 2 in the early morning, 2 in the afternoon, and 2 at night. But usually, it is about 4 hits, 2 in am, 2 in pm. I am no longer worried about it–because the alternatives are to be in the hospital again, or not go through with the pregnancy. The cannabis is really what is saving me–because I am able to eat and drink some, I can still work, although it is far from pleasant.

Unfortunately, in December 2000, I received the sad news that Gina miscarried as in her previous pregnancy. She stated: "The doctor said the fetus appeared to be about 13-14 weeks old, so I do not believe for a second that the cannabis or the Diclectin® caused the fetal demise. There's something else going on." She said that her obstetrician was going to follow up with different chromosome and blood tests so that she could see why her body was "rejecting the fetuses." In spite of the tragic ending, Gina wrote to me: "I want to thank you for your support. I still believe in the medicinal value of cannabis for hyperemesis." I mourned Gina's miscarriage not because I had lost a potential candidate to study the use of cannabis for HG, but because she had lost a much-wanted child, a heartbreaking process that many, many mothers with HG too often endure. Fortunately, Didi's baby was birthed in health and wellness.

CONCLUSION

In retrospect, I wonder if my home-based, underground, pilot study on HG and cannabis was more depressing than it was encouraging. While my findings revealed some promise, I am left feeling deeply frustrated by the social and legal impossibilities of engaging in a formal clinical study in present-day America. What grieves me most is the knowledge that women with HG continue to suffer with no medically (and legally) efficacious treatment when I am convinced that we already have the cure. The stories I have been privileged to know have left me with images that continue to haunt me: of Sofia with her thighs dwindled to the width of my thin arms, interchangeably crying and vomiting as she watches the food channel on television because she wants so much to be able to eat, but cannot in the devastation of hyperemesis; of Maria threatening suicide because she is given no choice but to be bound to endless machinery with tubes surgically inserted into her abdomen for feeding and drainage for the sake of keeping her baby alive; of Sarah, whose husband deserted her because she appeared like a "skeletal with a belly," looking like "death," smelling like "poison," and wanting to die every waking hour; of Gina, devastated with the discovery that she had lost a much wanted baby for the second time. These real-life tragedies bombard me with a dispirited, *"Why?"* Why do HG women continue to suffer, even amidst pharmaceutical and hospitalized treatments that can cost over hundreds of thousand of dollars of insurance money per pregnancy?

Why was I so blessed to have found a cure, one that cost no more than $90 for the entire duration of my HG? If it were not for the study of Jamaican pregnant women who used cannabis safely with positive effects on their babies, and if it were not for my Taiwanese obstetrician who reassured me that birthing women in China have commonly used cannabis to alleviate their nausea and vomiting, and if it were not for Dr. Grinspoon at Harvard Medical School, with his extensive research on the medicinal properties of cannabis, who found credibility and value in my anecdote, I would definitely be filled with self-doubt in the face of surrounding fear, persecution, and paranoia. While I should simply let the issue pass, a part of me is unwilling to give up so easily, partially because cannabis is an important, but lost, part of my cultural heritage. Having experienced severe hyperemesis, I can empathize with all the women who also endure its debilitating effects. If one could imagine surviving the nausea and retching of food poisoning combined with vertigo and motion-sickness non-stop for four to nine months straight, night and day, than one could possibly begin fathoming the physical and psychological trauma of living with HG.

In summary, it is relevant to ask: What are the rites and rights of birth offered to a woman with hyperemesis within the realm of modern medicine? The rites are obvious: *the ritual of isolation,* when the woman is attached to tubes and machines in the hospital, sometimes for the entire nine month duration, torn from her community of family and friends; *the ritual of sacrifice,* when the woman's body, viewed as an "object" rather than a "subject," is poked and prodded, severed and bloodied as she is merely treated as the container who must somehow "produce" the baby, the "product" (Davis-Floyd 1992, pp. 160-161); *the ritual of denial,* when the woman's incessant and tenacious nausea and vomiting is downplayed as being "all in the head," or accused as a way for her to "vomit out her baby" or disguise her "bulimia" disorder; *the ritual of suffering*, when the woman is expected to withstand the tortures of highly gruesome medical procedures that involve the surgical cutting and ripping of flesh without anesthesia, bear the pangs of long term starvation, and endure the end result of a "chronically collapsed digestive system"; *the ritual of silence*, when the woman's voice is not heard, in spite of her cries for help, and her body is not acknowledged, in spite of its emaciation. And finally, within these rites is simply her right to give birth with much medical intervention but no real cure.

REFERENCES

Abel, E.L. 1982. *A marihuana dictionary: Words, terms, events, and persons relating to cannabis*. Westport, CT: Greenwood Press.

Abel, E.L. 1980. *Marihuana: The first 12,000 years*. New York: Plenum Press.

Arms, S. 1975. *Immaculate deception: A new look at women and childbirth in America*. New York: Bantam Books.

Arms, S. 1994. *Immaculate deception II: Myth, magic, and birth*. Berkeley, CA: Celestial Arts.

Askling, J., G. Erlandsson, M. Kaijser, O. Akre, and B. Anders. 1999. Sickness in pregnancy and sex of child. *Lancet* 354(9195):2053-2055.

Benet, S. 1975. Early diffusion and folk uses of hemp. *Cannabis and culture*. Edited by V. Rubin. Chicago: Mouton Publishers.

Boyd, S.C. 1999. *Mothers and illicit drug use: Transcending the myths*. Toronto: University of Toronto Press.

Brady, E. (Ed.). 2001. *Healing logics: Culture and medicine in modern health belief systems*. Utah: Utah State University Press.

Browner, C.H. and N. Press. 1997. The production of authoritative knowledge in American prenatal care. *Childbirth and authoritative knowledge: Cross-cultural perspectives*. Berkeley: University of California Press.

Carlson, K.J., S.A. Eisenstat, and T. Ziporyn. 1996. *The Harvard guide to women's health*. Cambridge: Harvard University Press.

Chêng, T.-K.. 1959. *Archaeology in China (Volume 1): Prehistoric China*. Cambridge, UK: W. Heffer and Sons.

Christ, C.P. 1997. *Rebirth of the goddess: Finding meaning in feminist spirituality*. New York: Routledge Press.

Christy, C.P. 1978. Why women need the goddess: Phenomenological, psychological, and political reflections. *Heresies* (Spring):273-287.

Davis-Floyd, R.E. 1992. *Birth as an American rite of passage*. Berkeley: University of California Press.

Davis-Floyd, R.E. and C.F. Sargent (Eds.). 1997. *Childbirth and authoritative knowledge: Cross-cultural perspectives*. Berkeley: University of California Press.

Dick-Read, G. 1959. *Childbirth without fear: The principals and practice of natural childbirth*. New York: Harper and Brothers.

Dreher, M.C. 1997. Cannabis and pregnancy. *Cannabis in medical practice: A legal, historical and pharmacological overview of the therapeutic use of marijuana*, edited by M.L. Mathre. Jefferson, NC: McFarland.

Du Toit, B.M. 1980. *Cannabis in Africa: A survey of its distribution in Africa, and a study of cannabis use and users in multi-etnic [sic] South Africa*. Rotterdam, Netherlands: A.A. Balkema.

England, P. and R. Horowitz. 1998. *Birthing from within: An extra-ordinary guide to childbirth preparation*. Albuquerque, NM: Partera Press.

Erick, M. 1997. Nutrition via jejunostomy in refractory hyperemesis gravidarum: A case report. *J Amer Dietetic Assoc* 97(10):1154-1156.

Fleming, M.P. and R.C. Clarke. 1998. Physical evidence for the antiquity of *Cannabis sativa* L. (Cannabaceae). *J Internat Hemp Assoc* 5(2):80-92.

Foucault, M. 1973. *The birth of the clinic: An archeology of medical perception*. New York: Vintage Books.

Foucault, M. 1995. *Discipline and punishment: The birth of the prison*. New York: Vintage Books.

Foucault, M. 1980. *Power/Knowledge: Selected interviews and other writings 1972-1977*. Edited/translated by C.G.L. Marshall, J. Mepham, K. Soper. New York: Pantheon Books.

Gaskin, I.M. 1990. *Spiritual midwifery*. 3rd ed. Summertown, TN: The Book Publishing Company.

Ginsburg, F.D. and R. Rapp (Eds.). 1995. *Conceiving the new world order: The global politics of reproduction*. Berkeley: University of California Press.

Ginsburg, F.D. and R. Rapp. 1991. The politics of reproduction. *Annual Review Anthropol* 20:311-43.

Glenn, E.N., G. Chang, and L.R. Forcey (Eds.). 1994. *Mothering: Ideology, experience, and agency*. New York: Routledge.

Grinspoon, L., and J.B. Bakalar. 1997. *Marihuana: The forbidden medicine*. New Haven: Yale University Press.

Hillborn, M.J., V. Pylvenen, and K. Sotaniemi. 1999. Pregnant, vomiting, and coma (Wernicke's encephalopathy): Case report. *Lancet* 353(9164):1584.

Hufford, D.J. 1994. Folklore and medicine. *Putting folklore to use*, edited by M.O. Jones. Lexington: University Press of Kentucky.

Jordan, B. 1993. *Birth in four cultures: A cross-cultural investigation of childbirth in Yucatan, Holland, Sweden, and the United States*. 4th ed. Prospect Heights, IL: Waveland Press.

Jordan, B. 1997. Authoritative knowledge and its construction. *Childbirth and authoritative knowledge: Cross-cultural perspectives*. Berkeley: University of California Press.

Lamaze, F. 1956. *Painless childbirth*. Translated by L.R. Celestin. Chicago: H. Regnery Company.

Leavitt, J.W. 1986. *Brought to bed: Childbearing in America 1750-1950*. New York: Oxford University Press.

Leboyer, F. 1975. *Birth without violence*. New York: Alfred A Knopf.

Li, H.-L. 1975. The origin and use of cannabis in Eastern Asia: Their linguistic-cultural implications. In *Cannabis and culture*. Edited by V. Rubin. Chicago: Mouton Publishers.

Lichtmann, R. 1988. Medical models and midwifery: The cultural experience of birth. In *Childbirth in America: Anthropological perspectives*. Edited by K. Michaelson. South Hadley, MA: Bergin and Garvey.

Jones, M.O. (Ed.). 1994. *Putting folklore to use*. Lexington: University Press of Kentucky.

Mallon, C.L. 1997. Unnatural childbirth: A feminist sociology of birth in America. Ph.D. dissertation in Comparative Culture, University of California, Irvine.

Mathre, M.L. 1997. *Cannabis and medical practice: A legal, historical, and pharmaceutical overview of the therapeutic use of marijuana*. Jefferson, NC: McFarland & Co., Inc.

Meltzer, D.I. 2000. Complementary therapies for nausea and vomiting in early pregnancy. *Fam Pract* 17(6):570-573.

Murcott, A. 1988. On the altered appetites of pregnancy: Conceptions of food, body and person. *Sociological Rev* 36(4):733-764.

Murphy, S., and M. Rosenbaum. 1999. *Pregnant women on drugs: Combating stereotypes and stigma*. New Brunswick, NJ: Rutgers University Press.

Panesar, N.S., C.-Y. Li, and M.S. Rogers. 2001. Are thyroid hormones or hCG responsible for hyperemesis gravidarum? A matched paired study in pregnant Chinese women. *Acta Obstetricia et Gynecologica Scandinavica* 80:519-524.

Peterson, A. and R. Bunton (Eds.). 1997. *Foucault, health, and medicine*. New York: Routledge.

Rubin, V. (Ed.). 1975. *Cannabis and culture*. Netherlands: Mouton Publishers.

Schoenberg, F.P. 2000. Summary of data on hyperemesis gravidarum. *The Birthkit* (Spring):4-8.

Schultes, R.E., and A. Hofmann. 1979. *Plants of the gods: Origins of hallucinogenic use*. New York: McGraw-Hill Book Company.

Simpson, S.W., T. M. Goodwin, S.B. Robins, A.A. Rizzo, R.A. Howes, D.K. Buckwalter, and J.G. Buckwalter. 2001. Psychological factors and hyperemesis gravidarum. *J Women's Health and Gender-Based Med* 10(5):471-477.

Tesfaye, S., V. Achari, Y.C. Yang, S. Harding, A. Bowden, and J.P. Vora. 1998. Pregnant, vomiting, and going blind. *Lancet* 352(9140):1594.

Thompson, L. 1999. *The wandering womb: A cultural history of outrageous beliefs about women*. Amherst, NY: Prometheus Books.

University of California, Los Angeles. 2001. Folk Medicine Archive. Website: <http://www.folkmed.ucla.edu>.

Van de Ven, C.J.M. 1997. Nasogastric enteral feeding in hyperemesis gravidarum. *Lancet* 349(9050):445-446.

W. B. Saunders Dictionary Staff. 1994. *Dorland's illustrated medical dictionary*. 28th ed. Philadelphia: W.B. Saunders Company.

Wright, T.L. 1862. Correspondence. *Cincinatti Lancet and Observer* 5(4):246-247.

The Consequences
of Marijuana Use During Pregnancy:
A Review of the Human Literature

Peter A. Fried

SUMMARY. In spite of marijuana being the most widely used illegal drug among women of reproductive age there is a relative paucity of literature dealing with this topic. Of the data available, particularly in offspring beyond three years of age, most is generated by two ongoing cohort studies with very different populations. Both have reported similar findings. Up to approximately 3 years of age there appears to be very little impact upon the offspring. Beyond that age, *in utero* cannabis exposure does not impact upon standardized derived IQ scores but is negatively associated with attentional behavior and visual analysis/hypothesis testing. These findings are hypothesized as prenatal marijuana exposure having a negative influence on aspects of executive function–a "top-down," multifaceted cognitive construct involved in organizing and integrating specific cognitive and output processes over a interval of time. The results and their interpretation are examined in terms of behavioral teratogenic effects (or lack of effects) during the various developmental

---

Peter A. Fried, PhD, is Professor of Psychology, Carleton University, Ottawa, Ontario, Canada K1S 5B6 (E-mail: peter_fried@carleton.ca).

The author thanks the wonderfully cooperative families in the OPPS who have been participating for over two decades. The author also thanks his long-time research associates, B. Watkinson, R. Gray, and H. Linttell.

The OPPS has been and continues to be supported by grants from the National Institute on Drug Abuse.

[Haworth co-indexing entry note]: "The Consequences of Marijuana Use During Pregnancy: A Review of the Human Literature." Fried, Peter A. Co-published simultaneously in *Journal of Cannabis Therapeutics* (The Haworth Integrative Healing Press, an imprint of The Haworth Press, Inc.) Vol. 2, No. 3/4, 2002, pp. 85-104; and: *Women and Cannabis: Medicine, Science, and Sociology* (ed: Ethan Russo, Melanie Dreher, and Mary Lynn Mathre) The Haworth Integrative Healing Press, an imprint of The Haworth Press, Inc., 2002, pp. 85-104. Single or multiple copies of this article are available for a fee from The Haworth Document Delivery Service [1-800-HAWORTH, 9:00 a.m. - 5:00 p.m. (EST). E-mail address: getinfo@haworthpressinc.com].

stages of the offspring, the non-unitary nature of executive function, cannabis receptors, and the consequences of chronic marijuana use in the non-pregnant population. *[Article copies available for a fee from The Haworth Document Delivery Service: 1-800-HAWORTH. E-mail address: <getinfo@haworthpressinc.com> Website: <http://www.HaworthPress.com> © 2002 by The Haworth Press, Inc. All rights reserved.]*

KEYWORDS. Prenatal marijuana exposure, pregnancy, executive function, prefrontal lobe, longitudinal studies, IQ, visual perception, attention

In the ongoing debate about the role of cannabis and health as well as the increased interest in amending laws pertaining to the legal status of marijuana there is one area that appears noteworthy for its lack of inclusion: the possible short- and long-term consequences on the offspring of women who use marijuana during pregnancy. Particularly as applied to the long-term cognitive and behavioral outcomes, the absence of this issue reflects, at least in part, the relatively sparse body of information available on this topic. Contributing to this paucity are a myriad of complex pragmatic, logistic and interpretative difficulties that are part and parcel of the longitudinal behavioral teratological research that is required to examine this question. These design issues have been the subject of a recent review (Fried 2002) and will not be reiterated in the present paper. In spite of the difficulties involved in the gathering of information, the indisputable fact that marijuana is the most commonly used illicit drug among women of reproductive age (Johnston et al. 1994; 1996) emphasizes the need for the gathering and dissemination of data from well controlled studies.

In NIDA's most recently completed National Pregnancy and Health Survey (1996), self-reported marijuana use during pregnancy was 2.9 percent which, incidentally, is approximately three times the frequency of cocaine/crack usage. Among high school seniors (those entering reproductive years), a December 2000 Monitoring the Future press release (*http://www.monitoringthefuture. org/data/00data/pr00t2.pdf*) reported that marijuana had been used by 22% of grade 12 students in the past 30 days. In our own work (the Ottawa Prenatal Prospective Study–OPPS), which will be described briefly later in this paper, among 120 predominantly middle-class 18-20 years olds, the rate of smoking a minimum of one joint in the past week, determined by self-report coupled with a urine analysis, was 34% and smoking at least that amount on a regular basis at some time during the past five years was 45% (unpublished data). In addition to the relatively extensive use of marijuana by both women who are pregnant and women of child-bearing age, among both heavy (e.g., Hurt et al.

1995) and social (e.g., Graham et al. 1992) maternal cocaine users, marijuana is frequently smoked. This adds additional importance to the determination of marijuana's possible prenatal impact for, in order to disentangle cocaine's potential effects, marijuana's role must be understood.

The purpose of the present paper, portions of which have recently appeared elsewhere (Fried 2001; Fried and Smith 2001; Fried 2002), is to objectively summarize the present state of knowledge pertaining to marijuana and pregnancy, an issue highly pertinent to the theme of this edition of the Journal.

Only two longitudinal cohort studies with very different sample characteristics have focused upon the possible consequences of prenatal marijuana in offspring beyond early school age. In our own work, the OPPS, the objective has been to examine the association between marijuana (and other socially used drugs) consumed during pregnancy and effects upon offspring in the areas of growth, cognitive development and behavior. This longitudinal work has been underway since 1978 with the sample consisting of low-risk, white, predominantly middle-class families. Details of the recruitment procedures, interview protocol and drug use ascertainment have been described elsewhere (Fried et al. 1980). In essence subjects within the sample, representative of the English-speaking Ottawa population, were interviewed once during each of the trimesters remaining in their pregnancy. Birth data have been collected from 682 women in the Ottawa area but, for pragmatic reasons, approximately 180 offspring were chosen to be followed beyond the neonatal period.

During each of the pregnancy interviews, information was collected concerning socio-demographic status, mother's health (both current and prior to the pregnancy), father's health history, previous obstetrical history, a 24-hour dietary recall, and past and present drug use with particular emphasis upon marijuana, cigarettes and alcohol. For the drug histories, information was gathered pertaining to the year before pregnancy and each trimester of pregnancy. During the pregnancy, neonatal, childhood and adolescent time frames for which data have been published, the OPPS has collected over 4000 variables. Further details describing the assessment procedures at various ages are presented throughout this paper.

The second longitudinal study that has reported on a number of outcomes of prenatal exposure to marijuana in children ranging in ages from infancy to early adolescence is the Maternal Health Practices and Child Development Study (MHPCD) based in Pittsburgh (Goldschmidt et al. 2000). This study was initiated in 1982 and has focused upon the consequences of prenatal use of marijuana, alcohol and cocaine. The subjects in this high-risk cohort are of low socioeconomic status and just over half are African-American. Growth, cognitive development, temperament and behavioral characteristics have been reported in offspring up to the age of 10 and the marijuana findings reported are those noted after controlling for other drug use.

In the discussion of the OPPS and MHPCD findings as well as other studies, unless otherwise stated, the results described have been reported in the original articles as being statistically significant after controlling for potential confounding, mediating or moderating variables. In the present review, the use of the term significant refers to probability levels reported as > .05 whereas the term highly significant refers to probability levels of .01 or greater.

COURSE OF PREGNANCY

Over the centuries, in many parts of the world, marijuana has been anecdotally reported to hasten childbirth, with the drug increasing the frequency and intensity of contractions (Abel 1980). Contemporarily, Fried, Watkinson and Willan (1984) found a statistically significant reduction of approximately one week in the gestational age of infants born to mothers who used marijuana six or more times per week. A report (Greenland et al. 1982) that precipitate labor was significantly more frequent among women who reported using marijuana is consistent with the folk medicine and may be related to the shortened gestation noted in the OPPS sample. The approximate one week reduction in gestation length observed is of questionable clinical significance in and of itself. However, as the effect was dose related, the shortened gestation length may take on clinical significance if large amounts of the drug is consumed, if the $\Delta 9$-tetrahydrocannabinol levels are higher than those used in the early eighties, and/or if life-style habits include other risk factors such as alcohol. Some (Gibson et al. 1983; Hatch and Bracken 1986) but not all researchers (Tennes et al. 1985; Day et al. 1991) have reported an association between marijuana use during pregnancy and preterm delivery.

In the OPPS, no association with marijuana use and subjects' miscarriage rates, types of presentation at birth, Apgar status, and the frequency of neonatal complications or major physical abnormalities (Fried 1982; Fried et al. 1983) were found. No patterns of minor physical anomalies were noted among the offspring of marijuana users although two anomalies, true ocular hypertelorism and severe epicanthus, were observed only among children of heavy users of cannabis (O'Connell and Fried 1984). In general, researchers have not reported an association between prenatal marijuana use and morphologic abnormalities in offspring (e.g., Day et al. 1991) and, as reviewed elsewhere (Dalterio and Fried 1992; O'Connell and Fried 1984), the few reports of increased physical abnormalities may reflect a lack of control for confounding factors (e.g., prenatal exposure to alcohol) and/or the relative risk status of the women in the study.

The life-style and concomitant risk status are factors that appear to interplay with prenatal marijuana outcomes. For example, in the low-risk sample of the

OPPS, no evidence of increased meconium staining was noted among the newborns of the heavy marijuana users (Fried et al. 1983). This observation contrasts with the first but not second of two reports by Greenland and associates (1982; 1983). One of the primary differences between the two Greenland studies was the generally higher standard of living and health among the sample in the later (1983) report with these subjects being quite similar, demographically, to the OPPS sample. A study that manipulated non-marijuana factors and that utilized pregnant rats (Charlebois and Fried 1980) indirectly supports the critical role that life-style factors may have in interacting with the teratogenic effects of the drug. Briefly, different groups of pregnant rats were exposed to marijuana smoke while receiving diets varying in protein content. Compromised pregnancies were markedly potentiated when marijuana smoke was combined with a low-protein diet but, conversely, if marijuana smoke was coupled with a high-protein diet some risks associated with the cannabis exposure were attenuated.

GROWTH

The role of life-style interacting with marijuana's prenatal effect can be observed upon fetal growth (Fried et al. 1999). Most studies have not found marijuana to have a negative impact in this domain but, in some samples drawn from high-risk environments, a small but significant negative relationship between first trimester marijuana use and birth length (Day et al. 1991; Tennes et al. 1985) or birth weight and length (Zuckerman et al. 1989) have been reported. Intriguingly, in both the MHPCD and OPPS cohorts, prenatal marijuana use was associated with an increased weight: Day et al. (1994) found this association at birth between heavy third trimester use and birth weight in a minority, high risk sample, although it was not found with a combined marijuana and alcohol cohort (Day et al. 1994a) and Fried and O'Connell (1987) reported a positive relationship between marijuana use during each trimester and weight at 24 months in the low-risk, middle-class OPPS sample.

Of the few studies that have examined offspring beyond the newborn stage, no significant negative association with growth parameters was noted at 8 months (Day et al. 1992), 1 year (Fried et al. 1999; Tennes et al. 1985), 2 and 3 years (Fried and O'Connell 1987; Fried et al. 1999), 4 years (Fried et al. 1999), and 6 years (Day et al. 1994a; Fried et al. 1999). One growth parameter in the OPPS sample, a smaller head circumference, observed as a trend in all ages (birth, 1, 2, 3, 4 and 6 years) reached statistical significance among early adolescents (Fried et al. 1999) born to daily marijuana users but was not significant during mid-adolescence (Fried, James and Watkinson 2001). Maternal marijuana use was not associated with the timing of pubertal milestones in either adolescent males or females (Fried, James and Watkinson 2001).

NEUROBEHAVIORAL/COGNITIVE OUTCOMES IN NEWBORNS

The literature describing the neurobehavioral effects of prenatal marijuana use on the newborn, although provocative, is far from definitive. In the Ottawa sample, using the Brazelton Neonatal Assessment Scale (Brazelton, 1973), at less than one week of age, marijuana was associated with increased fine tremors typically accompanied by exaggerated and prolonged startles, both spontaneous and in response to mild stimuli (Fried et al. 1980; Fried 1982; Fried and Makin 1987). In the same sample, maternal marijuana use was associated with relatively similar observations in 9 and 30 day old infants (Fried et al. 1987). At 9 days, hand-to-mouth behaviour was associated with marijuana use during pregnancy. Many of the behaviours seen both in the newborn and at 9 and 30 days are consistent with, but milder in degree, than found among infants undergoing opioid withdrawal. Although these particular indicants of impairments in nervous system state regulation were not detected by some researchers (Richardson et al. 1995; Tennes et al. 1985), reports of altered autonomic arousal in other outcome measures have been reported. Neonates of maternal cannabis users have been noted as having an increased likelihood of exhibiting a high-pitched cry (Lester and Dreher 1989) and to spend less time in quiet sleep (Scher et al. 1988).

Habituation, which in infants is an indicator of nervous system functioning and integrity, was associated, in some studies, with prenatal marijuana exposure. In the OPPS sample, newborns of less than a week born to marijuana users have poorer habituation to visual, but not auditory, stimuli (Fried, 1982; Fried and Makin 1987). It is noteworthy that in a primate study (Golub et al. 1981), behaviour distinguishing marijuana offspring from controls was the failure to habituate to novel visual stimuli. At 9 and 30 days of age, no association in the OPPS sample was apparent between maternal marijuana use and visual outcome measures such as pupil dilation and nystagmus. Compared to the remainder of the sample, more marijuana babies demonstrated a lack of visual habituation but the increased incidence did not reach statistical significance (Fried et al. 1987). No negative relationship between infant behaviour and maternal marijuana use was found in three reports describing a Jamaican cohort (Hayes et al. 1988; Dreher, Nugent and Hudgins 1994; Dreher 1997), nor in two different American studies (Tennes et al. 1985; Richardson et al. 1989). However, the possible vulnerability of aspects of visual system functioning in the neonate is a theme that recurs both in the longer term evaluation of offspring of maternal marijuana users in the OPPS and MHPCD cohorts as well as in a polydrug study (Griffith et al. 1994). This recurrent pattern will be discussed later in this paper.

NEUROBEHAVIORAL/COGNITIVE OUTCOMES IN LATE INFANCY AND PRESCHOOLERS

Findings pertaining to the impact of prenatal marijuana exposure on offspring between the ages of 1 and 4 are quite limited but, in what is available, there is a degree of consistency that is intriguing. In the OPPS (Fried and Watkinson 1988), using the Bayley Scales of Infant Development (Bayley 1969), no association between marijuana use during pregnancy and infant mental or motor development was observed at 1 year of age. No relationship between Bayley outcomes and prenatal marijuana exposure has been reported by other workers (Astley and Little 1990; Tennes et al. 1985). In the high-risk MHPCD cohort, the use of 1 or more joints per day during the third trimester was associated with lowered mental scores on the Bayley at 9 months of age but no longer at 18 months (Richardson et al. 1995).

The failure to find an association between prenatal marijuana exposure and a variety of cognitive outcomes persisted in the OPPS sample until the offspring were 4 years of age. At 2, although there was a negative association with language comprehension, this relationship did not retain significance when the home environment was statistically controlled (Fried and Watkinson 1988). At 3 years of age, after controlling for confounding factors, prenatal marijuana exposure was not associated with language expression and comprehension or decreased cognitive scores (Fried and Watkinson 1990).

However, one year later, an association with prenatal marijuana exposure that remained significant after controlling for confounding factors, was observed. These four year old children in the OPPS, born to women who had used marijuana on a regular basis during pregnancy (more than 5 joints a week), scored significantly lower than the remainder of the sample on a number of verbal and memory outcome measures (Fried and Watkinson 1990) derived primarily from the McCarthy Scales of Children's Abilities (McCarthy 1972). These findings were similar to results from the MHPCD cohort when the children were 3 years of age (Day et al. 1994b) in that, among the offspring of women who had used marijuana on a daily basis, an impairment on the short-term memory, verbal and abstract/visual reasoning subscales of the Stanford-Binet Intelligence Test (Thorndike et al. 1986) was noted. In a study investigating the interaction between prenatal cocaine use and a number of drugs including marijuana in 3 year old offspring, maternal marijuana use of an unspecified amount was related to poorer performance on the abstract/visual reasoning subscale of the Stanford-Binet test (Griffith et al. 1994). In all three studies with these preschoolers there was no marijuana effect on the composite, intelligence scores. As will be emphasized below, this has important interpretative and theoretical consequences in evaluating the findings in school aged children prenatally exposed to marijuana.

Reports focusing upon the behavioral and cognitive outcomes in offspring beyond 36 months of age exposed prenatally to marijuana are limited to that of the OPPS and MHPCD. Within these two cohorts, as there was at younger ages, there is a considerable degree of concordance in the findings in the children beyond 3 years of age. Furthermore, in these longitudinal studies, as the offspring get older, the observations are consistent with and logically extend, in a number of ways, the outcomes reported at earlier stages of development. One sphere of functioning, which may be impacted by prenatal marijuana in the school-aged children, is within the behavioral/cognitive construct of executive function (EF). The hypothesis of a negative association between *in utero* marijuana exposure and facets of EF in older offspring has been developed elsewhere in detail (Fried 1998) and will be described briefly in the following sections of this paper.

EXECUTIVE FUNCTION (EF)

The nature of EF involves the interplay of subordinate cognitive operations and thus may be viewed as an overarching, "top-down" cognitive domain. EF involves the ability to organize and integrate specific cognitive and output processes over an interval of time (Denckla 1993). The mental control processes involved in carrying out such future oriented behaviors include cognitive flexibility in problem solving, sustained, focused attention, inhibition of prepotent responses, monitoring, evaluating and adjusting self-directed responses and working memory (the temporary storage of information while processing incoming data). EF therefore describes a multiple, non-unitary set of functions needed to successfully carry out effortful, non-routine, goal-oriented tasks (Fried 1998). In evaluating the adequacy of this higher-order, integrative mental control process in the offspring of marijuana users, competency in the underlying specific domains that are to be mentally manipulated and integrated must be ascertained (Fried and Smith 2001).

From both clinical and empirical research (e.g., Fuster 1989; Lezak 1995), EF has been shown to be primarily subserved by the prefrontal region of the brain although other structures such as the hippocampus and cerebellum are involved (e.g., Diamond 2000; Lezak 1995). Reflecting the prolonged developmental course of the prefrontal lobes, most EF behaviors are not apparent until the children approach or reach school age (Fried 1998; Levin et al. 1991; Welsh et al. 1991). It may be noteworthy that upon examining the distribution and concentration of cannabinoid receptors in the fetal, neonatal and adult human brain using autoradiographic procedures (Glass et al. 1997), binding sites were identified throughout the regions of the adult neocortex with the greatest density being in the middle gyrus of the frontal lobe, cingulate gyrus and temporal lobe. Although frontal cortex from either fetal or neonatal tissue was not available for analysis, based on the material that was examined, the authors found that the receptor distribution was similar in the fetal and neonatal brain to the adult human brain except that the density of receptor binding was markedly higher in the developing brain. The conclusion reached by the authors was that one of the major cannabinoid receptor sites in the human brain is in that part of the forebrain associated with higher cognitive functions.

The role of the prefrontal lobes in human intelligence is complex. One must distinguish between intelligence as a capacity to engage in adaptive, goal directed behavior and intelligence as defined by performance on standard psychometric instruments (Fried 1998). Data derived from clinical studies in which injury to the prefrontal area has occurred (e.g., Damasio and Anderson 1993; Fuster 1989; Stuss 1992) suggest that the former but not the latter type of intelligence is vulnerable to prefrontal dysfunction. Underlying this disassociation, at least in part, is that traditional intelligence tests set up specific tasks and goals thus obscuring the assessment of such key aspects of EF as integration of domains of functioning, goal setting, planning and self-monitoring.

From the maturational perspective, the observations, summarized earlier, that no effects of the drug were observed in offspring beyond the neonatal period until the children were 3 (Day et al. 1994; Griffith 1994) or 4 years of age (Fried and Watkinson 1990) is consistent with the developmental course of executive functioning. Further, from a functional perspective in these studies of the preschoolers, the combination of an absence of a lowering of global IQ scores but a negative association with such subtests that assess memory and abstract/visual reasoning is also consistent with the hypothesis that *in utero* marijuana exposure impacts negatively on particular facets of EF.

NEUROBEHAVIORAL/COGNITIVE OUTCOMES IN SCHOOL-AGED CHILDREN

The data available on school-aged offspring born to women who used marijuana during pregnancy suggests an interesting, but certainly incomplete emerging picture. It is important to note that as of this writing, in neither the OPPS nor the MHCPD longitudinal studies has an analysis been completed to determine whether the children that were impacted at one stage of development were those that continued to be impacted at a later age.

At 5 and 6 years of age, no differences were noted in the prenatally marijuana exposed and non-exposed children in the OPPS when assessed with global tests of cognition and language (Fried et al. 1992). As mentioned above with respect to EF and intelligence, it is possible that the instruments used in this work (Fried et al. 1992) provide a general and broad description of cognitive abilities and may not be capable of identifying nuances in neurobehavior that discriminate between marijuana-exposed and non-marijuana-exposed children. In order to determine whether this absence of an association was due to the limited assessment in the standardized intelligence test of such key aspects of EF as integration of domains of functioning, goal setting, planning and self-monitoring, two studies were undertaken to examine specific cognitive characteristics and strategies.

Both of these investigations involved the OPPS cohort when the subjects were between 9 and 12 years of age. In the first (Fried et al. 1998), a neuropsychological battery was administered that included tests that assessed various aspects of EF as well as tests designed to assess global intelligence. The second was a direct investigation of the possible influence of prenatal marijuana exposure on "top-down" visuoperception (Fried and Watkinson 2000).

In the report evaluating aspects of cognition (Fried et al. 1998) the assessment battery utilized included the Wechsler Intelligence Scale for Children-III (WISC-III) (Wechsler 1991) with its 13 subtests and 6 additional tests designed to evaluate aspects of EF. Included among the latter were tests of sustained attention and inhibition of prepotent responses (Gordon and McClure 1984), a problem solving task that required visually deducing abstract categories while adjusting responses on the basis of negative and positive feedback (Reitan and Davison 1974), a timed, difficult tactile, self-monitoring task (Reitan and Davison 1974), a measure of oral fluency (Spreen and Strauss 1991), and a working memory task (Siegel and Ryan 1989).

The results of the WISC-III were intriguing. As with the data collected from the OPPS sample at earlier ages, there was no association between the Full Scale IQ and *in utero* marijuana exposure. Among the 13 WISC-III subtests only 2, the Block Design and Picture Completion subtests, significantly differentiated among levels of prenatal marijuana exposure suggesting that *in utero* marijuana affects particular rather than global aspects of intelligence.

In the Block Design subtest, the children are directed to assemble blocks to form a design identical to one presented in a picture. This non-verbal, concept formation task requires the ability of perceptual organization, spatial visualization and abstract conceptualization (Wechsler 1991). The Picture Completion subtest requires the subject to identify a missing portion of an incompletely drawn picture and tests the ability to differentiate essential from nonessential details (Wechsler 1991).

These two subtests of the WISC are multifaceted, involving basic visuospatial and visuo-motor abilities as well as higher order cognitive processes. The latter likely include planning, impulse control, visuo-construction and visuo-analysis. Importantly, the marijuana findings on the two WISC subtests persisted after statistically controlling for basic spatial and motor abilities thus supporting the interpretation that the impact of prenatal marijuana exposure on these WISC subtests is upon "higher-order" or "top-down" cognitive processes. Although not the subject of this paper, it deserves mentioning that these findings are in considerable contrast to those found among the offspring of cigarette smokers. Both the IQ scores and virtually all of the WISC subtests (particularly those with a verbal aspect) served to discriminate across levels of prenatal cigarette exposure (Fried et al. 1998). This disassociation between the prenatal consequences of marijuana and cigarettes suggests quite strongly that the findings pertaining to marijuana are not some sort of artifact within the OPPS sample that, in a generic sense, would be found as a consequence to *in utero* exposure to any drug.

The finding that prenatal marijuana exposure impacted upon two subtests of the WISC-III that required complex visual analysis is consistent with observations noted in the two other reports mentioned earlier that focused upon prenatal marijuana exposure (Day et al. 1994; Griffith et al. 1994). At 3 years of age in both of those cohorts, the children of marijuana users were reported to have poorer abstract/visual reasoning skills based on the pre-schooler having to complete a formboard and replicate different block designs. This consistency of findings among different cohorts persisted at 10 years of age in the MHCPD cohort where prenatal marijuana use continued to be negatively associated with abstract/visual reasoning (Richardson and Day, 1997). At that age, this cognitive domain was assessed by performance on a block design task, a progressive matrices task and the ability to copy geometric shapes. As described in the "Neurobehavioral/Cognitive Outcomes in Newborns" portion earlier in this paper, it may be noteworthy, from a longitudinal perspective, that when the children in the OPPS were less than a week old, prenatal marijuana exposure was associated with poorer visual habituation (Fried 1982; Fried and Makin 1987).

Among the 9 to 12 year olds in the OPPS cohort (Fried et al. 1998), the results of the non-WISC outcome measures, which assessed aspects of EF, were consistent with and extend the observations for the marijuana groups gleaned from the WISC tasks. Of the two non-WISC-III tests that maximally discriminated among the marijuana groups was one that required the application of visual deduction to a problem solving task and the other was an assessment of impulsivity. Thus, of the six tests thought to assess aspects of EF, the two that were found to be associated with marijuana involve impulse control, visual analysis and hypothesis testing. This is consistent with the WISC results as the two subtests in that battery associated with prenatal marijuana use–Block Design and Picture Completion–require visual analysis and hypothesis testing.

This combination of visual analysis and impulsivity, but not other aspects of EF being vulnerable to prenatal marijuana, has been interpreted (Fried 1998, Fried and Smith 2001) as being consistent with conceptualizing EF as a non-unitary process. Developmental research not involving prenatal exposure to drugs and utilizing a factor analytic approach examining EF in children at different ages (Welsh et al. 1991) provides an important avenue of support for the marijuana findings from two perspectives. It both reinforces the general notion that successful executive functioning is a multifaceted process and also yielded findings that are consistent with the specific facets of EF that appear impacted by prenatal marijuana exposure (visual analysis/hypothesis testing and impulsivity). Welsh et al. (1991), using an extensive battery of tests with a normative sample, identified three independent factors in the developmental course of EF reflecting planning, verbal fluency, and hypothesis testing while controlling prepotent responding. The latter was derived from a convergence of cognitive processes based on visual hypothesis testing and impulse control. These components contributing to this factor labeled "Hypothesis Testing and Impulse Control" are strikingly similar to those neurobehavioral outcomes negatively associated with prenatal marijuana exposure in the 9 to 12 year old OPPS subjects (Fried et al. 1988). On the other hand, the other two factors which Welsh et al. (1991) labeled as a "Fluid and Speeded Response" (including a verbal fluency and a tactile performance task) and "Planning" (including a working memory and a tactile task) were not found to be associated with maternal marijuana use.

In terms of the developmental time course of the "Hypothesis Testing and Impulse Control" factor, competence is achieved at around 10 years of age (Welsh et al. 1991). This is consistent with the observation that marijuana's negative effect in this dimension of EF manifested itself in the 9-12 year olds.

In another report based on the 9-12-year-old OPPS subjects, persuasive evidence was obtained for the notion that prenatal marijuana may impact upon "top-down" neurocognitive functioning (Fried and Watkinson 2000), a major interpretative cornerstone of EF. In this study, visuoperceptual tasks ranging from those that required basic capabilities to those that required considerable integration and cognitive manipulation were utilized. Further, in order to ascertain whether any change in visuoperceptual functioning may in fact be due to demands upon nonvisual facets such as attentional, memory and/or motor components, tasks were included to assess and control for these underlying behaviors.

The consequences of prenatal marijuana use on the performance of visuoperceptual tasks varied, depending upon the nature of the demands of the tests (Fried and Watkinson 2000). No association was noted between maternal marijuana use and those tasks that required basic, fixed, functional visuoperceptual abilities with little or no analytical or integrative skills. Where *in utero* marijuana exposure did have a negative impact was on tasks that required the application of these basic visuoperceptual skills to problems involving planning, integration, analysis and synthesis. This negative association remained after statistically taking into consideration prenatal confounds plus both basic visuoperceptual abilities and the non-perceptual variables described above. Interestingly, once again the findings pertaining to prenatal marijuana exposure were disassociated from maternal use of cigarettes during pregnancy. In contrast to the marijuana findings, prenatal cigarette smoking was negatively associated with both the fundamental capabilities and the application of those basic "building blocks" to the resolution of complex, visual tests–a "bottom-up" impact.

The results of this study, linking *in utero* marijuana exposure to a poorer performance on complex visuoperceptual tasks were interpreted as being consistent with earlier theorizing that prenatal marijuana exposure impacts negatively upon certain facets of EF and by association reflecting aspects of altered prefrontal activity (Fried and Watkinson 2000). The clinical literature describing individuals with damage to this neuroanatomical region is consistent with the proposed marijuana hypothesis linking prenatal exposure with an impact upon the prefrontal area. Patients with injury to this area of the brain are not impaired on basic visuoperceptual tasks but are markedly impacted on tests requiring visuoperceptual planning and integration (Luria 1973; Stuss 1992).

A further line of evidence suggesting a link between prenatal marijuana exposure and aspects of EF can be derived from studies that have focused upon attention–a complex, multidimensional behavior (Denckla 1996; Barkely 1996; Mirskey 1996) with attributes that have considerable commonality with aspects of EF (Barkely 1997). This overlap includes the ability to withhold prepotent but unsuited response tendencies, the capacity to screen out distracting or irrelevant stimuli while focusing on the task at hand, and the faculty of both flexibility and sustainability of focus when appropriate.

The OPPS and MHCPD cohorts have been used at various ages with a number of outcome measures to investigate this domain of functioning. Although different aspects of attention appeared to be impacted, prenatal marijuana use was associated with a negative effect upon attentional processes in both cohorts. Children in the two studies were given a Continuous Performance Task (CPT) (Greenberg and Kindschi 1996).

Both the OPPS (Fried et al. 1992) and MHCPD (Leech et al. 1999) offspring were assessed in this domain at age 6. In the OPPS offspring, prenatal marijuana use was significantly predictive, in a dose response fashion, of increased inattentiveness. In the children born to women who had used more than 5 joints of marijuana per week during pregnancy, inattentiveness increased as the CPT progressed, suggesting that among these more heavily exposed children sustained attention may be particularly vulnerable.

Among the 6 year olds in the MHPCD cohort (Leech et al. 1999), prenatal marijuana exposure was also found to impact upon attentional processes in terms of increased impulsivity. The authors speculated that prenatal marijuana exposure may slow processing speed and that the deficit would become more pronounced over a longer task and if time pressure demands were increased. The CPT results were interpreted by Leech et al. (1999) to be consistent with Fried's (Fried 1996; Fried et al. 1998) speculation that prenatal marijuana exposure impacts upon aspects of EF.

Facets of attention have been the focus of a recent report of the 13 to 16 year olds participating in the OPPS (Fried and Watkinson 2001). The assessment battery that was used in this study permitted the investigation of a number of components of attention which were similar to those described in a multifactorial model of attention developed by Mirsky (1996). Five different elements of attention were identified by factor analytical procedures in Mirsky's model. These included the ability to focus, shift, and maintain attention, consistency of attentional effort over time ("stability") and a process that is conceptually very similar to working memory (Halperin 1996). Among the adolescents in the OPPS study, prenatal marijuana exposure was significantly related with that element of attention described as "stability." Subjects who had been exposed more than 5 times per week *in utero* manifested CPT reaction times that became less consistent as the test proceeded.

The negative impact of prenatal marijuana exposure upon attention noted in the adolescents (Fried and Watkinson 2001) is similar to the findings in the same cohort on a CPT at 6 years of age (Fried et al. 1992). The wide range of ages over which this relationship has been found is consistent with the developmental course of sustained attention which, unlike some other elements of attention, continues to develop throughout childhood and adolescence (McKay et al. 1994).

In the OPPS work when the children were 6 years of age (Fried et al. 1992), in addition to the CPT assessment, the mothers were asked to rate their offspring using a behavioral symptom checklist (Conners 1989). Consistent with the findings on the experimental task, the children exposed prenatally to marijuana were rated by the parent as more impulsive and hyperactive. Paralleling the OPPS observations, a recent report of the MHPCD cohort at 10 years of age (Goldschmidt et al. 2000) noted an association between prenatal marijuana exposure in the first and third trimester and increased parental reports of hyperactivity, inattention and impulsivity.

In this MHPCD study, based on both maternal ratings of child behavior and teachers' reports, an association between increased levels of delinquency and externalizing behavior associated with prenatal marijuana exposure was observed. Using a path analysis, poor attentional skills were interpreted as mediating the association between the mothers' report of delinquency and prenatal marijuana use. This relationship between prenatal marijuana exposure and the behavioral problems in the offspring is similar to an earlier trend noted in the OPPS cohort when the children were between 9 and 12 years of age (O'Connell and Fried 1991). Mothers who had used marijuana regularly during pregnancy rated their children as having a higher rate of conduct disorders but this difference did not retain significance after extraneous variables were controlled.

OVERALL CONCLUSIONS

Although predicated upon a limited body of literature, a suggestive, relatively consistent albeit nascent theoretical picture may be derived. The apparent effects of prenatal marijuana exposure upon offspring are subtle. The emergent picture is that such exposure *in utero* may impact upon particular aspects of a complex higher-order cognitive process termed executive function. Although it is not possible to control all of the host of complex factors that possibly influence the outcomes of interest (Fried and Smith 2000; Fried 2002), the major studies cited have considered and have attempted to take into statistical account such potential confounders and moderating variables as other drug use, parenting socioeconomic status and the home environment. In the longitudinal OPPS and MHPCD studies, in spite of the marked difference in their racial and socioeconomic backgrounds, a considerable degree of similarity in findings is evident lending both validity and reliability to the findings.

The observations and interpretations of the data reviewed in this paper can be synthesized and summarized as follows. After the moderating effects of other risk factors are taken into account, the course of pregnancy, fetal and postnatal growth, and behavior during the neonatal and toddler stages appears relatively unaffected by prenatal marijuana exposure. However, starting at approximately 3 years of age, there are converging findings from a number of researchers implicating that such exposure negatively affect facets of EF, a multifaceted, higher-order cognitive process mediated primarily by the prefrontal cortex. In particular, aspects of EF which appear impacted in the older offspring by maternal marijuana use are in two domains: (1) problem solving tasks that require complex visuoperceptual integration and (2) attention/impulsivity. Consistent with this proposed association is the developmental literature which has identified, via factor analysis, that these two cognitive processes follow a single maturational course.

Although there is a degree of consistency in the extant literature relating prenatal marijuana exposure and the consequences in offspring, the paucity of studies from which the data have been derived (particularly in children older than 3) coupled with the issues raised in the opening paragraphs combine to emphasize the continued need for well-controlled investigations in this topic.

REFERENCES

Abel, E.L. 1980. *Marihuana: The First Twelve Thousand Years*. New York: Plenum Press.

Astley, S., and R. Little. 1990. Maternal marijuana use during lactation and infant development at one year. *Neurotoxicol Teratol* 12:161-168.

Bayley, N. 1989. *Bayley Scales of Infant Development*. New York: Psychological Corporation.

Barkley, R.A. 1996. Critical issues in research on attention. In *Attention, Memory, and Executive Function*. Edited by G.R. Lyon, and N.A. Krasnegor. Baltimore: Paul H. Brookes.

Barkley, R.A. 1997. Behavioral inhibition, sustained attention, and executive functions: Constructing a unifying theory of ADHD. *Psychol Bull* 121:65-94.

Brazelton, T.B. 1973. *Neonatal Behavioral Assessment Scale*. London: William Heinemann and Sons.

Charlebois, A.T., and P.A. Fried. 1980. The interactive effects of nutrition and cannabis upon rat perinatal development. *Dev Psychobiol* 13:591-605.

Conners, C. 1989. *Manual for Conners Rating Scales*. Toronto: MultiHealth Systems.

Dalterio, S.L., and P.A. Fried. 1992. The effects of marijuana use on offspring. In *Perinatal Substance Abuse*. Edited by T.B. Sonderegger. Baltimore: Johns Hopkins University Press.

Damasio, A.R., and S.W. Anderson. 1993. The frontal lobes. In *Clinical Neuropsychology, 3rd ed.* Edited by K.M. Heilman and E. Valenstein. New York: Oxford University Press.

Day, N., M. Cornelius, L. Goldschmidt, G. Richardson, N. Robles, and P. Taylor. 1992. The effects of prenatal tobacco and marijuana use on offspring growth from birth through 3 years of age. *Neurotoxicol Teratol* 14:407-414.

Day, N.L., G.A. Richardson, D. Geva, and N. Robles. 1994a. Alcohol, marijuana, and tobacco: Effects of prenatal exposure on offspring growth and morphology at age six. *Alcohol Clin Exper Res* 18:786-794.

Day, N.L., G.A. Richardson, L. Goldschmidt, N. Robles, P. Taylor, D.S. Stofer, M.D. Cornelius, and D. Geva. 1994b. Effect of prenatal marijuana exposure on the cognitive development of offspring at age three. *Neurotoxicol Teratol* 16:169-175.

Day N., U. Sambamoorthi, P. Taylor, G. Richardson, N. Robles, Y. John, M. Scher, D. Stoffer, M. Cornelius, and D. Jasperse. 1991. Prenatal marijuana use and neonatal outcomes. *Neurotoxicol Teratol* 13:329-334.

Denckla, M.B. 1993. Measurement of executive function. In *Frames of Reference for the Assessment of Learning Disabilities: New Views on Measurement Issues*. Edited by G.R. Lyon. Baltimore: Paul H. Brookes.

Denckla, M.B. 1996. A theory and model of executive function. In *Attention, Memory, and Executive Function*. Edited by G.R. Lyon and N.A. Krasnegor. Baltimore: Paul H. Brookes.

Diamond, A. 2000. Close interrelation of motor development and cognitive development of the cerebellum and prefrontal cortex. *Child Develop* 71:44-56.

Dreher, M. 1997. Cannabis and pregnancy. In *Cannabis in Medical Practice: A Legal, Historical and Pharmacological Overview of the Therapeutic Use of Marijuana*. Edited by M.L. Mathre. Jefferson, NC: McFarland.

Dreher, M.C., Nugent, K. and R. Hudgins. 1994. Prenatal marijuana exposure and neonatal outcomes in Jamaica: An ethnographic study. *Pediatrics* 93:254-260.

Fried, P.A. 1982. Marihuana use by pregnant women and effects on offspring: An update. *Neurotoxicol Teratol* 4:451-454.

Fried, P.A. 1996. Behavioral outcomes in preschool and school-age children exposed prenatally to marijuana: A review and speculative interpretation. In *Behavioral Studies of Drug-Exposed Offspring: Methodological Issues in Human and Animal Research*. Edited by C.L. Wetherington, V.L. Smeriglio, and L.P. Finnegan. National Institute on Drug Abuse Research Monograph 164. Washington: U.S. Government Printing Office.

Fried, P.A. 1998. Behavioral evaluation of the older infant and child. In *Handbook of Developmental Neurotoxicology*. Edited by W. Slikker Jr. and C.W. Chang. San Diego: Academic Press.

Fried, P.A. 2002. Conceptual issues in behavioral teratology and their application in determining long-term sequelae of prenatal marihuana exposure. *J Child Psychol Psychiat* 43:81-102.

Fried, P.A. 2001 Schwangerschaft. In *Cannabis und Cannabinoide. Pharmakologie, Toxikologie und therapeutisches Potenzial*. Edited by F. Grotenhermen. Bern, Switzerland: Verlag Hans Huber.

Fried, P.A., M. Buckingham, and P. Von Kulmiz. 1983. Marijuana use during pregnancy and perinatal risk factors. *Amer J Obstet Gynecol* 144:922-924.

Fried, P.A., and C.M. O'Connell. 1987. A comparison of the effects of prenatal exposure to tobacco, alcohol, cannabis and caffeine on birth size and subsequent growth. *Neurotoxicol Teratol* 9:79-85.

Fried, P.A., D.S. James, and B. Watkinson. 2001. Growth and pubertal milestones during adolescence in offspring prenatally exposed up to cigarettes and marihuana. *Neurotoxicol Teratol* 23:431-436.

Fried, P.A., and J.E. Makin. 1987. Neonatal behavioural correlates of prenatal exposure to marihuana, cigarettes and alcohol in a low risk population. *Neurotoxicol Teratol* 9:1-7.

Fried, P.A., C.M. O'Connell, and B. Watkinson. 1992. 60-and 72-month follow-up of children prenatally exposed to marijuana, cigarettes and alcohol: Cognitive and language assessment. *J Dev Behav Pediatr* 13:383-391.

Fried, P.A., and A. Smith. 2001. A literature review of the consequences of prenatal marihuana exposure. An emerging theme of a deficiency in aspects of executive function. *Neurotoxicol Teratol* 23:1-11.

Fried, P.A., and B. Watkinson. 1988. 12-and 24-month neurobehavioural follow-up of children prenatally exposed to marihuana, cigarettes and alcohol. *Neurotoxicol Teratol* 10:305-313.

Fried, P.A., and B. Watkinson. 1990. 36-and 48-month neurobehavioral follow-up of children prenatally exposed to marijuana, cigarettes and alcohol. *J Dev Behav Pediatr* 11:49-58.

Fried, P.A., and B. Watkinson. 2000. Visuoperceptual functioning differs in 9-to 12-year olds prenatally exposed to cigarettes and marihuana. *Neurotoxicol Teratol* 22:11-20.

Fried, P.A., and B. Watkinson. 2001. Differential effects on facets of attention in adolescents prenatally exposed to cigarettes and marihuana. *Neurotoxicol Teratol* 23:421-430.

Fried, P.A., B. Watkinson, R.F. Dillon, and C.S. Dulberg. 1987. Neonatal neurological status in a low-risk population after prenatal exposure to cigarettes, marijuana and alcohol. *J Dev Behav Ped* 8:318-326.

Fried, P.A., B. Watkinson, A. Grant, and R.K. Knights. 1980. Changing patterns of soft drug use prior to and during pregnancy: A prospective study. *Drug Alcohol Depend* 6:323-343.

Fried, P.A., B. Watkinson, and R. Gray. 1992. A follow-up study of attentional behavior in 6-year-old children exposed prenatally to marihuana, cigarettes and alcohol. *Neurotoxicol Teratol* 14:299-311.

Fried, P.A., B. Watkinson, and R. Gray. 1998. Differential effects on cognitive functioning in 9-to 12-year olds prenatally exposed to cigarettes and marihuana. *Neurotoxicol Teratol* 20:293-306.

Fried, P.A., B. Watkinson, and R. Gray. 1999. Growth from birth to early adolescence in offspring prenatally exposed to cigarettes and marihuana. *Neurotoxicol Teratol* 21:513-525.

Fried, P.A., B. Watkinson. and A. Willan. 1984. Marijuana use during pregnancy and decreased length of gestation. *Am J Obstet Gynecol* 150:23-27.

Fuster, J.M. 1989. *The Prefrontal Cortex: Anatomy, Physiology, and Neuropsychology of the Frontal Lobe, 2nd ed.* New York: Raven Press.

Gibson, G.T., P.A. Bayhurst, and G.P. Colley. 1983. Maternal alcohol, tobacco and cannabis consumption and the outcome of pregnancy. *Aust N Z J Obstet Gynaec* 23:15-19.

Glass, M., M. Dragunow, and R.L.M. Faull. 1997. Cannabinoid receptors in the human brain: A detailed anatomical and quantitative autoradiographic study in the fetal, neonatal and adult human brain. *Neuroscience* 77:299-318.

Goldschmidt, L., N.L. Day, and G.A. Richardson. 2000. Effects of prenatal marijuana exposure on child behavior problems at age 10. *Neurotoxicol Teratol* 22:325-336.

Golub M.S., E.N. Sassenrath, and C.F. Chapman. 1987. Regulation of visual attention in offspring of female monkeys treated chronically with delta-9-tetrahydrocannabinol. *Dev Psychobiol* 14:507-512.

Gordon, M., and D.F. McClure. 1984. *Gordon Diagnostic System: Interpretative Supplement.* Golden, CO: Clinical Diagnostics.

Graham, K., A. Feigenbaum, A. Pastuszak, I. Nulman, R. Weksberg, T. Einarson, S. Goldberg, S. Ashby, and G. Koren. 1992. Pregnancy outcome and infant development following gestational cocaine use by social cocaine users in Toronto, Canada. *Clin Investigative Med* 15:384-394.

Greenberg, L.M., and C.L. Kindschi. 1996. *T.O.V.A.® Clinical Guide.* Los Alamitos: Universal Attention Disorders.

Greenland, S., G.A. Richwald, and G.D. Honda. 1983.The effects of marijuana use during pregnancy. II. A study in a low risk home-delivery population. *Drug Alcohol Depend* 11:359-366.

Greenland, S., K.J. Staisch, N. Brown, and S.J. Gross. 1982. The effects of marijuana use during pregnancy. I. A preliminary epidemiologic study. *Amer J Obstet Gynecol* 143:408-413.

Griffith, D.R., S.D. Azuma, and I.J. Chasnoff. 1994. Three-year outcome of children exposed prenatally to drugs. *J Amer Acad Child Adolesc Psychiat* 33:20-27.

Halperin, J.M. 1996. Conceptualizing, describing, and measuring components of attention. A summary. In *Attention, Memory, and Executive Function*. Edited by G.R. Lyon and N.A. Krasnegor. Baltimore: Paul H. Brookes.

Hatch, E.E., and M.R. Bracken. 1986. Effects of marijuana use in pregnancy on fetal growth. *Amer J Epidemiol* 124:986-993.

Hayes, J., M. Dreher, and K. Nugent. 1988. Newborn outcomes with maternal use in Jamaican women. *Pediatr Nurs* 14:107-110.

Hurt, H., N.L. Brodsky, L. Betancourt, L.E. Braitman, E. Malmud, and J. Giannetta. 1995. Cocaine-exposed children: Follow-up through 30 months. *Dev Behav Ped* 16:29-35.

Johnston, L., P. O'Malley, and J. Bachman. 1994. *National survey results on drug use from Monitoring the Future study, 1975-1993, vol. 2 College Students and Young Adults*. NIDA, Rockville, MD, NIH Publication Number 94-3809.

Johnston, L., P. O'Malley, and J. Bachman. 1996. *National survey results on drug use from the Monitoring the Future study, 1975-1994, vol. 2 College Students and Young Adults*. NIDA, Rockville, MD, NIH Publication Number 96-4027.

Leech, S.L., G. Richardson, L. Goldschmidt, and N.L. Day. 1999. Prenatal substance exposure: Effects on attention and impulsivity of 6-year-olds. *Neurotoxicol Teratol* 21:109-118.

Lester, B., and B.M. Dreher. 1989. Effects of marihuana use during pregnancy on newborn cry. *Child Dev* 60:765-771.

Levin, H.S., K.A. Culhane, J. Hartman, K. Evankovich, A.J. Mattson, H. Harward, G. Ringholtz, L. Ewing-Cobbs, and J.M. Fletcher. 1991. Developmental changes in performance on tests of purported frontal lobe functioning. *Develop. Neuropsychol* 7: 377-395.

Lezak, M.D. 1995. *Neuropsychological Assessment, 3rd ed.* New York: Oxford University Press.

Luria, A.R. 1973. *The Working Brain. An Introduction to Neuropsychology*. London: Penguin Press.

McKay, K.E., J.M. Halperin, S.T. Schwartz, and V. Sharma. 1994. Developmental analysis of three aspects of information processing: Sustained attention, selective attention, and response organization. *Dev Neuropsychol* 10:121-132.

McCarthy, P. 1972. *McCarthy Scales of Children's Abilities*. New York: The Psychological Corporation.

Mirsky, A.F. 1996. Disorders of attention. A neuropsychological perspective. In *Attention, Memory, and Executive Function*. Edited by G.R. Lyon and N.A. Krasnegor. Baltimore: Paul H. Brookes.

National Pregnancy and Health Survey. 1996. *Drug use among women delivering live births, 1992*. NIDA, Rockville, MD, NIH Publication Number 96-3819.

O'Connell, C.M., and P.A. Fried. 1984. An investigation of prenatal Cannabis exposure and minor physical anomalies in a low risk population. *Neurotoxicol Teratol* 6:345-350.

O'Connell, C.M., and P.A. Fried. 1991. Prenatal exposure to cannabis: A preliminary report of postnatal consequences in school-age children. *Neurotoxicol Teratol*, 13:631-639.

Reitan, R., and L. Davison. 1974. *Clinical Neuropsychology*. New York: John Wiley and Sons.

Richardson, G.A., and N.L. Day. 1997. A comparison of the effect of prenatal marijuana, alcohol, and cocaine use on 10-year child outcome. *Neurotoxicol Teratol* 19:256.

Richardson, G., N. Day, and P. Taylor. 1989. The effect of prenatal alcohol, marijuana, and tobacco exposure on neonatal behavior. *Infant Behav Dev* 12:199-209.

Richardson, G.A., N.L. Day, and L. Goldschmidt. 1995. Prenatal alcohol, marijuana, and tobacco use: Infant mental and motor development. *Neurotoxicol Teratol* 17:479-487.

Scher, M., G. Richardson, P. Coble, N. Day, and D. Stoffer. 1988. The effects of prenatal alcohol and marijuana exposure: Disturbances in neonatal sleep cycling and arousal. *Pediatr Res* 24:101-105.

Siegel, L.S., and E.B. Ryan. 1989. The development of working memory in normally achieving and subtypes of learning disabled children. *Child Dev* 60:973-980.

Spreen, O., and Strauss, E. 1991. *A Compendium of Neuropsychological Tests: Administration, Norms and Commentary*. London: Oxford University Press.

Stuss, D.T. 1992. Biological and psychological development of executive functions. *Brain Cognit* 20:8-23.

Tennes, K., N. Avitable, C. Blackard, C. Boyles, B. Hassoun, L. Holmes, and M. Kreye. 1985. Marijuana: Prenatal and postnatal exposure in the human. In *Current Research on the Consequences of Maternal Drug Abuse*. Edited by T.M. Pinkert. NIDA Research Monograph No. 59. Rockville: U.S. Department of Human Health and Services.

Thorndike, R.L., E. Hagan, and J. Sattler. 1986. *The Stanford-Binet Intelligence Scale: 4th ed*. Chicago: Riverside Publishing.

Welsh, M.C., B.F. Pennington, and D.B. Groisser. 1991. A normative-developmental study of executive function: A window on prefrontal function in children. *Develop Neuropsychol* 7:131-149.

Wechsler, D. 1991. *Wechsler Intelligence Scale for Children 3rd ed*. New York: The Psychological Corporation.

Zuckerman, B., D. Frank, R. Hingson, H. Amaro, S. Levenson, H. Kayne, S. Parker, R. Vinci, K. Aboagye, L. Fried, H. Cabral, R. Timperi, and H. Bauchner. 1989. Effects of maternal marijuana and cocaine use on fetal growth. *N Eng J Med* 320:762-768.

Cannabis and Harm Reduction: A Nursing Perspective

Mary Lynn Mathre

SUMMARY. The goal of nursing care is to promote health and reduce harm caused by injury, disease, or poor self-care. Harm reduction is a public health model, which is gaining popularity as an effective modality to help persons reduce the negative consequences associated with their drug use. The harm reduction model blends well with the core principles of nursing. When viewed from a nursing perspective, cannabis could be an effective harm reduction agent based on its high benefit-low risk ratio when compared to other standard medications/drugs. As a medicine, cannabis has demonstrated a high therapeutic potential with relatively few side effects or adverse reactions. As a social/recreational drug, cannabis has a wide margin of safety with relatively few risks. The greatest risks from cannabis use are the legal consequences, which are the result of the cannabis prohibition rather than the drug itself. The therapeutic relationship between individuals and their health care providers is severely compromised by the cannabis prohibition. *[Article copies available for a fee from The Haworth Document Delivery Service: 1-800-HAWORTH. E-mail address: <getinfo@haworthpressinc.com> Website: <http://www.HaworthPress. com> © 2002 by The Haworth Press, Inc. All rights reserved.]*

KEYWORDS. Cannabis, medical marijuana, harm reduction, nursing, social drug use, recreational drug use, adolescent drug use, cannabis prohibition, marijuana prohibition

Mary Lynn Mathre, RN, MSN, CARN, is Addictions Consult Nurse, University of Virginia Health System, Charlottesville, VA, and President and Cofounder of Patients Out of Time, 1472 Fish Pond Road, Howardsville, VA 24562 (E-mail: ML@ medicalcannabis.com).

[Haworth co-indexing entry note]: "Cannabis and Harm Reduction: A Nursing Perspective." Mathre, Mary Lynn. Co-published simultaneously in *Journal of Cannabis Therapeutics* (The Haworth Integrative Healing Press, an imprint of The Haworth Press, Inc.) Vol. 2, No. 3/4, 2002, pp. 105-120; and: *Women and Cannabis: Medicine, Science, and Sociology* (ed: Ethan Russo, Melanie Dreher, and Mary Lynn Mathre) The Haworth Integrative Healing Press, an imprint of The Haworth Press, Inc., 2002, pp. 105-120. Single or multiple copies of this article are available for a fee from The Haworth Document Delivery Service [1-800-HAWORTH, 9:00 a.m. - 5:00 p.m. (EST). E-mail address: getinfo@haworthpressinc.com].

INTRODUCTION

Nursing is the art and science of caring. Since 1999 when nurses were included in the Gallup "Honesty and Ethics" poll, nurses have been rated as one of the most trusted professional groups by the American public (http://www.gallup.com/poll/releases/pro011205.asp). What is it about nurses that the public is willing to trust? Could it be that nurses often see people in their most vulnerable states and during that time treat them with respect and provide a safe environment to nurture them back to a more independent self-caring state? Nursing is much more than simply caring and providing comfort; it involves the art of knowing how to give the right kind of care and comfort to facilitate the healing process, and this knowledge is based in science. The goal of nursing care is to promote health and reduce the harm caused by injury, disease, or poor self-care.

Nurses are the largest group of health care professionals, and are keenly aware of the potential risks related to medications. While pharmacists dispense medications and physicians prescribe medications, nurses administer them to countless numbers of patients and monitor the effects of the medications. Nurses are in a key position to see not only the beneficial effects of a particular medication, but also the side effects or adverse reactions that can accompany medications even when used as recommended. Safe administration of medication is a critical skill all nurses must master because any error could cost a patient added suffering, organ damage, or could result in death.

Harm reduction is a public health approach to human behaviors, which involves helping persons learn to make better personal choices to minimize the potential risks associated with their behavior. Examples of harm reduction practices include using condoms properly during intercourse to avoid STDs, wearing a seatbelt when traveling in a motor vehicle, or using a helmet when riding a motorcycle. Today, harm reduction is gaining popularity as a more effective and realistic modality for helping persons who use drugs to reduce negative consequences associated with their drug use. Such harm reduction strategies include needle exchange programs for intravenous drug users to prevent blood-borne infections, use of a designated driver for persons consuming alcohol away from home, overdose prevention education, and offering a variety of drug treatment options (www.harmreduction.org).

Harm reduction is based on the premise that people are responsible for their behavior, that they make personal choices that affect their health and well-being, and that they can make safer and better decisions if given useful and honest information. The harm reduction approach accepts the fact that individuals will use drugs for various reasons and offers to help them "where they're at." In contrast, the War on Drugs is based on the premise that certain drugs are "bad" and that the government has the paternal right and duty to prohibit the use of these drugs. This "zero tolerance" or "just say no" approach condemns the use of certain drugs and punishes those who use them. Acceptance comes after transgressors admit their wrongful ways and adhere to the abstinence option.

The underlying flaw in the war on drugs is the belief that some drugs are inherently bad and therefore deserve to be prohibited for the greater good of society. A drug is not simply good or bad, right or wrong, but rather the manner of use of a drug by an individual may be helpful or harmful. The harm reduction approach is based on science and the respect of others, while the war on drugs is based on moralistic ideology and the control of others. Drug use will always have the potential of causing sequelae. Harm reduction strives to minimize the harmful effects from drug use, while the drug prohibition creates more harmful effects from drug use.

Cannabis is an herbal agent that has been used as a medicine, a recreational drug, as well as a source of food and fiber. It is environmentally friendly, essentially non-toxic, yet currently forbidden by our federal government. US citizens are prohibited from growing this plant or possessing any of its leaves, seeds, stems or flowers. Physicians are forbidden to prescribe it for medical use. When the cannabis plant is examined in a scientific and logical manner, its therapeutic value becomes apparent. From a nursing perspective cannabis could be a useful harm reduction tool, yet the laws prohibiting its use present contrived risks that can cause more harm than the drug itself.

This article will examine cannabis as a harm reduction agent from a nursing perspective. Cannabis as medicine is not a magic bullet that will work for everyone, and is not without potential risks. Cannabis as a recreational drug is not enjoyable for everyone and is not harmless, but when put in the broader perspective and compared to standard medicines or common recreational drugs, cannabis offers greater benefit with fewer relative risks.

CANNABIS WAS A MEDICINE IN THE US

Prior to the prohibition of marijuana, cannabis products were widely used by physicians. By the 1930s there were 23 pharmaceutical companies producing cannabis preparations. In 1937, the passage of the Marihuana Tax Act marked the beginning of the cannabis prohibition. The head of the Federal Bureau of Narcotics (now the Drug Enforcement Administration or DEA), Harry Anslinger, led this legislative effort using exaggerations and lies (Bonnie and Whitebread 1974). During the congressional hearings the American Medical Association (AMA) opposed the Act and supported cannabis as a therapeutic agent. The lawmakers won and the AMA has since given up the fight.

The Controlled Substances Act of 1970 furthered the cannabis prohibition when it called for a system to classify psychoactive drugs according to their risk potential. Five Schedules were created, with Schedule I being the most restrictive category. Under the Act, cannabis was initially placed in Schedule I, but Congress called for a National Commission on Marihuana and Drug Abuse to determine whether or not that placement was appropriate. President Nixon appointed most of the commissioners including the former Republican Governor of Pennsylvania, Raymond Shafer, as the chairman. The "Shafer Commission" completed their study in 1972, and it remains the most comprehensive review of marijuana ever conducted by the federal government. In the end, the Shafer Commission concluded that cannabis did not belong in Schedule I and stated (National Commission on Marihuana and Drug Abuse 1972, p. 130), "Marihuana's relative potential for harm to the vast majority of individual users and its actual impact on society does not justify a social policy designed to seek out and firmly punish those who use it." The recommendations were ignored and cannabis remained in Schedule I, a forbidden drug.

Now, thirty years later, the infamous Nixon tapes of Oval Office conversations from 1971 to 1972 have been declassified and made available to the public (transcripts available at www.csdp.org). It is clear that Nixon used his political power to influence the outcome of the Shafer Commission, and when that didn't work he simply dismissed their recommendations and launched the war on drugs. Curiously, at the same time, the Bain Commission in The Netherlands (with a similar mission) issued its report with similar findings. The government of The Netherlands acted on the recommendations of the Bain Commission, and today the Dutch have half of the per capita cannabis use as the U.S., with far fewer drug-related problems at much lower drug enforcement costs (Zeese 2002).

CANNABIS AS A HARM REDUCTION MEDICINE

Compared to standard medications, cannabis has a remarkably wide margin of safety. In 1988, after a lengthy legal battle to reschedule cannabis, the DEA Administrative Law Judge, Francis Young, ruled that marijuana should be assigned to Schedule II and thus available for physicians to prescribe. In his summary he noted that (p. 57), "Marijuana in its natural form is one of the safest therapeutically active substances known to man." Throughout the centuries of its use, there has never been a death from cannabis (Abel 1980). In contrast, there are more than 32,000 deaths per year associated with prescription medications in hospitalized patients (Lazarou, Pomeranz and Corey 1998). All opioids carry the risk of overdose. Even over-the-counter (OTC) medications can be lethal. There are approximately 120 annual deaths from aspirin.

Cannabis has been studied extensively in regard to determining its health risks. General McCaffrey called upon the Institute of Medicine (IOM) to study the therapeutic value of marijuana in 1997. In March of 1999 the IOM released its 18-month study, which concluded that cannabis does have therapeutic value and is safe for medical use (Joy, Watson and Benson 1999). Concern was noted about the potential risks related to smoking medicine, but the study concluded that for patients suffering from cancer or AIDS, the potential pulmonary risks were minimal when compared to the benefits. The study also noted that while more research is warranted, cannabis is safe enough for physicians to conduct N-of-1 studies on their patients who they believe could benefit from cannabis if other medications are not effective.

The IOM report put health risks associated with cannabis in perspective noting (p. 5), ". . . except for the harms associated with smoking, the adverse effects of marijuana use are within the range of effects tolerated for other medications." A recent study of the chronic effects of cannabis on four of the seven federally provided medical marijuana patients showed minor bronchitis in 2 of the patients (Russo et al. 2002). These patients smoked from 5 to 10 low-grade (2% to 4% THC content) cannabis cigarettes on a daily basis for 10 to 20 years. No other attributable long-term problems were noted, but rather a reduction in their use of other medications and a feeling of well-being was experienced by the patients.

While smoking cannabis may cause lung damage after chronic use, there are various actions that can be taken to reduce the harm from smoking. Patients can smoke less if using a high potency product (THC content greater than 10%) and can easily adjust the dosage by decreasing the number of inhalations. Also, when smoking cannabis, patients should limit their breath holding to less than ten seconds to avoid lung damage (Tashkin 2001). Vaporizers are being developed that heat the plant material to the point of vaporization without combustion, thus avoiding smoke inhalation (Gieringer 2001, Whittle, Guy and Robson 2001). Finally patients may use cannabis in alternative delivery forms such as pills, sublingual spray, eye drops, suppository, dermal patch, or salve, thereby eliminating pulmonary risks.

The federal government claims that cannabis is harmful to the immune system. When reviewing the published animal studies that reported harm to the immune system the reader should note that most of the researchers used delta-9-tetrahydrocannabinol (THC) rather than natural cannabis and that extremely high doses were used. A review of the active ingredients in cannabis suggests that some of these constituents act synergistically to enhance the beneficial effects of THC, while others may mitigate the harmful side effects of THC including possible immunosuppression (McPartland and Russo 2001). Given the thousands of immuno-compromised patients who have used cannabis there have been no reports of direct damage to the immune system from cannabis except when the patient has used a contaminated supply. Many AIDS patients who, by virtue of their disease have a severely compromised immune system, do not show any decline in their health status related to cannabis. In fact, a recent study of cannabis use by AIDS patients showed that cannabis did not interfere with protease inhibitors and helped increase weight gain for a significant number of patients (Abrams et al. 2000).

Another cannabis risk has been an allegation that it causes brain damage. Although the federal government continues to use this scare tactic, modern research has not confirmed such findings. A Johns Hopkins study examined cannabis' effects on cognition on 1318 subjects over a 15-year period (Lyketsos et al. 1999). The researchers found no significant differences in cognitive decline between heavy users, light users, and nonusers of cannabis. They concluded that the results provided strong evidence of the absence of long-term residual effects of cannabis use on cognition.

Perhaps the most illogical argument the federal government uses to prohibit the therapeutic use of cannabis is that to allow its medical use would "send the wrong message to our youth." General Barry McCaffrey openly fought the growing popular opinion and scientific findings that cannabis has medical value. In response to the passage of state initiatives allowing the medical use of marijuana, McCaffrey dismissed its therapeutic value and declared that state laws allowing medical use of cannabis would increase the rate of drug use among teenagers. He stated, "While we are trying to educate American adolescents that psychoactive drugs are bad, now we have this apparent message that says 'No they're medicine. They're good for you'" (Substance Abuse Report 1996). That is nonsense. Teenagers don't think, "Insulin is medicine. It must be good for me." A persistent message that parents and health care professionals should demonstrate and reinforce with children and teenagers is that medicine is for sick people and that all medicine should be used with caution based upon an awareness of the risks and benefits.

Since nurses are advocates and health educators for patients, families, and communities, they have a key role in helping others learn to use medications safely. With more than 400,000 medication preparations available in the U.S. it is unlikely that any person can know everything about these medications. However, the user can reduce harm from medications by following some general guidelines designed to ensure that the risks are minimized. Mothers Against Misuse and Abuse (MAMA) has developed medication guidelines that persons may follow when using any OTC, prescribed medication, or recreational drug. The premise for these guidelines is that no medication is completely risk-free, but harm can be minimized if the user has appropriate information to make an informed decision. MAMA seeks opportunities to teach these guidelines to parents to help them set a good example for their children when it comes to the use of medications or recreational drugs (www.

mamas.org). This includes essential information that nurses include in their patient education, such as the name of the medication, desired effect, possible side effects or adverse reactions, proper dosage and route of administration, risk of tolerance, dependence or drug interactions.

Pain is the most frequent symptom for patients seeking medical care. Cannabis analgesia provides a good example of its potential as a harm reduction medication. Innumerable chronic pain patients have found it difficult to find a balance between managing their pain and being able to function in daily life. Opiates are frequently used for management of severe pain, however they sometimes leave the patient feeling "drugged" and come with the risk of overdose and side effects such as constipation, nausea and vomiting. Increasingly, patients are acting on the advice of others and are trying cannabis as an analgesic.

Per numerous reports (Mathre 1985, Corral, Black and Dalotto 2002, Russo et al. 2002, Rosenblum and Wenner, 2002), the introduction of cannabis into pain management regimens has been very helpful. Most patients report a significant reduction in the use of opioids or need them on occasion for acute exacerbations; this reduction in the use of opioids lessens the risk for physical dependence. Cannabis is an effective antiemetic, and is not constipating. In summary, many chronic pain patients who use cannabis report that they feel better, experience fewer untoward side effects, are able to reduce their use of opioids and other medications, and are thereby able to eliminate additional side effects that may accompany those medications as well as the added risks from drug interactions.

Margo McCaffery (1968) has taught us that pain "is whatever the experiencing person says it is, existing whenever he says it does." Pain is a subjective experience and patient feedback is essential to effective pain management. Current national guidelines for pain management endorse McCaffery's standard (Jacox et al. 1994). Given patients' reports of pain control with cannabis and its relative safety, nurses recognize that cannabis should be an option for patients. To date 11 state nurses associations (AK, CA, CO, HI, MS, NJ, NM, NY, NC, VA, and WI) have passed formal resolutions supporting patient access to this medicine (www.medicalcannabis.com). In addition, the American Nurses Association's Congress on Nursing Practice issued a statement in 1996 calling for the education of all RNs on evidence-based therapeutic indications for cannabis.

CANNABIS AS A SOCIAL/RECREATIONAL DRUG

While the federal government may be waging a war on certain drugs, it is clear to onlookers that America is a drug using society. Americans are constantly bombarded with advertisements for drugs that can take care of any of life's problems. We have pills to help us sleep, to help us stay awake, to help us calm down, to help us feel better, to take away our pain, to regulate our bowels, and on and on. We tend to call these drugs, *medications*, and that identifies them as "good" drugs. Americans don't even consider caffeine as a drug, but for many a cup of coffee in the morning is a must to start their day. Caffeinated drinks are even marketed to our youth with such lines as: "Do the Dew"–as though kids need any more energy. (For children with too much energy, we simply drug them with a "medication" such as Ritalin®.) We also have regulated drugs that are acceptable for adult usage. Alcohol can be used for enjoyment: "This Bud's for you." The tobacco industry is struggling with the mandated health warnings and their advertisement ploys. "Smoking may cause lung cancer" versus "You've come a long way baby" or the "Joe Camel" character.

Psychoactive drug use has and will be a part of our society. In the American culture, drug experimentation among adolescents is considered normative behavior (Newcomb and Bentler 1988, Shedler and Block 1990). Adolescence is a time of transition, when young people are trying to determine their identity. Testing limits are part of their developmental process and the "forbidden" drugs are for many a temptation too great to resist. A longitudinal study investigated the psychological characteristics and drug use patterns in children studied from age 3 to 18 (Shedler and Block 1990). Those adolescents who experimented with drugs (primarily cannabis) were the "best-adjusted" compared to abstainers and frequent users.

These children were tested prior to the initiation of drug use and there were notable antecedent personality differences. The frequent users were found to be relatively maladjusted as children, unable to form good relationships, insecure and showed signs of emotional distress. The abstainers were relatively over controlled, timid, fearful, and morose. Authors described (p. 617), ". . . the picture of the frequent user that emerges is one of a troubled adolescent, an adolescent who is interpersonally alienated, emotionally withdrawn, and manifestly unhappy, and who expresses his or her maladjustment through uncontrolled, overtly antisocial behavior." In contrast, they noted (p. 618), ". . . the picture of the abstainer that emerges is of a relatively tense, overcontrolled, emotionally constricted individual who is somewhat socially isolated and lacking in interpersonal skills." The experimenters were found to be psychologically healthy, sociable, and reasonably inquisitive individuals. Twenty years earlier Hogan et al. (1970) compared marijuana users with non-users in a college population. They found that users (p. 63) "are more socially skilled, have a broader range of interests, are more adventuresome, and more concerned with the feelings of others." Nonusers were found to be (p. 61) "too deferential to external authority, narrow in their interests, and overcontrolled."

Shedler and Block (1990) also examined the quality of parenting the children received through direct observations of mother-child interactions when the children were 5 years old. Compared to the mothers of the experimenters, the mothers of the frequent users and abstainers (p. 624) "were perceived to be cold, critical, pressuring, and unresponsive to their children's needs." They found no noteworthy findings involving the fathers of frequent users. However, when compared to the fathers of experimenters, the fathers of abstainers were seen (p. 625) "as relatively unresponsive to their children's needs and as authoritarian, autocratic, and domineering."

The researchers caution readers not to misinterpret their findings as an encouragement for adolescents to use drugs. The findings do indicate that problem drug use is a symptom, not a cause of personal and social maladjustment. It is also helpful to understand that experimentation with certain behaviors can be expected with healthy adolescents. When it comes to the potential risks of drug experimentation, cannabis is a relatively safer drug choice.

The federal government has historically used the *stepping stone* hypothesis and *gateway drug* hypothesis as valid reasons for the marijuana prohibition. The stepping stone hypothesis presumes that there are pharmacological properties in cannabis that lead the user to progress to other drugs, while the gateway theory presumes that as an illicit drug cannabis serves as an entry to access other illicit drugs. The premise of both theories is that cannabis use leads to harder, more dangerous drug *abuse*. There is no question that cocaine, methamphetamine, heroin or other hard drug users may have used cannabis in their earlier stages of drug use, but there has never been a causal relationship established. In fact, most drug users begin with alcohol and nicotine, usually when they are too young to do so legally. The Shafer Commission noted (p. 88), "No verification is found of a causal relationship between marihuana use and subsequent heroin use." The IOM report found that (Joy, Watson and Benson 1999, p. 6), "There is no conclusive evidence that the drug effects of marijuana are causally linked to the subsequent abuse of other illicit drugs." More recently, a study by Jan van Ours of Tilberg University in The Netherlands, which will be published by the Centre for Economic Policy Research in London, also concluded that cannabis is not a gateway drug (Sunday Times 2001). It is not the cannabis that is associated with progression to other illicit drugs, but rather its illegal status that makes it a gateway drug.

When compared to the legal and regulated drugs such as alcohol and tobacco, cannabis is much less harmful. I have worked as a registered nurse for more than 25 years in acute care facilities and during the past 10, I have served as the addictions consult nurse in a university hospital setting. During that time I have had the typical nursing experience of caring for persons who were hospitalized as a result of their drug use. Common reasons for admissions related to alcohol abuse include: traumatic injuries secondary to acute intoxication (motor vehicle accidents, falls, fights, etc.), overdose with alcohol alone or in combination with other drugs/medications, life-threatening alcohol withdrawal, pancreatitis, liver disease, gastro-intestinal bleeding, cardiomyopathy, cardiac arrhythmias secondary to acute intoxication, depression, suicide attempts, various cancers, and malnutrition. Common admissions related to tobacco dependence include: heart attacks, vascular diseases, pulmonary problems, and various cancers. Hospital admissions for cannabis related health problems are rare. Alcohol is responsible for more than 100,000 annual deaths, nicotine for more than 430,700 (Schneider Institute for Health Policy, 2001), while use of cannabis has never killed anyone due to toxicity.

Driving under the influence of alcohol is the second leading cause for motor vehicle accidents after fatigue. While driving under the influence of any psychoactive drug is not recommended, several studies have shown that cannabis use does not seem to significantly impair driving performance and thus is not associated with an increase in accidents (National Commission on Marihuana and Drug Abuse 1972, Hunter et al. 1998, Bates and Blakely 1999, Frood 2002). It seems that drivers on cannabis tend to be aware of their intoxicated state and therefore drive more cautiously to compensate. The new study by the Transport Research laboratory in England did find that drivers under the influence of cannabis showed impairment in their tracking ability (being able to hold a constant speed while following the middle of the road), but those with a blood alcohol level of 50 mg/dl (0.05 g) showed even more impairment (Frood 2002).

In 1996, two leading experts in psychoactive drugs rated 6 commonly used drugs (Hilts 1994) (Table 1). Henningfield and Benowitz ranked nicotine, heroin, cocaine, alcohol, caffeine, and marijuana according to their potential risks for withdrawal symptoms, reinforcement, tolerance, addiction, and intoxication. They rated marijuana as the least serious risk, except for intoxication in which they both ranked it above caffeine and nicotine.

In recent years, treatment programs have had an increase in admissions for "marijuana dependence." The reason for this increase seems to be due to the fact that individuals charged with marijuana offenses (usually simple possession) are offered a choice of incarceration or treatment. Most choose to stay out of prison and enter treatment for "marijuana dependence." Just recently, the current director of the Office of National Drug Control Policy (ONDCP), John Walters, spoke to 4,500 teens and adults at the Pride World Drug Prevention Conference in Cincinnati. He told the audience that 65% of drug-dependent people have a primary or secondary dependence on marijuana and that (Kranz 2002), "Marijuana is two-thirds of the addiction problem in America today . . . We have too many people trapped in addiction to marijuana because they thought it couldn't happen, or they were told it couldn't happen." Where did

TABLE 1. Ranking of Risk of 6 Commonly Used Drugs

	Withdrawal		Reinforcement		Tolerance		Dependence		Intoxication	
	NIDA	UCSF	NIDA	UCSF	NIDA	UCSF	NIDA	UCSF	NIDA	UCSF
Nicotine	3	3	4	4	2	4	1	1	5	6
Heroin	2	2	2	2	1	2	2	2	2	2
Cocaine	4	3	1	1	4	1	3	3	3	3
Alcohol	1	1	3	3	3	4	4	4	1	1
Caffeine	5	4	6	5	5	3	5	5	6	5
Marijuana	6	5	5	6	6	5	6	6	4	4

Ranking scale: 1 = Most serious 6 = Least serious

Explanation of terms
Withdrawal–Presence and severity of characteristic withdrawal symptoms.
Reinforcement–Substance's ability, in human and animal tests, to get users to take it repeatedly, and instead of other substances.
Tolerance–Amount of substance needed to satisfy increasing cravings, and level of plateau that is eventually reached.
Dependence (Addiction)–Difficulty in ending use of substance, relapse rate, percentage of people who become addicted, addicts self-reporting of degree of need for substance, and continued use in face of evidence that it causes harm.
Intoxication–Level of intoxication associated with addiction, personal, and social damage that substance causes.

By Dr. Jack E. Henningfield of the National Institute of Drug Abuse (NIDA) and Dr. Neal L. Benowitz of the University of California at San Francisco (UCSF), data from an article in the *New York Times* (August 2, 1994, p. C3).

these numbers originate? Drug experts Henningfield and Benowitz ranked marijuana as the least likely to lead to addiction or dependence. Inquiries made to the ONDCP asking for the source of these figures have remained unanswered. The IOM report (1999) concluded that marijuana is not highly addictive. Hopefully the American public will not accept these gross exaggerations.

One must ask the question that given the health and social risks related to alcohol and tobacco, which are regulated drugs for adult use, why isn't cannabis regulated for adults to use as well? Politicians, such as Representative Barr and Senator Feinstein, have justified the continued marijuana prohibition by rationalizing that we simply shouldn't add another *dangerous* drug for adults. From a harm reduction perspective one would have to ask, why wouldn't it make sense to allow adults to choose to use cannabis, a drug that is much less harmful (this is not to say it is *harmless*) to individuals and society?

CANNABIS PROHIBITION CAUSES MORE HARM
THAN THE DRUG

Cannabis is the most commonly used illicit recreational/social drug in the US. Today, at least 76 million Americans have tried it (Substance Abuse and Mental Health Services Administration 2000, p. G-4). Many of those Americans who have risked "breaking the law" by using cannabis have suffered harsh consequences. In 2000, 46.5% (or 734,497) of the 1,579,566 total arrests for drug abuse violations were for cannabis. Of those, 88% (or 646,042 people) were arrested for possession alone (Federal Bureau of Investigation 2001). With mandatory minimums for drug offenses, the prison sentences for cannabis convictions can be as long as several decades to life. Why are we willing to spend so much on prison terms for non-violent marijuana offenders? Are they truly such a danger to society that we are willing to take away their freedom and pay up to $40,000 per year per individual in prison costs? Would it not be wiser to allow them to continue to work and pay taxes? Couldn't this money be better spent by using it for drug addicts who are seeking treatment?

Children may be removed from their homes because a parent has been convicted of cannabis possession. Family members convicted of cannabis possession have been sent hundreds to thousands of miles away to serve time in overcrowded out-of-state prisons. These non-violent cannabis prisoners are often at the mercy of hardened criminals and suffer rapes, assaults and even death while in prison. Are they such a danger to society that we are willing to destroy the lives of these individuals and break up their families?

The Shafer Commission was very clear in their conclusions that such punishment was unwarranted (p. 78): "Neither the marihuana user nor the drug itself can be said to constitute a danger to public safety," and (p. 96), "Most users, young and old, demonstrate an average or above average degree of social functioning, academic achievement, and job performance." The Commission concluded (p. 41), "The most notable statement that can be made about the vast majority of marihuana users–experimenters and intermittent users–is that they are essentially indistinguishable from their non-marihuana using peers by any fundamental criterion other than their marihuana use." Yet hundreds of thousands of Americans remain behind bars separated from their families because of the marijuana prohibition. Readers may consult the web site of Families Against Mandatory Minimums (FAMM) for more information (www.famm.org).

Drug testing in the workplace remains a controversial issue. Most government organizations and private companies that perform drug testing conduct urine drug screens. To many this testing is an invasion of privacy, especially when done as a pre-employment requirement or random on-the-job testing. Urine testing is not a screen for drug abuse, it only tests for past drug use. There are numerous issues associated with drug testing, but cannabis poses a particular problem. The metabolites from THC are fat-soluble and can remain in the body for up to a month after the last use. Alcohol, in contrast, can be out of the system in a day (and is often not even included in the urine screen). Countless numbers of citizens have lost an opportunity for employment or been fired from their job based solely on a drug screen positive for cannabis.

There are waiting lists at many drug treatment facilities. Cannabis users who have been coerced into treatment by threat of incarceration or job loss are filling the openings that could and should be available for persons whose lives have been destroyed by their drug addiction. This is not to say that no cannabis users may be in need of help, but rather there are alcoholics, IV drug addicts, crack cocaine addicts and others who have lost all control and are desperate for help that are turned away because there is no room for them.

The policy of prohibition interferes with the procedures necessary for quality control of this medication/drug necessary to prevent the risks of infection or other untoward reactions resulting from a contaminated product. Patients (especially AIDS patients) can suffer from a respiratory tract infection if the cannabis becomes moldy with the *Aspergillus* fungus (Krampf 1997, McPartland, Clarke and Watson 2000). Patients/users can also suffer toxic effects of other contaminants such as Paraquat, a highly toxic herbicide that was used by the federal government to destroy marijuana crops (McPartland, Clarke and Watson 2000).

The therapeutic use of cannabis could greatly reduce the financial costs to patients when they are able to eliminate other medications. The cost of therapeutic cannabis should be minimal in a regulated environment. However, prohibition has inflated the price of cannabis to that of gold. More important than the financial costs, patients who could benefit from the therapeutic use of cannabis are denied this medicine that may help them when all other medications have failed. There is no excuse for denying them the option of trying this medicine.

Denying patients access to therapeutic cannabis does nothing to prevent substance use/abuse among adolescents. The government claims they are concerned about drug abuse among our children and that by acknowledging the therapeutic potential of cannabis they would be sending the wrong message to our youth. Rather, the continued prohibition sends other more chilling messages to our youth: Their government is willing to put patients in prison simply for taking a medicine to ease their suffering. Their government will ignore, try to cover up, or lie about scientific studies that do not support its unjust policies/laws. If their government is lying about cannabis, what else is it lying about?

Finally, cannabis prohibition interferes with open communication between patients and their healthcare providers (Mathre 1985). Patients fear talking to their primary care provider because of possible negative reactions. Patients don't want their use noted in their health record because they fear there may be legal consequences. This fear of admitting to cannabis use to their healthcare provider interferes with the development of a trusting relationship. Healthcare professionals cannot adequately monitor the effects of cannabis if they aren't aware of its use. Health care professionals cannot educate the cannabis user about the potential risks of cannabis if they are unaware of its use.

CONCLUSIONS

The possibility of a "drug free" society is unrealistic. People seek and use drugs to feel better. Medications/drugs are not risk free, but the risks can be minimized only with accurate and readily available information on the harmful effects prior to their use. Compared to most medications available today, cannabis is remarkably safe and effective and therefore should be available as an initial option to patients. As a social/recreational drug, the effects of cannabis are pleasant for many with little personal or societal risks and therefore may be the safer choice compared to other social/recreational drugs used by adults. While concern is justified about the dangers related to children and teenagers using drugs, the lies and cruelty of the marijuana prohibition are confusing to young people who learn not to trust their government. The harm resulting from the prohibition of cannabis costs individuals and our society as a whole much more than the drug itself.

When viewed from a nursing perspective, cannabis can be a useful therapeutic agent if it were legally available. Cannabis could be a useful harm reduction agent for substance abuse if it were regulated. The greatest harm from cannabis is the threat of legal consequences related to its illegal status. Nurses and other health care providers can play a vital role in reducing the harmful effects from medication/drug use. Health care professionals can teach patients and the public how to minimize the potentially harmful effects of cannabis when it is used as a medicine or social/recreational drug, but as long as cannabis remains in Schedule I, health care providers will be reluctant to talk with their patients about this drug. The role of the health care provider is severely compromised by cannabis prohibition and society suffers from this unjust, cruel, and costly policy.

REFERENCES

Abel, E.L. 1980. *Marihuana: The first twelve thousand years.* New York: Plenum Press.
Abrams, D.I., S.B. Leiser, S.B. Shade, J. Hilton, and T. Elbeik. 2000. Short-term effects of cannabinoids on HIV-1 viral load. Poster presentation at the 13th International AIDS Conference, Durban, South Africa. 13 July 2000.

Bates, M.N. and T.A. Blakely. 1999. Role of cannabis in motor vehicle crashes. *Epidemiol Rev* 21(2): 222-232.

Bonnie, R.J. and C.H. Whitebread. 1974. *The marihuana conviction: A history of the marihuana prohibition in the United States*. Charlottesville, VA: University Press of Virginia.

Compton, D.R., W.O. Dewey, and B.R. Martin. 1990. Cannabis dependence and tolerance production. *Adv Alcohol Subst Abuse* 9(1-2):129-147.

Corral, V.L., H. Black, and T. Dalotto. 2002. Medical cannabis providers. Panel presentation at The Second National Conference on Cannabis Therapeutics, Analgesia and Other Indications, Portland, OR, 4 May 2002.

Federal Bureau of Investigation. 2001. *Uniform Crime Reports for the United States 2000*. U.S. Government Printing Office: Washington, DC.

Frood, A. 2002. Alcohol impairs driving more than marijuana. *New Scientist (UK)*. March 20.

Gieringer, D.H. 2001. Cannabis "vaporization": A promising strategy for smoke harm reduction. *J Cannabis Therap* 1(3/4):153-170.

Herkenham, M. 1992. Cannabinoid receptor localization in the brain: Relationship to motor and reward systems. *Ann Amer Acad Sci* 654:19-32

Hilts, P.J. 1994. Is nicotine addictive? Depends on whose criteria you use. *New York Times*. 2 August 1994, C3.

Hogan, R., D. Mankin, J. Conway, and S. Fox. 1970. Personality correlates of undergraduate marijuana use. *J Consult Clin Psychol* 35:58-63.

Hunter, C.E., R.J. Lokan, M.C. Longo, J.M. White, and M.A. White. 1998. *The prevalence and role of alcohol, cannabinoids, benzodiazepines and stimulants in non-fatal crashes*. Adelaide, South Australia: Forensic Science, Department for Administrative and Information Services.

Jacox, A., D.B. Carr, R. Payne, C.B. Berde, W. Brietbart, J.M. Cain, C.R. Chapman, C.S. Cleeland, B.R. Ferrell, R.S. Finley et al. 1994. *Management of cancer pain: Clinical practice guideline #9*. AHCPR Publication No. 94-0592: Rockville, MD.

Jones, R.T., N.M. Benowitz, and J. Bachman. 1976. Clinical studies of cannabis tolerance and dependence. *Ann NY Acad Sci* 282:221-239.

Joy, J.E., S.J. Watson, and J.A. Benson, Jr. 1999. *Marijuana and medicine: Assessing the science base*. Washington, DC: Institute of Medicine, National Academy Press.

Krampf, W. 1997. AIDS and the wasting syndrome. In *Cannabis in medical practice: A legal, historical and pharmacological overview of the therapeutic use of marijuana*. Edited by M.L. Mathre. Jefferson, NC: McFarland & Company Publishers.

Kranz, C. 2002. U.S. drug chief waves the flag. *Cincinnati Enquirer*. 11 April 2002.

Lazarou, J., B.H. Pomeranz, and P.N. Corey. 1998. Incidence of adverse drug reactions in hospitalized patients: A meta-analysis of prospective studies. *J Amer Med Assoc* 279:1200-1205.

Lyketsos, C.G., E. Garrett, K. Liang, and J.C. Anthony. 1999. Cannabis use and cognitive decline in persons under 65 years of age. *Amer J Epidem* 149(9):794-800.

Mathre, M.L. 1985. *A survey on disclosure of marijuana use to health care professionals*. (Thesis). Cleveland, OH: Frances Payne Bolton School of Nursing, Case Western Reserve University.

McCaffery, M.1968. *Nursing practice theories related to cognition, bodily pain, and man-environment interactions.* Los Angeles: UCLA Students Book Store.

McPartland, J.M., R.C. Clarke, and D.P. Watson. 2000. *Hemp diseases and pests: Management and biological control.* New York: CABI Publishing.

McParland, J.M. and E.B. Russo. 2001. Cannabis and cannabis extracts: Greater than the sum of their parts? *J Cannabis Therap* 1(3/4):103-132.

National Commission on Marihuana and Drug Abuse. 1972. *Marihuana: A signal of misunderstanding.* Washington, DC: Government Printing Office.

National Commission on Marihuana and Drug Abuse. 1973. *Drug use in America: Problem in perspective.* Washington, DC: U.S. Government Printing Office.

Newcomb, M. and P. Bentler. 1988. *Consequences of adolescent drug use: Impact on the lives of young adults.* Newbury Park, CA: Sage.

Office of Technology Assessment, U.S. Congress. 1993. *Biological components of substance abuse and addiction.* Washington, DC: U.S. Government Printing Office (OTA-BP-BBS-117).

Rosenblum, S. and W. Wenner. 2002. OR and HI clinical case studies. Panel presentation at The Second National Clinical Conference on Cannabis Therapeutics, Analgesia and Other Indications, Portland, OR, 3 May 2002.

Russo, E., M.L. Mathre, A. Byrne, R. Velin, P.J. Bach, J. Sanchez-Ramos, and K.A. Kirlin. 2002. Chronic cannabis use in the compassionate investigational new drug program: An examination of benefits and adverse effects of legal clinical cannabis. *J Cannabis Therap* 2(1):3-57.

Schneider Institute for Health Policy. 2001. *Substance abuse: The nation's number one health problem.* Princeton, NJ: Robert Wood Johnson Foundation.

Shedler, J. and J. Block. 1990. Adolescent drug use and psychological health: A longitudinal inquiry. *Amer Psychologist* 45(5):612-630.

Substance Abuse and Mental Health Services Administration. (2000). *Summary of findings from the 1999 National Household Survey on Drug Abuse.* Rockville, MD: Department of Health and Human Services.

Substance Abuse Report. 1 December 1996. Medical marijuana laws will increase teen drug use: Drug czar. Boston: Warren, Gorham & Lamont.

Sunday Times. 16 December 2001. Science: Cannabis no gateway drug. London.

Tashkin, D.I. 2000. Potential health risks of therapeutic cannabis–pulmonary effects. Oral presentation at The First National Conference on Cannabis Therapeutics, Medical Marijuana: Science Based Clinical Applications, University of Iowa, Iowa City. 8 April 2000.

Whittle, B.A., G.W. Guy and P. Robson. 2001. Prospects for new cannabis-based prescription medicines. *J Cannabis Therap* 1(3/4):183-205.

Wiesbeck, G.A., M.A. Schuckit, J.A. Kalmijn, J.E. Tipp, L.K. Bucholz, and T.L. Smith. 1996. An evaluation of the history of marijuana withdrawal syndrome in a large population. *Addiction* 91(10):1469-1478.

Wikler, A. 1976. Aspects of tolerance and dependence on cannabis. *Ann NY Acad Sci* 282:126-147.

Young, F.L. 6 September 1988. *In the matter of marijuana rescheduling petition* (Docket #86-22). Washington, DC: U.S. Department of Justice, Drug Enforcement Administration.

Zeese, K. 26 March 2002. Once secret "Nixon tapes" show why the U.S. outlawed pot. <AlterNet.org>. Story ID-12666.

Crack Heads and Roots Daughters:
The Therapeutic Use of Cannabis in Jamaica

Melanie Dreher

SUMMARY. An ethnographic study of women and drug use in inner city neighborhoods in Kingston, Jamaica, revealed that cannabis is commonly used in conjunction with crack cocaine to minimize the undesirable effects of crack pipe smoking, specifically paranoia and weight loss. According to 33 current or former crack using women, who were followed for a period of nine months, cannabis cigarettes ("spliffs") constitute the cheapest, most effective and readily available therapy for discontinuing crack consumption. The findings of this research suggest the need to reframe "multiple drug use" within the cultural meanings that attend cannabis in Jamaica as a medicine and a sacrament. *[Article copies available for a fee from The Haworth Document Delivery Service: 1-800-HAWORTH. E-mail address: <getinfo@haworthpressinc.com> Website: <http://www. HaworthPress.com> © 2002 by The Haworth Press, Inc. All rights reserved.]*

KEYWORDS. Cannabis, ganja, culture, crack, cocaine, Jamaica, women, self-treatment, Rastafarians, multiple drug use

There are only two illicit substances that are widely used in Jamaica, marijuana (or "ganja," as it is called locally) and crack cocaine. This paper describes the use of cannabis as a cheap, available therapy for the treatment of

Melanie Dreher, PhD, FAAN, is Dean and Professor, University of Iowa College of Nursing, 101D Nursing Building, 50 Newton Road, Iowa City, IA 52242-1121 (E-mail: melanie-dreher@uiowa.edu).

[Haworth co-indexing entry note]: "Crack Heads and Roots Daughters: The Therapeutic Use of Cannabis in Jamaica." Dreher, Melanie. Co-published simultaneously in *Journal of Cannabis Therapeutics* (The Haworth Integrative Healing Press, an imprint of The Haworth Press, Inc.) Vol. 2, No. 3/4, 2002, pp. 121-133; and: *Women and Cannabis: Medicine, Science, and Sociology* (ed: Ethan Russo, Melanie Dreher, and Mary Lynn Mathre) The Haworth Integrative Healing Press, an imprint of The Haworth Press, Inc., 2002, pp. 121-133. Single or multiple copies of this article are available for a fee from The Haworth Document Delivery Service [1-800-HAWORTH, 9:00 a.m. - 5:00 p.m. (EST). E-mail address: getinfo@haworthpressinc.com].

121

cocaine addiction by working class women in Kingston, Jamaica. The findings reported here are derived from an ethnographic study of crack-using women in Kingston (Dreher and Hudgins 1992). The purposes of this study were to identify the social and economic conditions that promote and reinforce cocaine use and generate implications for treatment and prevention. Complementing the earlier large-scale opinion survey that had influenced drug policy in Jamaica (Stone 1990), the ethnographic design was deployed to: (1) observe the actual drug-linked behavior of crack using women in the natural settings of home and community, (2) permit a longitudinal examination of the processes embedded in drug careers over several months, and (3) overcome the potential mistrust of investigators that often accompanies research on illegal and socially sensitive activities.

Participant observation in inner city Kingston provided opportunities to witness, first hand, the social interactions and behavior associated with crack consumption and procurement, the daily routine of crack users, the techniques of crack cocaine ingestion, and the role and status of crack users in their communities. In addition to the general observations in the homes, yards, and community establishments of a Kingston neighborhood, 33 women who had ever used cocaine and its derivatives were followed for a period of nine months, in which their drug use and life events were monitored and recorded. An unstructured interview schedule served as a guide for the investigators, ensuring the comparability of the data while not constraining the responses of informants. As their histories unfolded, probes by the investigator generated new factors that were added to the interview schedule and explored in repeat visits to all participants.

The data derived from both interviews and observations included: (1) sociodemographic characteristics such as age, place of birth, residence, transience, religion, education, employment, marital status, health status and ethnicity; (2) past and present social relationships including family of origin, conjugal unions, children, household composition, friends, and recreational activities; (3) major life events; and (4) drug use careers including the circumstances surrounding initiation to crack, current use patterns, perceived short-term and long-term effects of crack use and their opinions of crack as both a personal and social phenomenon. Their wealth of experience and their willingness to share it provided us with a window into the drug related behavior of women in Jamaica.

GANJA

Although the use and distribution of ganja (cannabis) are illegal in Jamaica, the substance has been part of Jamaican working class culture for over a century (Rubin and Comitas 1975; Dreher 1982). There is a strong cultural tolerance for ganja and for most of the working class, it simply is not regarded as a "drug" (Dreher and Shapiro 1994). The Rastafarian community has adopted ganja as its sacrament–substance "from the earth," in harmony with the environment, natural (or "ital") and indigenous. Even heavy cannabis users, such as Rastafarians, are accepted because they do not threaten the social fabric of the community.

The use of cannabis for therapeutic purposes is not new in Jamaica. For over a century, the health-rendering properties of cannabis have enjoyed widespread endorsement (Rubin and Comitas 1975; Dreher 1997). Ganja tonics, teas and other infusions are household medicines used both curatively and prophylactically by Jamaicans of all ages, both sexes and a wide range of socioeconomic levels. Believed to improve health, stimulate the appetite, enhance work, promote a calm, meditative approach to life, reduce violence and augment sexual performance, ganja is a substance that symbolizes and promotes enduring values about health and behavior in Jamaica. Over the years, socially generated rules have evolved regarding who can use ganja, when, where, in what form and how much, creating a "complex" of social institutions that have served to guide the use of ganja and inhibit its abuse.

For example, since its introduction to Jamaica in the mid-nineteenth century by indentured laborers from India, ganja smoking, either in a "spliff" (ganja cigarette that is sometimes mixed with tobacco) or a pipe (also called a "chillum" or "chalice"), has been almost universally a male-dominated activity. Indeed, the early anthropological studies of cannabis use in Jamaica, conducted in the late sixties and early seventies, focused on ganja smoking as a working class, male social activity (Dreher 1976, 1982; Rubin and Comitas 1975). The female ganja smoker was rare, except in a pre-sexual context with their mates, and the few women that did smoke ganja outside of socially prescribed contexts were regarded as disreputable and often held in contempt by both men and women in their communities (Dreher 1984).

The organization of consumption based on sex was validated by the ethno-physiological explanation that ganja, when smoked, goes "directly to the brain," producing psychoactive effects that include the power to "reason" or engage in intellectual and philosophical discourse. In contrast, when drunk as teas or tonic, goes "directly to the blood," where it promotes health, prevents disease, and makes the body strong and ready to work. According to the men who smoked ganja, women "do not have the brains" for smoking and were excluded from the adult recreational and work groups in which ganja was used and exchanged socially. At the same time, however, it was usual and acceptable for women to cultivate and sell ganja, and even more common for women to prepare and administer ganja in the form of medicinal teas and tonics to their families and household members (Dreher 1984).

The institutionalized social rules that comprise the ganja "complex," including the widespread sanctions against female smoking, have continued to limit use among women. Within the past twenty years, however, increasing numbers of women have begun to smoke ganja routinely, in a manner not unlike their male counterparts. Partly due to the increase in Rastafarianism, not only are such women tolerated, but many have been given the commendatory title of "roots daughter" (Dreher 1987). The term "roots" has become part of the Rastafarian and youth vernacular in Jamaica to signify that which is real, natural, original, perhaps African, or at least, non-Western. The appellation "roots daughter" is used to identify women who come from a fine, if humble, tradition, who have "good brains," who can "smoke hard as a man" and with whom men can "reason" (discuss and debate) as they would with other men.

The roots daughter is not simply a ganja smoker but also a clear thinker and a woman of dignity. She "must keep a standard" and "go about properly." If she is involved in a stable union, her partner can expect her to be helpful and sexually faithful. As one informant explained, "if your woman is roots and you see her talking to another man, there is no reason to be jealous." Roots daughters are dignified, conservative, independent, non-promiscuous, hardworking and spiritual. They often are contemptuous of jewelry and make-up and may be recognizable by their hair, which frequently is styled in dread locks and covered. Finally, a roots daughter is a responsible, strict but nurturing mother who values education (both intellectual and moral) and who will forego her own ganja smoking to prepare ganja teas and tonics for her children to "make them smarter and stronger." Nevertheless, roots daughters are not the norm and the restrictions on female ganja use in the general population remain intact.

COCAINE

The presence of cocaine, especially in the form of crack, is relatively recent in Jamaica. Unlike the "ganja complex," with its institutionalized social rules that guide use, there is no "culture" for crack cocaine. Explosive rates of addiction have resulted in widespread social and economic dysfunction (Dreher and Hudgins 1992, Dreher 1995). Cocaine is chemically prepared, synthetic and not indigenous to Jamaica. Crack users, in general, are considered inherently "repulsive," straying from what is considered "normal" human behavior. For most Jamaicans, the use of crack cocaine is not only a violation of the law, but indicative of an undisciplined, lazy and even unhygienic person. In a society that values "clear" skin, fleshiness, sexual vigor, self-control and family loyalty, the "mawga" (skinny), debauched, impotent crack user is seen as fundamentally "bad," violent, self-serving, and the antithesis of everything that is good and important in Jamaica.

In Jamaica, crack is consumed in two ways: either directly in a pipe, or ground and sprinkled on a ganja cigarette, called a "seasoned" or a "dust up" spliff. In a seasoned spliff, the rock (crack) is mashed and spread over the mixture of ganja and tobacco, which is then rolled and smoked. Some users sprinkle the ashes from the pipe on the seasoned spliff so as not to waste any part of the crack. The seasoned spliff is of particular interest because it is the form of drug consumption in which two opposing Jamaican metaphors intersect: ganja (the wholesome multi-purpose herb) and crack (the noxious drug).

Opinions regarding the "seasoned spliff" are mixed and reflect the beliefs and behavior of the users. Rastafarians, with their ideological commitment to ganja as a sacrament, disdain the idea of mixing crack cocaine (a white man's poison, an unnatural substance) with a natural substance that is associated with physical and mental health and is considered indigenous to Jamaica. Almost universally, they regard the seasoned spliff as "defiled herb," alleging that it is the signature of "commercial Rastas" or "Rasta-tutes," who earned their livelihood by being the sexual partners of American and European female tourists.

Ironically, many crack pipe users were equally derisive of the seasoned spliff, claiming that herb (ganja) weakens the effects of the crack: "Real crack users aren't interested in the seasoned spliff." "Real crack addicts are not interested in ganja at all." "Wi' de pipe, you feel de effects instantly." "Me prefer de blow." According to one self-identified coke addict, she didn't like the seasoned spliff because when she smoked it, it made her feel like her "mind is beatin' (racing), but when you smoke it in a pipe it makes you feel numb."

Based on the results of his national survey, Stone (1990) attributed the increase in crack cocaine use to the seasoned spliff, asserting that ganja is the "gateway" to cocaine use. In the sense that ganja established inhalation as the primary mechanism by which to achieve a psychoactive experience (intravenous drug use is rarely, if ever, practiced in Jamaica), crack smoking clearly fit well into the existing Jamaican drug paradigm. The gateway explanation is further reinforced by reports of vendors "seasoning" ganja to create a more potent product and thus a market for cocaine. On the other hand, the almost universal presence of ganja smoking and the comparatively small percentage of crack cocaine users suggest that there is no direct or necessary relationship between ganja and crack and, at the very least, call for further analysis.

WOMEN AND CRACK

Unlike ganja, crack routinely is consumed with members of the opposite sex, and thus the most likely explanation for the higher proportion of women among crack smokers than that among ganja smokers. In some Jamaican communities women are reported to make up 25% of the crack users (Dreher and Shapiro 1994). Several women reported that they first were exposed to cocaine by "big men," such as entertainers, who allegedly are responsible for introducing literally hundreds of young women to cocaine. Women who are directly or indirectly associated with the tourist industry are most at risk (Broad and Feinberg 1995). As one study participant stated simply, "tourists like to try different drugs when they are on vacation." Thus, women who are hotel workers or waitresses, as well as exotic dancers and prostitutes, are recruited to procure crack for tourists and are likely to be invited to join them in smoking it. Women who are associated with men who work in tourism and the entertainment industry also are at risk. Taxi drivers, for example, often are asked to obtain crack/cocaine and then are invited to partake with their female tourist customers. They, in turn, may take some home for their girlfriends to try and even turn to selling crack/cocaine themselves.

In contrast to roots daughters, women who smoke crack are considered drug addicts and held in the very lowest esteem. To support their dependency, the vast majority of crack addicts become street prostitutes and engage in sexual practices that are outside normative behavior for Jamaicans, including oral sex, anal sex, and performance sex with other women. Female crack users in Jamaica suffer a life of peril and degradation. Prostitutes reported being beaten, stabbed, and robbed by their clients. In addition they are exposed to HIV infection and other sexually transmitted diseases. Moreover, their exposure to danger is increased at the very time that their ability to avoid or manage high-risk situations is most impaired.

Of the 33 women who were followed in the study (Table 1), 17 were using crack in some form at the time of the study while 14 were former users. Of the 17 current users, five were exclusively pipe smokers, 11 smoked both the pipe and seasoned spliff and only one smoked seasoned spliffs exclusively. Of the 14 former users, only one had used the pipe exclusively, 7 were exclusively seasoned spliff users and 5 used both pipe and seasoned spliff. The remaining former user was the only woman in the study who "snorted" cocaine powder while she lived abroad but had not used cocaine since she had returned to Jamaica and became a Rastafarian. The eight women who used the seasoned spliff exclusively, typically defined themselves not as crack *addicts* but rather as crack *users*, for whom the seasoned spliff was enhanced herb, with an extra "kick" or "boost." In contrast, all the pipe smokers, whether they used it exclusively or in addition to a seasoned spliff, identified themselves as addicts.

All the women in the study agreed that the two modes of ingestion produced very different effects. As one woman stated, "the pipe makes you more high than dust spliff." She recounted how she likes to smoke a seasoned spliff and that her capacity to "reason" was facilitated by the mixing of crack with ganja.

TABLE 1. Crack/Cocaine Using Women in Kingston, Jamaica According to Type of Use

	Current Users	Former Users	Total
Pipe	5	1	6
Seasoned Spliff	1	7	8
Combined	11	5	16
Intranasal	0	1	1

Another woman stated that the pipe made her feel "more drunk," "like a monster." She also said that it will make you "grow fine like a thread" (thin), if you continue to use it alone. The youngest user in the study, who smoked only seasoned spliffs, commented that the "pipe do you bad–mek you want it more often." Both kinds of crack users believed the pipe is more addicting than a seasoned spliff or even "snorting." Many of the women who had smoked crack in a seasoned spliff for several months or even years, reported that when they were exposed to the pipe, it quickly became their predominant and preferred mode of use. One woman described how cocaine was pushed on her by a "guy who dust up a cigarette" and gave it to her. She said she refused it several times but he was persistent and finally she tried it. Because she had experienced little danger in the seasoned spliff, she started smoking the pipe, which she now uses exclusively. Thus while crack and ganja commonly are thought of as linked in both consumption and distribution, participants in this study saw them as quite distinct. "The difference between ganja and coke is that with the ganja you can still work, cook and clean up . . . When you're high on ganja you want to eat but when you are high on coke you don't want to do anything. You are just afraid and want to hide."

The devastating impact of crack on their health and physical appearance, typical of crack users cross-culturally (Ratner 1993; Inciardi 1993), was a consistent complaint of participating women. Not only does crack "rob" them of their strength and ability to work, it impairs their appearance with dry hair, dark blotches and sores on their skin, burned and stained fingers, and, perhaps most important for this Jamaican population, severe weight loss. In addition to the physical effects of crack, the women reported a disregard for personal hygiene and grooming, including hair, skin and clothing. Regardless of their family history or social status, they reported stealing from and lying to their friends and relatives and being referred to as "coke heads" or "crack heads," universally despised and disrespected. Many of the women in the study were banished from their home communities and one woman reported that her mother threw a pail of boiling water at her as she approached her family home, where her children were living with their grandmother. As prostitutes, they engaged in sexual practices that others found repulsive and it was not unusual for young boys to call them names, e.g., "suck hood," or "lick 'im batty" (referring to fellatio and oral-anal sex), or even to stone them. The combination of community distrust and repulsion reinforced their social isolation and self-loathing.

Both current and former crack using women lamented their waste of money. Although they had the potential to generate comparatively large sums of money in a very short period of time through prostitution, they reaped no permanent benefits. They stated repeatedly that their need for crack supersedes all other needs, including food, clothing, housing and child support. Indeed, it is the impact on their children that was the most compelling source of guilt and remorse. Children had to be placed with other family members, friends or even neighbors because of the mother's inability to care for them. Women poignantly described having their children removed by police, subjected to ridicule by community members, neglected and abused both physically and sexually, often by their prostitution clients.

Consistent with the literature on women cocaine users in general (Pottieger and Tressell 2000), children were a primary motivation for these Jamaican women to discontinue cocaine use. One former crack user, for example, discontinued her habit one month before her first grandson was born because she did not want her grandchild to "come and find his granny a prostitute and a drug addict." During the interview, one of her children brought her grandchild in to her. As he sat on her lap during the interview, she caressed his head and smiled, "he's my drugs, I know I am not going back, I have control and I love my grandson and my kids." A few women reported that they had stopped smoking during their pregnancies because they heard that their addiction might kill the baby.

Also consistent with reports from other cultures (Labigalini et al. 1999), the drug histories of these women did not fall into a uniform trajectory, moving singly and consistently from non-use to addiction and then, if they recovered, back to non-use. It was not unusual, for example, to refrain from smoking for a few days, or even weeks, while they visited their families or when they felt that they were getting too thin. Many used a trip to their family home, usually outside of Kingston, as an opportunity to "stay clean" and "fatten up." Some women, who had been ostracized by their families, and thus could not go home, reported actually trying to get arrested so that they would be incarcerated and could sleep and get three meals a day. A short jail sentence was a welcome relief from sex work and provided an opportunity to gain weight.

While their children, family members, and communities were powerful motivators for these women to discontinue crack cocaine, they also reported that such motivators were insufficient to maintain abstinence for long periods of time. In most cases, the return to crack use generally was triggered by a personal problem or simply because they were depressed and wanted to feel better. One participant, for example, reported that her boyfriend got her pregnant to get her off coke and she was clean for one year and three months but she started using it again when he returned to Jamaica with his wife. Another woman, working as a prostitute, said that she had stopped for four months and then started back when a client paid her with crack.

With the exception of the youngest participant in the study, who used only the seasoned spliff, all current users longed to discontinue smoking crack permanently and get their lives in order. Most were uninformed of any treatment facilities available to them. Four had tried to enroll in the University of West Indies Hospital drug intervention program but had been put on waiting lists of several months. In fact, treatment and counseling programs in which these women could avail themselves of professional assistance were almost non-existent.

Given the unavailability of formal detoxification and recovery programs in Jamaica, the experience of the 14 former users is both important and cogent. Of the fourteen, one was an intranasal cocaine user while living abroad who became a Rastafarian on her return to Jamaica, gave up cocaine and now partakes of ganja as a religious sacrament. One was a woman who had never used ganja and was the only participant who had received professional assistance. Of the remaining 12, seven had been exclusively seasoned spliff users and five were pipe users who also smoked seasoned spliffs. Of these last five, three started using ganja for the express purpose of reducing the cravings, the paranoia and the loss of appetite associated with crack use.

Labigalini et al. (1990), reporting a similar folk therapy in Brazil, described the experience of several male patients in a treatment program who had used cannabis to reduce their craving for crack, thus helping them to overcome their addiction. According to these authors, the control of impulsive behavior and stabilization of the hunger mechanism is likely explained by the capacity of cannabis to increase the cerebral availability of serotonin that has been compromised by crack cocaine. Indeed, there were numerous reports from both ganja and crack users that ganja slows down the immediate effects of crack, and makes the overall high less intense but last longer and trail off more gradually. This avoids both the plummeting euphoria and subsequent paranoia that precipitate the need to smoke again. According to one woman:

> It makes me charged but not as strong as the pipe. It stays longer than the pipe–about 20 minutes to half an hour, while the pipe stays in your system for only ten minutes. The pipe is a killer . . . I was always wanting the next pipe. The seasoned spliff is much better to me than the pipe. You can eat and drink at the same time because the herb opens the appetite. When it wears off, I feel like I want a fresh (bath) and sleep. When you

smoke season spliffs, you don't feel "paro." It is a different meditation. Crack and coke are like demons and devils, they are not good and to how dem see de pipe mash up people, dem a turn to season spliff and some a dem nah touch de pipe.

The opinion of some of the users was that ganja simply reduces the volume of crack needed for a high while others claim it has a psychological role in counteracting the triggers in the environment that stimulate the need for crack cocaine.

It mek you meditate an' have an interest away from crack.

. . . when you want crack you should smoke a spliff instead.

. . . nuff time me would use crack but (ganja) mek me t'ink twice.

. . . herb helps me not want to smoke.

If you're trying to stop and you smoke weed, you nah wan de rock.

With two spliff, I can resist crack.

The use of ganja as a vehicle for getting through the stress and urgency associated with the need for a "lick" of cocaine was reported by almost all of the women who were followed in this study.

Among the current users, the women who combined ganja consumption with their crack consumption were much more "successful" users in terms of physical health and lifestyle. In addition to reducing the need to smoke large quantities of crack, and thus engage in extensive and depleting prostitution, the role of ganja as an appetite stimulant was mentioned by several women. Even committed pipe smokers smoked ganja to compensate for the weight loss that accompanies cocaine use. Among the eight users (current and former) who smoked crack only in a seasoned spliff and did not consider themselves to be true addicts, all claimed that they were able to discontinue crack consumption easily and that they smoked a seasoned spliff because they enjoyed it, not because they needed it.

While the intriguing, preliminary evidence supports the physiological capacity of ganja to promote cocaine abstinence, its *cultural role* as a health rendering substance that induces thoughtfulness, meditation and communion with "Jah" (God) also warrants mention. Roots women, especially those with definitive Rastafarian affiliations, rejected a lifestyle requiring prostitution and culturally deviant sexual practices. Although there is no explicit injunction against crack in Rastafarian doctrine, the "roots" concept provides a comprehensive plan for living that includes responsibility, dignity and a family orientation. As the one Rasta woman in the study stated:

> Me nah trouble dat ting . . . me a roots. Now I am proud and happy to state that I am completely cured from that sin, and indeed, I am ever so thankful to Jah. Surely, God is good . . . A very common saying is that cocaine addiction is uncurable. I have proved that saying to be completely wrong. My advice to all who want to quit using that garbage is to sincerely ask Jah for his help.

Being a roots daughter provides the motivation not only to discontinue the use of crack cocaine, but to reduce exposure to the drug in the first place. As such, Rastafarianism, with the ganja sacrament, has ideological value for prevention as well as treatment. The only roots daughter among the 33 women in the study was the one informant who had used cocaine intra-nasally when she lived abroad some years earlier. Since she became a Rastafarian, using ganja sacramentally, she speaks in great opposition to crack cocaine. The effectiveness of religious involvement in the treatment of alcohol and drug addiction has been long acknowledged (Buxton et al 1987), and the notion that one substance can be used as a deterrent to, or replacement for, others is not new. Historical evidence suggests that peyotism, for example, provided an alternative substance as well as an alternative lifestyle, thus serving as a deterrent to alcoholism among Native American populations (Hill 1990). Even Sefanek and Kaplan (1995) reevaluated their "stepping stone" theory in the light of Dutch heroin users who succeeded in controlling the damaging effects by smoking cannabis.

CONCLUSIONS

Although the evidence is preliminary, the reported success rate of self-cure, using the cheapest and most available psychoactive substance, is persuasive. It lends credence to the reports of male crack users in Brazil and heroin users in the Netherlands and, at the very least, deserves further investigation. The data certainly suggest that ganja is neither a precondition nor a gateway to crack use. In fact, nine of the 33 women had never used ganja at all and reported hating "even the smell of it." Although the majority of the participants in the study had smoked ganja prior to using crack cocaine, the number of years elapsing between initiating crack use ranged from one to thirteen, suggesting no automatic or direct linkage either physiologically or socially between ganja and crack. The youngest woman in the study (16 years old), said that she *started* using a seasoned spliff because her boyfriend wanted her to try it but spoke adamantly against pipe use. Moreover, for the women who were ganja users prior to becoming crack users, the number of years elapsing between initiating crack use ranged from one to thirteen, suggesting, again, no automatic or direct linkage.

Indeed, these findings indicate that rather than serving as a gateway to crack, cannabis may be instrumental in both the prevention and treatment of crack addiction. Of the 14 women who succeeded in discontinuing crack use, 13 attribute their success to the use of ganja, either because of its capacity to control the damage of crack cocaine use physiologically or, in one case, because of its religious value. Moreover, it is clear that the women who combined ganja and crack were at least able to maintain their weight and care for their children. At the very least, these findings beg the need to revisit the notion of multiple drug use in a more culture-specific context. Far from being the hedonistic multi-drug users that present so many challenges to prevention and treatment programs, the women in this study were actually self-medicating, either to modify the effects of pipe smoking or to relinquish the habit all together.

IMPLICATIONS

Crack is a highly addictive form of cocaine, with serious social consequences. The exponential increase in crack use worldwide has generated an urgent demand for treatment and prevention programs and international development agencies in the United States have invested considerable monetary and technical support to develop such programs in Jamaica as well as other countries. It is common knowledge, however, that health and social service programs are not automatically transferable from one society to another. Effectiveness requires that such programs be designed according to what is meaningful and important in the culture where it is to be applied. Thus the commitment to demand reduction and treatment programs by both the Jamaican and United States governments has created a need for continued monitoring of the knowledge, attitudes and practices surrounding substance consumption and distribution. Not only is ganja typically not thought of as a drug in Jamaica, it has assumed a positive value for limiting the ravages of cocaine as an appetite stimulant that counteracts the anorexia of cocaine addiction, and as an assistive substance in relinquishing cocaine addiction. Yet the tendency to include ganja, often as a starting point, for drug prevention and intervention in Jamaica continues to exist. Whether or not the use of ganja is a remedy for crack addition in the biological, psychological or sociological sense, programs that fail to acknowledge the different cultural meanings and experiences attached to these two illicit substances ultimately will lose credibility with the very population they need to serve. The experience of women who have managed to relinquish their cocaine habit without expensive professional intervention would appear to be highly consequential for the design of effective, low cost, culture-specific treatment programs both in the United States and internationally.

REFERENCES

Broad, K. and B. Feinberg. 1995. Perceptions of ganja and cocaine in urban Jamaica. *J Psychoactive Drugs* 27(3):261-276.
Buxton, M., D. Smith, and R. Seymour. 1987. Spirituality and other points of resistance to the 12-step recovery process. *J Psychoactive Drugs* 19:275-286.
Dreher, M. 1982. *Working men and ganja*. Philadelphia: Institute for the Study of Human Issues.
Dreher, M. 1984. Marijuana use among women–An anthropological view. *Adv Alcohol Subst Abuse* 3(3):51-64.
Dreher, M. 1987. The evolution of a roots daughter. *J Psychoactive Drugs* 19(2):165-170.
Dreher, M. 1995. Women and drugs: Case studies from Jamaica. *Drugs: Education, Prevention and Policy* 2(2):167-176.
Dreher, M. 1997. Cannabis and Pregnancy. In, *Cannabis in medical practice: A legal, historical and pharmacological overview of the therapeutic use of marijuana.* Edited by M.L. Mathre. Jefferson, NC: McFarland & Co.
Dreher, M. and C. Rogers. 1976. Getting high: The ganja man and his socioeconomic milieu. *Caribbean Studies* 16(2):219-231.
Dreher, M. and R. Hudgins. 1992. *Women and crack in Jamaica.* Report submitted to U.S. Department of State, United States Embassy. Kingston, Jamaica.
Dreher, M. and D. Shapiro. 1994. *Drug consumption and distribution in Jamaica: A national ethnographic study.* Report submitted to U.S. Department of State, United States Embassy, Kingston, Jamaica.
Hill, T. 1990. Peyotism and the control of heavy drinking: The Nebraska Winnebago in the early 1900s. *Human Organization* 49(3):255-265.
Inciardi, J., Lockwood, D., and A. Pottieger 1993. *Women and crack cocaine.* New York: MacMillan.
Labigalini, E., Rodrigues, L.R. and D.X. DaSilviera. 1999. Therapeutic use of cannabis by crack addicts in Brazil. *J Psychoactive Drugs* 31(4):451-455.
Pottieger, A.E. and P.A. Tressell. 2000. Social relationships of crime-involved women cocaine users. *J Psychoactive Drugs* 32(4):445-460.
Ratner, M. (ed). 1993. *Crack pipe as pimp: An ethnographic investigation of sex-for-crack exchanges.* New York: Lexington Books.
Rubin, V., and L. Comitas. 1975. *Ganja in Jamaica.* The Hague: Mouton.
Sefaneck, S.J. and C.D. Kaplan. 1995. Keeping off: Stepping on and stepping off: The stepping stone theory reevaluated in the context of the Dutch cannabis experience. *Contemp Drug Problems* 22(8):483-512.
Stone, C. 1990. *National survey on the use of drugs in Jamaica.* Mona: University of West Indies.

One Woman's Work in the Use of Hashish in a Medical Context

Mila Jansen
Robbie Terris

SUMMARY. This article provides a brief introduction to the process of producing hashish with the Pollinator® and Ice-O-Lator® devices. Both are systems designed to separate the most active parts of the cannabis plant, the glandular trichomes, or "resin glands," from the plant material. The highly concentrated product of these systems has great value to medical users of cannabis, as they only need to employ a fraction of the amount of material otherwise necessary. The systems can also be used to pre-process cannabis or hemp for laboratory work that requires solely the active substances. The article also gives a brief introduction to Mila Jansen, the inventor of the Pollinator and the Ice-O-Lator. *[Article copies available for a fee from The Haworth Document Delivery Service: 1-800-HAWORTH. E-mail address: <getinfo@haworthpressinc.com> Website: <http://www. HaworthPress.com> © 2002 by The Haworth Press, Inc. All rights reserved.]*

KEYWORDS. Hashish, Pollinator, Ice-O-Lator, cannabis genetics, medical marijuana

There are several definite benefits to employing hashish as opposed to herbal cannabis, especially in a medical context. If one examines a female can-

Mila Jansen and Robbie Terris are affiliated with the Pollinator Company, Nieuwe Herengract 25, 1011 RL Amsterdam, Holland (E-mail: info@pollinator.nl) (Web: www.pollinator.nl).

[Haworth co-indexing entry note]: "One Woman's Work in the Use of Hashish in a Medical Context." Jansen, Mila, and Robbie Terris. Co-published simultaneously in *Journal of Cannabis Therapeutics* (The Haworth Integrative Healing Press, an imprint of The Haworth Press, Inc.) Vol. 2, No. 3/4, 2002, pp. 135-143; and: *Women and Cannabis: Medicine, Science, and Sociology* (ed: Ethan Russo, Melanie Dreher, and Mary Lynn Mathre) The Haworth Integrative Healing Press, an imprint of The Haworth Press, Inc., 2002, pp. 135-143. Single or multiple copies of this article are available for a fee from The Haworth Document Delivery Service [1-800-HAWORTH, 9:00 a.m. - 5:00 p.m. (EST). E-mail address: getinfo@haworthpressinc.com].

nabis flower under a microscope (20X), the bulk is the plant material with several thin pedestals on the surface called glandular trichomes. Atop of each stalk is a tiny clear resin gland, or head, that is the component of the flower that contains approximately 90% of the active cannabinoid ingredients: tetrahydrocannabinol (THC), cannabidiol (CBD), other cannabinoids and essential oils with a variety of therapeutic terpenoid components (Clarke 1998). The concentration of these tiny resin glands into what is traditionally called hashish is a logical step when seeking a medical application of cannabis. The chemical potency will be enhanced, and levels of active ingredients will be consistent throughout all of the collected material, therefore making it easier to administer accurately in precise dosages. Extraneous fiber components unnecessary to therapeutic effects are also eliminated.

Hashish was traditionally made in many eastern countries. The primary author was lucky enough to be in Morocco in 1965 and in Turkey, Afghanistan, Northern Pakistan, India and Nepal in 1968-69. The techniques for making hashish were distinct in each of these areas. We learned to make our own, either sifting or hand rubbing the flower buds. There were government hashish shops and temples in Nepal where patrons smoked the *goolies* (balls) of hand rubbed hashish with the *babas* and *saddhus* (holy men, wandering ascetics on life long pilgrimages, smoking hashish, devoting their lives to Shiva, the Hindu God of destruction of ignorance). There, hashish is a holy sacrament. There are rituals, mantras, *mudras*, meditations and visualizations connected with the smoking of a chillum (straight clay pipe). Hashish is an age-old medicine that is also used by many cultures as a means of social and spiritual development.

Eventually, I settled in Northern India with my four children for a number of years. After coming to live in Amsterdam in 1988, I found that most cannabis users smoked marijuana and there was very little good hashish available, so we set about trying to make some of our own. We would store all the dried leaf material until the coldest nights in winter, the extreme cold being ideal for extracting the resin glands, making them easier to isolate. The leaf material would then be gently tossed over a silk screen to knock off the resin glands for collection on a smooth surface beneath. This process, taken from the ancient method employed in Afghanistan for thousands of years, was time consuming and laborious. We continued the technique until 1993, when inspired by my clothes drier, I invented the Pollinator® machine.

The Pollinator machine is a dry method of resin gland separation, which contains a removable drum that is opened for the insertion of leaf material (Figure 1). Inside the rim of the drum are several horizontal rods which further aid the tumbling of the leaf material. The drum is closed and placed back inside the Pollinator where it is turned by an electric motor. Low temperature and low humidity are crucial when using the Pollinator machine, as both these factors

FIGURE 1. Mila Jansen with Pollinator® drums.

greatly increase the yield and the quality of the collected product. Quality of any hashish or other cannabis based product is primarily genetically determined. The chemical make up, yield and other such traits are all genetically influenced. The main concern is how to extract the resin glands from the plants as cleanly and efficiently as possible. By placing the leaf material in an airtight container, which is then placed in a freezer for two hours, one may approximate the low temperature necessary but the humidity will not be sufficiently low. We discovered that when the outside temperature was − 10°C the Pollinator produced the best quality product in the shortest time period. Extreme low humidity combined with literal freezing of the resin glands produces a very clean removal of the glandular trichome heads from their brittle stalks. In an environment with a warmer working temperature, there will be a significant decrease in the quality of hashish collected as a result of a greater proportion of stalks and other small pieces of plant material being present in the subsequent collection.

The resin glands from the cannabis leaves fall through the precise fine screen around the drum onto the bottom of the Pollinator container for later collection. The size of screen employed for the Pollinator is 147 μ, so as to allow the largest resin glands to fall through freely. The quality of the hashish is dependent on the length of time the drum is allowed to turn. A session of three to five minutes produces top quality hashish (containing only glandular trichomes without plant material, dirt or other impurities); longer turning results in a lower quality as the plant material is broken down and falls through the screen, mixing with the separated resin glands. The five minute turning of the Pollinator produced hashish that would have taken hours of labor-intensive work by traditional methods. This allowed Dutch growers of cannabis to make a small amount of excellent hashish easily from plant material previously considered waste.

The Pollinator was the first modern machine to be designed for the production of hashish. The industry was previously unchanged for thousands of years due to the fact that silk screens used for sieving had not been improved until the creation of modern technology. The first Pollinator machines were sold from home, but after a couple of years, I opened a shop as there was a clear demand by many cannabis growers who had marvelled at the first public demonstration of the Pollinator machine by Robert C. Clarke at C.I.A. Amsterdam, during the 1994 High Times Cannabis Cup event. This gave us more time and space to work on the development of methods to improve the technique of pure hashish production, as previously all the testing was done at the kitchen table. It was in this shop where I made my second breakthrough, the creation of the "Ice-O-Lator®," a water and ice method of making hashish.

In 1997, we practiced at home with jugs of water, but had no satisfactory results. The big revelation did not come until we saw the Extractor®. Designed in the USA, and manufactured in Yugoslavia, this system tended to break down within 8 months, and was very heavy and expensive. All over the world, people could buy buckets and mixing machines. In the summer of 1998, I sewed my first Ice-O-Lator bags.

This method of extracting the resin glands from the leaf material involved the use of water and ice (Figure 2). Leaf material is placed in cold water (4°C), where it is agitated causing the glandular trichomes to separate from the plant material. Temperature is again of great importance. As the herbal material is agitated in the cold water, hardened resin glands are dislodged more cleanly. Gravity then plays its part as the trichomes sink, and the plant material is left floating on the surface. With the aid of two precise screens (one for the leaf material and the other for the resin) the desirable mature glands and leaf material are separated. One factor that influences the resin glands are ideal growing conditions. Resin glands from plants grown indoors are slightly larger than those grown outdoors, as the plants have more light, nutrients and water. For outdoor growers of cannabis (or older plants where the resin glands have shrivelled with drying), I prefer a 187 µ screen on top. This will allow the resin glands to pass through while containing the rest of plant material. A pore sized screen of 62 µ as a lower screen will trap the extracted glandular heads. For growers of indoor plants with larger sized glands, I recommend a top screen of 210 µ and a 77 µ screen for the lower bag.

FIGURE 2. Washing machine Ice-O-Lator® with open drum, ice and cannabis in filter bag.

The Ice-O-Lator process is very simple, quick and efficient. The process begins by hanging both Ice-O-Lator bags (making sure the bag with the larger pore sized screen is on the top of the fine screened bag) in a bucket and then adding the plant material, ice blocks and enough cold water to 3/4 fill the bucket. A temperature of between 2-4°C is set before starting to agitate the plant material and ice. After twenty minutes of agitation, the water is left to settle for twenty minutes. In this period, the resin glands sink and any plant material rises to the surface. The top bag may then be gently raised out of the bucket, allowing the water and resin glands to drain. Lifting the lower bag out of the bucket reveals the collected trichomes once the water has drained. The inside of the bag is then rinsed with water to collect all the resin glands from the top of the screen. The outside of the bag is the wrapped in kitchen paper and pressed to remove the water. The resin glands are then sufficiently dry enough to remove from the Ice-O-Lator bag.

The collected resin glands are then placed into a metal kitchen sieve and filtered onto paper below. The resin glands are then ready for complete drying, as moisture may quickly lead to a deterioration of quality due to fungal growth. Once the resin glands are fully dried, they can be stored by pressing, or left in granular form (Figure 3). The Ice-O-Lator has proved to be the most efficient method of separation when taking into consideration factors such as time, purity and quantity. In the "coffee shops" of Amsterdam, the hashish made by this process is highly sought, as its potency and purity have become legendary. Ice-O-Lator bags have been sold throughout the world.

The Dutch Government awarded a research subsidy to the Pollinator Company in 2001 for the sole purpose of investigating resin separation methods for use in medical marijuana. As a medical commodity, cannabis has been found to aid a wide-ranging number of conditions. Demand for it in a medical context is growing due to government recognition. This subsidy has enabled us to expand our small research area and conduct tests on a daily basis. Some such experiments include sonic separation, and various wet and dry methods of sieving. Varieties of cannabis strains and growing methods are also factors to take into consideration. Cannabis strains, their yields and the potency of the resin glands also vary greatly. Lighting conditions also affect glandular trichome size. All these factors must be taken into consideration when assessing techniques of resin gland collection. Microscopy, laboratory tests, chromatography and several other methods of examination should always be employed to assess the true condition of hashish (Figure 4).

Hashish is a considerably easier substance to distribute than herbal cannabis. Storage, longevity, and consistency are all extremely important factors for medical patients who would have to administer it in precise quantities. Herbal cannabis may have little consistency in active components. Cropped buds of the cannabis plant contain varying amount of stalks, leaves and other plant ma-

FIGURE 3. Processed "water hash" after Ice-O-Lator® treatment.

terial that have no beneficial therapeutic properties, and may be harmful when smoked. Moreover, as the resin glands coat the buds, heavy handling or pruning can knock off the active trichomes, diminishing potency. Once pressed, hashish is concentrated and compact, easy to store and simpler to divide into measurable doses. As many patients using "medical marijuana" require long-term treatment where variations in dosage are important, hashish represents a considerably more practical therapeutic product.

For a number of years, both the Ice-O-Lator and Pollinator products have been used to create very pure and potent hashish from drug strains of cannabis. Recently we have begun working using hemp strains of cannabis, which have very low levels of THC and very high levels of CBD. The resulting hashish product is very useful to laboratories that are involved in the synthesis of THC from CBD (Gould 2001), a process described by Gold (1973). By using these products, pre-processing of plant material is easily achieved, ensuring that the laboratories have the best possible plant material to employ, as they may utilize only the resin glands instead of whole plants. As the laboratory work is very expensive, there are huge potential cost-saving benefits in ensuring total efficiency in all aspects of the production. This is of great interest to me, as I

FIGURE 4. GC/MS of a random Ice-O-Lator® hashish sample (performed by Thomas Herkenroth, THC Pharm, Frankfurt, Germany).

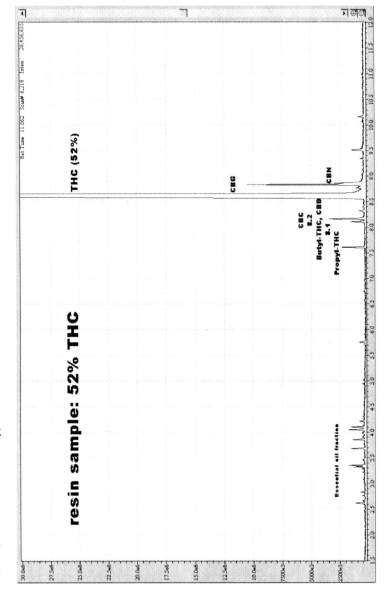

feel that hashish is a powerful medicine that has helped many people in cultures all over the world for hundreds of years. I am very happy to be involved in the production of medicines that can help many people.

At the Pollinator Company in spring 2002 there is much activity, as the level of interest in our products has enabled us to expand our shop space while also allowing the space to set up a dedicated research and development area. Issues concerning processing methods and medical issues will be discussed and addressed in our ongoing research of medicinal hashish production and its subsequent uses.

REFERENCES

Clarke, R.C. 1998. *Hashish!* Los Angeles, CA: Red Eye Press.
Gould, J. 2001. Personal Communication. THC Pharm, Frankfurt, Germany.
Gold, D. 1973. *Cannabis Alchemy–The art of modern hashmaking: Methods for preparation of extremely potent cannabis products.* Berkeley, CA: Ronin.

Combined Treatment of Tourette Syndrome with Δ⁹-THC and Dopamine Receptor Antagonists

Kirsten R. Müller-Vahl
Udo Schneider
Hinderk M. Emrich

SUMMARY. Animal studies suggest that cannabinoid receptor agonists might enhance the effect of dopamine receptor antagonists (neuroleptics, NL) in hyperkinetic movement disorders. In Tourette syndrome, NL are the most effective drugs for the treatment of tics. Recent clinical trials demonstrated that delta-9-tetrahydrocannabinol (Δ⁹-THC) also produces a tic-suppressing effect. In this single case study in a 24 years old female suffering from TS with extreme tics, it is suggested for the first time that Δ⁹-THC may be useful in augmenting the pharmacological response to atypical NL such as amisulpride and risperidone in TS patients. No serious adverse reactions occurred. Controlled studies are necessary to confirm this initial report. *[Article copies available for a fee from The Haworth Document Delivery Service: 1-800-HAWORTH. E-mail address: <getinfo@ haworthpressinc.com> Website: <http://www.HaworthPress.com> © 2002 by The Haworth Press, Inc. All rights reserved.]*

Kirsten R. Müller-Vahl, MD, Udo Schneider, MD, and Hinderk M. Emrich, MD, are affiliated with the Department of Clinical Psychiatry and Psychotherapy, Medical School Hannover, Germany.

Address correspondence to: Dr. Kirsten R. Müller-Vahl, Department of Clinical Psychiatry and Psychotherapy, Medical School Hannover, Carl-Neuberg-Str. 1, D-30625 Hannover, Germany (E-mail: mueller-vahl.kirsten@mh-hannover.de).

[Haworth co-indexing entry note]: "Combined Treatment of Tourette Syndrome with Δ⁹-THC and Dopamine Receptor Antagonists." Müller-Vahl, Kirsten R., Udo Schneider, and Hinderk M. Emrich. Co-published simultaneously in *Journal of Cannabis Therapeutics* (The Haworth Integrative Healing Press, an imprint of The Haworth Press, Inc.) Vol. 2, No. 3/4, 2002, pp. 145-154; and: *Women and Cannabis: Medicine, Science, and Sociology* (ed: Ethan Russo, Melanie Dreher, and Mary Lynn Mathre) The Haworth Integrative Healing Press, an imprint of The Haworth Press, Inc., 2002, pp. 145-154. Single or multiple copies of this article are available for a fee from The Haworth Document Delivery Service [1-800-HAWORTH, 9:00 a.m. - 5:00 p.m. (EST). E-mail address: getinfo@ haworthpressinc.com].

145

KEYWORDS. Tourette syndrome, tics, cannabis, THC, amisulpride, neuroleptics

INTRODUCTION

Tourette syndrome (TS) is a chronic neuropsychiatric spectrum disorder characterized by multiple motor and one or more vocal tics. The pathology is still unknown but there is evidence for an involvement of the dopaminergic system (Singer 1997). Dopamine blocking drugs (neuroleptics, NL) are considered the first-line pharmacotherapy for tics. However, these drugs are not effective in all patients, and their usage is limited due to dose dependent side effects such as sedation, weight gain, depression, and irritability (Kurlan 2001).

From animal studies carried out over many years, it is well known that cannabinoids influence motor behavior. It has been demonstrated that acute administration of cannabinoid receptor agonists induces catalepsy and immobility and attenuates turning behavior (Pertwee and Wickens 1991, Souilhac et al. 1995). Central CB_1 cannabinoid receptors are found at very high density in neurons of the basal ganglia. Therefore, there is considerable evidence that cannabinoids modulate the outflow of information from the basal ganglia.

To date the physiological role of the central cannabinoid receptor system is not well understood. However, there is evidence that cannabinoids might be of therapeutic value in different neurological movement disorders. Single case studies and an open uncontrolled trial in five patients suffering from focal and generalized dystonia suggested that cannabidiol (CBD), a non-psychoactive ingredient of *Cannabis sativa*, might be effective in the treatment of different forms of dystonia (Snider and Consroe 1984, Sandyk et al. 1986, Consroe et al. 1986). A pilot study in seven patients suffering from Parkinson's disease (PD) demonstrated that the cannabinoid receptor agonist nabilone reduces levodopa-induced dyskinesia (Sieradzan et al. 2001). In patients suffering from multiple sclerosis (MS) there is evidence that both smoked cannabis and oral delta-9-tetrahydrocannabinol (Δ^9-THC), the major psychoactive ingredient of cannabis sativa, improves tremor (Consroe et al. 1997, Clifford 1983, Meinck et al. 1989).

In TS, anecdotal reports as well as two randomized double-blind placebo-controlled clinical trials in 12 and 24 patients, respectively, demonstrated that cannabis and Δ^9-THC reduce motor and vocal tics (Sandyk and Awerbuch 1988, Hemming and Yellowlees 1993, Müller-Vahl et al. 1998, Müller-Vahl et al. 1999, Müller-Vahl et al. 2001, Müller-Vahl et al. in press). Several years ago, Moss et al. (1989) suggested that in TS, cannabinoid receptor agonists might enhance the effect of NL in the treatment of tics because animal studies had demonstrated that cannabinoids like Δ^9-THC increase NL-induced hypokinesia (Moss et al. 1984).

In this open uncontrolled single case study in a 24 years old female with TS, we report a successful treatment of motor and vocal tics with a combination of oral Δ^9-THC and amisulpride, an atypical dopamine receptor antagonist.

CASE STUDY

Ms. R. is a 24-year-old female suffering from TS. Motor and vocal tics started at age 9. At the age of 16 years, her clinical status deteriorated and medical treatment was initiated. Between age 16 and 21 several drugs had been prescribed, but either failed to improve tics or could not be tolerated due to significant side effects. The following drugs were used in monotherapy or combination: tiapride, pimozide, sulpiride, olanzapine, clonazepam, fluvoxamine, and clomipramine. At age 21, treatment with risperidone was started and tics improved. Although she complained of side effects such as acute dyskinesia (that required long-term treatment with biperiden), galactorrhea, and amenorrhea, she continued medication. However, by age of 23 years tics worsened again, and could no longer be controlled by risperidone even after the dosage was increased up to 8 mg/d.

At that time, she participated in a randomized double-blind placebo-controlled clinical trial investigating the effect of Δ^9-THC in TS over a 6-week period at our clinic. During the treatment period her tics clearly improved, and then deteriorated after study medication was stopped. During the course of the study, her treatment with risperidone remained unchanged. After completion of the study it turned out that she had received Δ^9-THC (10 mg/d). Therefore, she asked for a prescription of Δ^9-THC for long-term treatment. Unfortunately, her health insurance refused to cover the costs because in Germany Δ^9-THC is not approved for the treatment of TS.

This open uncontrolled study was carried out to reexamine the effect of oral Δ^9-THC in combination with an atypical NL. Tics were rated using examiner rating scales (Global Clinical Impression Scale (GCIS) (Leckman et al. 1988), Shapiro Tourette-Syndrome Severity Scale (STSS) (Shapiro et al. 1988), Yale Global Tic Severity Scale (YGTSS) (Harcherik et al. 1984) and a self-rating (Tourette-Syndrome Symptom List) (TSSL) (Leckman et al. 1988). Using the TSSL the patient was asked to rate not only tics, but also "premonitory experiences" prior to the occurrence of tics.

Baseline visit 1 was performed on monotherapy with 8 mg risperidone. At that time, she suffered from extreme vocal tics, including very loud and frequent yelling and severe coprolalia (compulsive swearing). In addition, she had moderate to severe motor tics with facial grimacing, head jerking, arm extension, jumping, and stamping feet. (For tic rating at visit 1 see Table 1 and Figure 1.)

In the first part of the study, combined treatment with risperidone (8 mg/d) and Δ^9-THC (up to 17.5 mg/d) was started. At a dose of 10 mg Δ^9-THC, tics clearly improved. Further dose increases, however, did not cause an additional improvement. Tic rating at visit 2 (week 6) was performed at a dose of 17.5 mg/d Δ^9-THC in combination with 8 mg/d risperidone (Table 1, Figure 1). The only reported adverse effect was a mild "high-feeling." Two weeks later, the patient herself reduced the dosage of risperidone at home, but felt that tics deteriorated and, therefore, resumed taking 8 mg/d.

After a treatment period of about 2 months with a combination of risperidone (8 mg/d) and Δ^9-THC (10 mg/d), tics slightly increased. Tic rating at visit 3 (week 12) documented that tics worsened, but did not reach the severity measured at baseline visit 1 (Table 1, Figure 1).

Therefore, treatment with risperidone was stopped and therapy with amisulpride, an atypical neuroleptic drug, was started. Treatment with Δ^9-THC (10 mg/d) was continued. The dose of amisulpride was slowly increased up to 600 mg twice a day. Tics improved in frequency and intensity (visit 4, week 17, for tic rating see Table 1 and Figure 1). The only side effect that occurred was minimal galactorrhea.

To exclude that this improvement was attributable only to the treatment with amisulpride and not to the combination of both drugs, treatment with Δ^9-THC was reduced and discontinued. Tics deteriorated after withdrawal

TABLE 1. Tic Rating at Visits 1-7

	visit 1	visit 2	visit 3	visit 4	visit 5	visit 6	visit 7
GCIS	5	4	5	4	4	4	4
STSS	5	4	5	4	4	3	4
YGTSS	81	67	74	64	70	46	59
TSSL	46	22	23	26	32	13	16
PE	23	17	23	12	16	6	9

GCIS = Global Clinical Impression Scale, STSS = Shapiro Tourette-Syndrome Severity Scale, YGTSS = Yale Global Tic Severity Scale, TSSL = Tourette-Syndrome Symptom List, PE = premonitory experiences (measured by the TSSL).
Visit 1: risperidone (8 mg) monotherapy, visit 2: combination of risperidone (8 mg) and Δ^9-THC (17.5 mg), visit 3: combination of risperidone (8 mg) and Δ^9-THC (10 mg), visit 4: combination of amisulpride (800 mg) and Δ^9-THC (10 mg), visit 5: amisulpride (1200 mg) monotherapy, visit 6: combination of amisulpride (1200 mg) and Δ^9-THC (10 mg), visit 7: combination of amisulpride (1200 mg) and Δ^9-THC (10 mg).

FIGURE 1. Self rating of tics and premonitory experiences (PE) using the Tourette-Syndrome Symptom List (TSSL). Visit 1: risperidone (8 mg) monotherapy, visit 2: combination of risperidone (8 mg) and Δ^9-THC (17.5 mg), visit 3: combination of risperidone (8 mg) and Δ^9-THC (10 mg), visit 4: combination of amisulpride (800 mg) and Δ^9-THC (10 mg), visit 5: amisulpride (1200 mg) monotherapy, visit 6: combination of amisulpride (1200 mg) and Δ^9-THC (10 mg), visit 7: combination of amisulpride (1200 mg) and Δ^9-THC (10 mg).

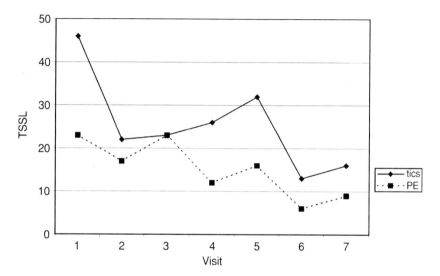

from Δ^9-THC (visit 5, week 19, Table 1, Figure 1) and improved again after resumption of Δ^9-THC (10 mg/d) (visit 6, week 20, Table 1, Figure 1).

One month later a final visit (visit 7, week 24, Table 1, Figure 1) was performed. The patient reported mild tic deterioration compared to visit 6, but still felt an improvement of motor tics in frequency and intensity and of extreme vocal tics, particularly with respect to their frequency.

Rating of "premonitory experiences" prior to the occurrence of a tic showed that the patient felt that in parallel with the tic improvement, there was a concomitant reduction in the urge to tic especially during combined treatment with Δ^9-THC and amisulpride (Table 1, Figure 1).

DISCUSSION

Anecdotal reports and two controlled clinical trials have suggested that Δ^9-THC is effective in the treatment of tics in TS (Sandyk and Awerbuch 1988, Hemming and Yellowlees 1993, Müller-Vahl et al. 1998, Müller-Vahl et al. 1999, Müller-Vahl et al. 2001, Müller-Vahl et al. in press). Although various other drugs have been found to be useful in the treatment of tics, at present there is general agreement that classic and atypical NL are the most effective anti-tic agents (Kurlan 2001). In this single case study, we report for the first time a successful treatment of tics with a combination of Δ^9-THC and the atypical NL amisulpride.

The patient suffered from extreme vocal tics in severe intensity, complexity, and frequency and moderate motor tics. Combined treatment with Δ^9-THC and amisulpride did not eliminate all the tics, but frequency of vocal tics decreased and motor tics improved significantly. A combination of Δ^9-THC and amisulpride was superior compared to a combination of Δ^9-THC and risperidone. Amisulpride was most effective at a high dose of 1200 mg/d, Δ^9-THC at a low dose of 10 mg/d. The only side effect was minimal galactorrhea.

Single case reports are always of limited meaning. However, this patient was followed for more than 6 months. Tics improved after medication was started, deteriorated after withdrawal from Δ^9-THC and improved again after continuation of combined treatment. A positive treatment effect could be observed using both global and complex measures, self and examiner rating scales. The patient herself noted not only a marked tic reduction but also an improvement of premonitory experiences prior to the occurrence of tics. One year before in this patient a comparable beneficial effect of Δ^9-THC had been observed when participating in our double-blind placebo-controlled study. It is worthy of note that the patient desired that no deterioration would occur after withdrawal from Δ^9-THC because a long-term treatment with Δ^9-THC was not possible. Her health insurance refused to cover the costs. She herself could not meet them, and, furthermore, declined to use illegal cannabis.

From these preliminary results, therefore, it is suggested that Δ^9-THC may augment the anti-tic effect of atypical NL such as risperidone and amisulpride. To the best of our knowledge, there is only one single report available suggesting a beneficial effect of amisulpride in TS (Trillet et al. 1990). To date, the neurobiology of TS is unknown. Most evidence, however, supports an active role of the dopaminergic system. It has been suggested that TS is due to dopaminergic hyperinnervation in the striatum or supersensitive postsynaptic dopamine receptors (Singer 1997). It has also been speculated that abnormalities within several neurotransmitter systems (including gamma-aminobutyric acid (GABA), acetylcholine, serotonin, opiates) contribute to TS pathology. Since it has been demonstrated that cannabinoids are effective in the treatment of tics, it can be speculated that the central cannabinoid receptor system might be involved in TS pathology as well (Müller-Vahl et al. in press).

In reserpine-treated rats, an animal model of PD, it has been demonstrated that Δ^9-THC increases hypokinesia (Moss et al. 1981). Another study has shown that hypokinesia induced by the dopamine receptor antagonist haloperidol significantly increase after co-administration of Δ^9-THC (Moss et al. 1984). It, therefore, has been suggested that cannabinoids in combination with NL might be of therapeutic value in hyperkinetic movement disorders such as TS (Moss et al. 1989).

Interpreting these data, different hypotheses can be advanced. The beneficial effect of a combination of NL and Δ^9-THC may be due to an interaction between cannabinoid and the dopaminergic system. Dopamine D1 and D2 receptors both are co-localized with CB_1 receptors in various combinations on the cell bodies and terminal axons of striatal efferent neurons projecting to globus pallidus lateralis (GPl), globus pallidus medialis (GPm), and substantia nigra (SN) (Glass et al. 2000). Several animal studies have demonstrated a highly complex interaction between these two systems within the basal ganglia (Navarro et al. 1993, Giuffrida et al. 1999). Dopaminergic and cannabinoid receptors are both located in the outflow nuclei of the basal ganglia. Therefore, there may be an interrelation of these receptors in the regulation of motor activity (Giuffrida et al. 1999). Repeated stimulation of D1 (but not D2) dopamine receptors enhances catalepsy induced by a potent cannabinoid receptor agonist (Rodriguez de Fonseca et al. 1994). Cannabinoid receptor stimulation attenuates rotational behavior induced by a dopamine D1 (but not a D2) agonist with unilateral lesions of the dopaminergic nigrostriatal pathway (Anderson et al. 1995). Turning behavior induced by cannabinoid agonists can be blocked by D1 and D2 receptor antagonists (Souilhac et al. 1995). In the reserpine-treated rat model of PD it could be demonstrated that cannabinoid receptor agonists reduce D2 (but not D1) dopamine receptor-mediated alleviation of akinesia (Maneuf et al. 1997). Local administration of a D2-like (but not a D1-like) receptor agonist resulted in an eightfold increase of the endogenous cannabinoid release in the dorsal striatum (Giuffrida et al. 1999). Therefore, it has been suggested that the CB_1 receptor system acts as an inhibitory feedback mechanism countering dopamine-induced facilitation of motor activity (Giuffrida et al. 1999).

On the other hand it has been demonstrated that cannabinoids enhance GABAergic transmission in the GPl (Maneuf et al. 1996) and, therefore, enhance inhibitory motor effects resulting in reduced voluntary movements and Parkinson-like symptoms (Wickens and Pertwee 1995). Cannabinoid receptors are located at high concentrations on GABAergic terminals projecting from the striatum to the globus pallidus (GP) and substantia nigra pars reticulata (SNr) (Herkenham et al. 1990). GABA is the major (inhibitory) transmitter in these two motor striatopallidal pathways ("direct" and "indirect" pathway). This circuit is modulated by dopaminergic inputs from substantia nigra pars compacta (SNc), cholinergic striatal interneurons, and serotonergic projections. In PD it has been speculated that cannabinoid agonists such as nabilone reduce levodopa-induced dyskinesia due to an increased GABA transmission in the GPl (Sieradzan et al. 2001).

The distribution of neurotransmitters within the basal ganglia circuits makes different hypotheses possible to explain tic reduction after treatment with a combination of Δ^9-THC and NL. It can be speculated that in TS, Δ^9-THC enhances GABA transmission in the GPl resulting in a reduction of basal ganglia motor output. On the other hand one might hypothesize that cannabinoids reduce tics by a functional interaction between the dopaminergic and the cannabinoid receptor system within the striatum. However, as long as TS pathology and the role of the central cannabinoid receptor system in this disease both are unknown, only speculation is possible.

In conclusion, from this single case it is suggested that the atypical NL amisulpride is effective in the treatment of tics in TS. Furthermore, there is evidence that this anti-tic effect can be augmented by additional treatment with Δ^9-THC. Previous reports about successful treatment of TS with cannabinoids predominantly included males, because there is higher disease prevalence in male than in female subjects (3-4:1). This study, therefore, suggests that cannabinoids are effective not only in males but also in females suffering from TS.

REFERENCES

Anderson, L.A., J.J. Anderson, T.N. Chase, and J.R. Walters. 1995. The cannabinoid agonists WIN 55,212-2 and CP 55,940 attenuate rotational behavior induced by a dopamine D1 but not a D2 agonist in rats with unilateral lesions of the nigrostriatal pathway. *Brain Res* 691(1-2):106-114.

Clifford, D.B. 1983. Tetrahydrocannabinol for tremor in multiple sclerosis. *Ann Neurol* 13(6):669-671.

Consroe, P., R. Musty, J. Rein, W. Tillery, and R. Pertwee. 1997. The perceived effects of smoked cannabis on patients with multiple sclerosis. *Eur Neurol* 38(1):44-48.

Consroe, P., R. Sandyk, and S.R. Snider. 1986. Open label evaluation of cannabidiol in dystonic movement disorders. *Int J Neurosci* 30(4):277-282.

Giuffrida, A., L.H. Parsons, T.M. Kerr, F. Rodriguez de Fonseca, M. Navarro, and D. Piomelli. 1999. Dopamine activation of endogenous cannabinoid signaling in dorsal striatum. *Nat Neurosci* 2(4):358-363.

Glass, M., M. Dragunow, and R.L. Faull. 2000. The pattern of neurodegeneration in Huntington's disease: a comparative study of cannabinoid, dopamine, adenosine and GABA(A) receptor alterations in the human basal ganglia in Huntington's disease. *Neuroscience* 97(3):505-519.

Harcherik, D.F., J.F. Leckman, J. Detlor, and D.J. Cohen. 1984. A new instrument for clinical studies of Tourette's syndrome. *Am J Acad Child Psychiatry* 23(2):153-160.

Hemming, M., and P.M. Yellowlees. 1993. Effective treatment of Tourette's syndrome with marijuana. *J Psychopharmacol* 7(4):389-391.

Herkenham, M., A.B. Lynn, M.D. Little, M.R. Johnson, L.S. Melvin, B.R. de Costa, and K.C. Rice. 1990. Cannabinoid receptor localization in brain. *Proc Natl Acad Sci USA* 87(5):1932-1936.

Kurlan, R. 2001. New treatments for tics? *Neurology* 56(5):580-581.

Leckman, J.F., K.E. Towbin, S.I. Ort, and D.J. Cohen. 1988. Clinical assessment of tic disorder severity. In *Tourette's Syndrome and Tic Disorders*, edited by D.J. Cohen, R.D. Bruun, and J.F. Leckman. New York: Wiley.

Maneuf, Y.P., A.R. Crossman, and J.M. Brotchie. 1997. The cannabinoid receptor agonist WIN 55,212-2 reduces D2, but not D1, dopamine receptor-mediated alleviation of akinesia in the reserpine-treated rat model of Parkinson's disease. *Exp Neurol* 148(1):265-270.

Maneuf, Y.P., J.E. Nash, A.R. Crossman, and J.M. Brotchie. 1996. Activation of the cannabinoid receptor by delta 9-tetrahydrocannabinol reduces gamma-aminobutyric acid uptake in the globus pallidus. *Eur J Pharmacol* 308(2):161-164.

Meinck, H.M., P.W. Schönle, and B. Conrad. 1989. Effect of cannabinoids on spasticity and ataxia in multiple sclerosis. *J Neurol* 236(2):120-122.

Moss, D.E., P.Z. Manderscheid, S.P. Montgomery, A.B. Norman, and P.R. Sanberg. 1989. Nicotine and cannabinoids as adjuncts to neuroleptics in the treatment of Tourette syndrome and other motor disorders. *Life Sci* 44(21):1521-1525.

Moss, D.E., S.B. McMaster, and J. Rogers. 1981. Tetrahydrocannabinol potentiates reserpine-induced hypokinesia. *Pharmacol Biochem Behav* 15(5):779-783.

Moss, D.E., S.P. Montgomery, A.A. Salo, and R.W. Steger. 1984. Tetrahydrocannabinol effects on extrapyramidal motor behaviors in an animal model of Parkinson's disease. In *The cannabinoids: chemical, pharmacologic, and therapeutic aspects*, edited by S. Agurell, W.L. Dewey, and R.E. Willette. New York: Academic Press.

Müller-Vahl, K.R., H. Kolbe, U. Schneider, and H.M. Emrich. 1998. Cannabinoids: Possible role in pathophysiology of Gilles de la Tourette-syndrome. *Acta Psychiat Scand* 98(6):502-506.

Müller-Vahl, K.R., U. Schneider, A. Koblenz, M. Jöbges, H. Kolbe, T. Daldrup, and H.M. Emrich. 2002. Treatment of Tourette-Syndrome with Δ^9-Tetrahydrocannabinol (THC). *Pharmacopsychiatry*, in press.

Müller-Vahl, K.R., U. Schneider, H. Kolbe, and H.M. Emrich. 1999. Treatment of Tourette-Syndrome with delta-9-tetrahydrocannabinol. *Am J Psychiatry* 156(3): 495.

Müller-Vahl K.R., U. Schneider, K. Theloe, H. Prevedel, H. Kolbe, and H.M. Emrich. 2001. Cannabinoids in the Treatment of Tourette-Syndrome. International Association for Cannabis as Medicine, 2001 Congress on Cannabis and Cannabinoids, 26-27 October, 2001, Berlin, Abstracts.

Navarro, M., J.J. Fernandez-Ruiz, R. De Miguel, M.L. Hernandez, M. Cebeira, and J.A. Ramos. 1993. Motor disturbances induced by an acute dose of delta 9-tetrahydrocannabinol: possible involvement of nigrostriatal dopaminergic alterations. *Pharmacol Biochem Behav* 45(2):291-298.

Pertwee, R.G., and A.P. Wickens AP. 1991. Enhancement by chlordiazepoxide of catalepsy induced in rats by intravenous or intrapallidal injections of enantiomeric cannabinoids. *Neuropharmacology* 30(3):237-244.

Rodriguez de Fonseca, F., J.L. Martin Calderon, R. Mechoulam, and M. Navarro. 1994. Repeated stimulation of D1 dopamine receptors enhances (−)-11-hydroxy-delta 8-tetrahydrocannabinol-dimethyl-heptyl-induced catalepsy in male rats. *Neuroreport* 5(7):761-765.

Sandyk, R., and G. Awerbuch. 1988. Marijuana and Tourette's syndrome. *J Clin Psychopharmacol* 8(6):444-445.

Sandyk, R., S.R. Snider, P. Consroe, and S.M. Elias. 1986. Cannabidiol in dystonic movement disorders. *Psychitry Res* 18(3):291.

Shapiro, A.K., E.S. Shapiro, J.G. Young, and T.E. Feinberg. 1988. Signs, symptoms, and clinical course. In *Gilles de la Tourette Syndrome*, 2nd ed., edited by A.K. Shapiro, E.S. Shapiro, J.G. Young, and T.E. Feinberg. New York: Raven Press.

Sieradzan, K.A., S.H. Fox, M. Hill, J.P. Dick, A.R. Crossman, and J.M. Brotchie. 2001. Cannabinoids reduce levodopa-induced dyskinesia in Parkinson's disease: a pilot study. *Neurology* 57(11):2108-2111.

Singer, H.S. 1997. Neurobiology of Tourette syndrome. *Neurol Clin* 15(2):357-379.

Snider, S.R., and P. Consroe. 1984. Treatment of Meige's syndrome with cannabidiol. *Neurology* 34(Suppl):147.

Souilhac, J., M. Poncelet, M. Rinaldi-Carmona, G. Le Fur, and P. Soubrie. 1995. Intrastriatal injection of cannabinoid receptor agonists induced turning behavior in mice. *Pharmacol Biochem Behav* 51(1):3-7.

Trillet, M., T. Moreau, J. Dalery, R. de Villard, and G. Aimard. 1990. Treatment of Gilles de la Tourette's disease with amisulpride. *Presse Med* 19(4):175.

Wickens, A.P., and R.G. Pertwee. 1995. Effect of delta 9-tetrahydrocannabinol on circling in rats induced by intranigral muscimol administration. *Eur J Pharmacol* 282(1-3):251-254.

Personal Account
of Medical Use of Cannabis

Clare Hodges

SUMMARY. The author provides a personal account of her sojourn with multiple sclerosis and its treatment with smoked and oral preparations of cannabis.

Additional information is provided as to the effects, dosing and delivery of cannabis employed by 250 members of the Alliance for Cannabis Therapeutics. *[Article copies available for a fee from The Haworth Document Delivery Service: 1-800-HAWORTH. E-mail address: <getinfo@haworthpressinc. com> Website: <http://www.HaworthPress.com> © 2002 by The Haworth Press, Inc. All rights reserved.]*

KEYWORDS. Cannabis, medical marijuana, multiple sclerosis, patient advocacy

I discovered I had multiple sclerosis (MS) 18 years ago when I was 25 years old. For several years I was only mildly affected. I carried on working as a television producer, married and had two children. Slowly my condition became worse, so that now I am constantly uncomfortable and tired. I am visually impaired and cannot sleep, eat or move very well.

Multiple sclerosis (MS) is a cruel disease. It develops when you're young and healthy, and slowly but surely you lose all your faculties, abilities and

Clare Hodges, MA, is affiliated with the Alliance for Cannabis Therapeutics, P.O. Box CR14, Leeds LS7 4XF, England (E-mail: clare@dallases.free-online.co.uk).

[Haworth co-indexing entry note]: "Personal Account of Medical Use of Cannabis." Hodges, Clare. Co-published simultaneously in *Journal of Cannabis Therapeutics* (The Haworth Integrative Healing Press, an imprint of The Haworth Press, Inc.) Vol. 2, No. 3/4, 2002, pp. 155-160; and: *Women and Cannabis: Medicine, Science, and Sociology* (ed: Ethan Russo, Melanie Dreher, and Mary Lynn Mathre) The Haworth Integrative Healing Press, an imprint of The Haworth Press, Inc., 2002, pp. 155-160. Single or multiple copies of this article are available for a fee from The Haworth Document Delivery Service [1-800-HAWORTH, 9:00 a.m. - 5:00 p.m. (EST). E-mail address: getinfo@haworthpressinc.com].

functions. Nowadays you can often expect to live your full life span until you become completely dependent, and of course this is a very depressing prospect. I began to get gloomy and introspective, as all my future seemed to hold was deteriorating health, since I had not found any medicines that really helped.

The medicines prescribed only gave limited relief and often with unacceptable side effects. Over the years I've been given steroids, tranquilisers, painkillers, muscle relaxants and antidepressants. At best they only helped in the short term, and many have intolerable side effects. My main problem, however, was that my bladder was in constant spasm and no prescribed medicines helped me. For several months I took oxybutinin to help my bladder. This didn't help the problem, but I persevered, hoping at some time it might. However, it gave me side effects of blurred vision and headaches. My nights were so disturbed by the bladder problems, I was given temazepam to help me sleep, which did get me off to sleep, but left me slow and 'hung-over' the following day. Using cannabis helped me gradually cut back on these medicines, so that I stopped oxybutinin, and cut down on temazepam. I much preferred using cannabis because not only did it seem just as effective, but also I felt I had control over my medication, which was very important.

In 1992 I read an article in a U.S. journal about how some doctors had observed cannabis could help people with MS. Before I did anything I talked to different doctors I saw. None of them knew much about it, but said they thought it wouldn't do me much harm in moderate quantities, and indeed it was probably safer than many of the medicines they could prescribe.

As I was a middle class mother of two very young children I had a bit of a problem obtaining cannabis. My life revolved around the local mothers and toddlers group and it was sometimes quite embarrassing asking people if they could assist me, but eventually I found someone who did help me get some and showed me how to use it. I had approached a woman I knew from when I was working who I'd been told used cannabis. I didn't know her very well, but decided to ask her for help. Like most people, she was happy to help someone in trouble, and came around one evening when the children were in bed. She brought some cannabis, tobacco and papers, and showed me how to roll a joint. She smoked some with me, talking me through what I might be experiencing, constantly telling me to take it slowly. I'd tried cannabis about twice when I was a student, but without much effect, so I was very naïve. I had smoked cigarettes for a few years when I was younger, and still have an occasional cigarette, so smoking tobacco was familiar to me. The advice she gave to go slowly was very good, as I now know it is easy to take too much if you're not careful.

When I did try cannabis, the physical relief was almost immediate. The tension in my spine and bladder was eased, and I slept well. I was comfortable with my body for the first time in years. Just as important, I felt happy that there was something, after all, that could help me. It was as if a huge weight had been lifted from me.

My MS symptoms vary considerably. Sometimes I can appear very well, and at other times I look and sound very handicapped. Similarly, I can be cheerful about my situation, but when the MS is bad I become very introspective and gloomy. Very simple tasks take enormous effort and leave me exhausted. Cannabis helps to stabilize my health and I find I can now do simple things that I hadn't been able to do, like go to the shops, or cook my children's dinner after school.

It took a couple of months to work out how to self-medicate. The main problem, which continues to this day, is working out how to use each new batch as strength and quality differ considerably. To begin with, it was easy to take too much or too little. If I took too much I became uncoordinated and confused, which distressed me and made it harder to deal with the condition. I have now established a routine that helps. I take 9 grams of herbal cannabis per week, drinking it in milky drinks during the day, and smoking it at night before I go to bed. To make the drink, I simmer the cannabis in milk for a few minutes, sieve the milk to remove the leaves, then drink the milk. I do not smoke it with tobacco, but dried herbs in a herbal tobacco mix you can buy in health food shops. I've found smoking is the easiest way of taking it to treat my disease, as it is much easier to regulate the dose. MS is a particularly unpredictable disease, not just in the long term, but from day to day, and almost hour to hour. Over 24 hours I would usually expect to take 4 joints (half cannabis, half herbal tobacco). However, the total number can be only two, or up to six or seven, depending on the state of health.

So, it's vitally important that MS patients have some kind of control over when and how much of the medicine they take, in the same way that patients often self-titrate for pain relief.

There was concern expressed by politicians and charities when medical use of cannabis was first talked about, that patients would become addicted to cannabis and would be tempted to take 'harder' drugs. I've never been able to take this very seriously, but I thought I'd say that I don't feel in any way addicted to cannabis. If for some reason I can't use it (such as when travelling abroad), I don't crave it or suffer withdrawal symptoms; the MS simply gets worse.

I've been prescribed nabilone, the only available cannabinoid preparation currently available in Britain. I took 1 mg daily for four nights, but it made me confused and clumsy. I persevered for four days, hoping it might be a substitute, but it wasn't. It's not clear to me whether a synthetic preparation will ever have the same therapeutic benefit as the natural plant.

My neurologist was very impressed by how much better I was. He put me in touch with two other patients with MS who also used cannabis. When we found out that cannabis in tincture form was available by medical prescription in Britain until 1973, we decided to start an organisation based on the U.S. Alliance for Cannabis Therapeutics (ACT) to press for cannabis to be moved from Schedule 1 to Schedule 2 and thereby restore it as a legal medicine. It has involved an enormous amount of work, dealing with thousands of letters from patients, doctors and politicians. The ACT has never pressed for legalisation of cannabis and has no 'hidden agenda.' I've always thought a great strength of our group is that it's been run and financed entirely by patients. We do not fund-raise nor have we applied for charitable status, but have remained quite independent. It was doubtless thanks to our independent status that official bodies have regularly consulted the ACT.

We were very involved in the British Medical Association report and were interviewed by the House of Lords Select Committee on cannabis. Led by Austin Mitchell, MP, we took two delegations of patients and doctors to talk to the Ministers of Health and the Home Office. These delegations were very distinguished, including Lord Whaddon, who suffers from MS, and Professor Patrick Wall, the specialist in pain control.

In 1997 we invited the director of a pharmaceutical company, GW Pharmaceuticals, to join our delegation when the doctors and politicians representing the ACT asked the Department of Health Minister, Paul Boateng, if his company could be granted a licence to grow cannabis for medical research. This was issued shortly afterwards and clinical trials are now proceeding with a preparation manufactured by the company and administered via a sublingual spray. Following this, the Medical Research Council has set up several trials around the country, using synthetic versions of cannabis.

I've been using cannabis for nine years. There is no doubt that my condition has improved in different ways. I do not have to take as many prescribed medicines. I now eat better, sleep better, and I feel more positive and motivated.

GENERAL OBSERVATIONS FROM PATIENTS

I've outlined my personal experience of using cannabis with MS, but I'm also in a position where I can give a broader overview as over the last nine years I've talked to or corresponded with many patients who use cannabis. Of the 3,000 letters the ACT has received, there are about 250 patients who have written about their use of cannabis in some detail. There have been more letters from women than men, and they have tended to be older rather than younger. I assume this reflects the general pattern of people with MS. Although most women are early or late middle-aged, a handful of much older people (70+) have also written about their experiences. Several of these I have followed up by visiting and talking to the people who wrote in.

Here are some thoughts I now want to pass based on these letters and conversations over the years.

PSYCHOACTIVITY

There is a recurring theme through all the letters patients write: cannabis helps them because it not only eases their physical problems, but also improves their mood, lifts their spirits, and gives them a better quality of life.

There's a large literature about the effects of cannabis, but when you're chronically ill your experience of all these effects is somewhat different.

Like all medicines and drugs cannabis has a mixture of physical and psychoactive effects. One common physical effect is that it relaxes muscles, which is one reason why people enjoy using it, but when you have MS relaxing muscles is not just fun–it is very important. For many of us it takes much effort and concentration just to move around and do ordinary things. I know this makes me slightly tense all the time which is very wearing and uncomfortable and can result in going into spasm. So relaxing muscles is not just a way of 'chilling out,' but can mean people are able to function more normally.

Similarly, the more I talk to ill and disabled people who use cannabis, the more I think the psychoactive effects are vital to its therapeutic value. There's been great interest in developing drugs that will affect the physical progress of the disease, but for many sufferers and their families being depressed and demoralised is the hardest aspect of the disease to live with and can be extremely debilitating. In the same way that your physical strength diminishes, your mental powers and spirit weaken. One person who wrote to our group put the benefits of the psychoactive effects very well. He said that "people in good health who smoke cannabis get high, while if you've got MS, you're under par all the time, you don't move properly, see properly, have much energy, and cannabis lifts you to normality."

It has been slightly disheartening when some people say we need to find a version of cannabis without the psychoactive effects. This could only work well for a type of MS that produces no psychological effects. The effort to eliminate mood-altering effects seems to me to be a fundamental misunderstanding of how it helps us.

DELIVERY METHODS

Most people choose to smoke cannabis, for the reasons I've mentioned, but many don't like smoking. I've been very impressed by how inventive people are about how to take the cannabis. Two of the people I went to see in the Orkney Islands have developed a skin patch. They simply put some home-grown cannabis on their skin and cover with cling film and a surgical waterproof bandage. They say this gives them a regular, low dose of cannabis that keeps them going for a couple of days. Several people bake it in cakes, but often have a problem as they don't know how it is distributed. I went to see a lady in my home county, Yorkshire, who has got around this by baking little buns with just a tiny pinch in each bun. This simple, neat solution really appealed to me. Someone else has tried to use it as a suppository, but seemed very primitive. This lady with MS did not continue with the suppositories, finding smoking much easier, if more wasteful.

DOSAGE

It is remarkable the very different amounts people use to find relief. For some, an ounce of herbal cannabis may last four months, for others only two weeks. Similarly the amount used can vary considerably in the same patient. Research could be more flexible in amounts tested on patients, acknowledging the unpredictability of the disease.

In general, patients who use cannabis now outside the law are a rich source of information. Their experiences could help direct any further research.

Cannabis in Multiple Sclerosis: Women's Health Concerns

Denis J. Petro

SUMMARY. Women's health has received greater attention with the recognition of significant differences in disease expression and drug action in men and women. Multiple sclerosis is a neurological disorder with important gender differences. MS patients have employed cannabis to treat a number of symptoms associated with the disease including spasticity, pain, tremor, fatigue, and autonomic dysfunction. The scientific literature includes supportive case reports, single-patient (N-of-1) trials and randomized clinical trials. Large-scale clinical trials are underway to answer questions concerning the efficacy and safety of cannabis in patients with MS. While these studies will answer important questions concerning the actions of cannabinoids on the nervous system, additional studies in female MS patients will be needed to address issues such as gender-specific actions on symptoms such as pain and autonomic dysfunction along with studies in menopausal and post-menopausal women. Since the drug-drug interactions have been reported with cannabinoids, the effects of cannabis on the actions of other centrally-acting drugs should be explored. *[Article copies available for a fee from The Haworth Document Delivery Service: 1-800-HAWORTH. E-mail address: <getinfo@ haworthpressinc.com> Website: <http://www.HaworthPress.com> © 2002 by The Haworth Press, Inc. All rights reserved.]*

KEYWORDS. Multiple sclerosis, cannabis, cannabinoids, spasticity, women's medicine

---

Denis J. Petro, MD, 1550 Clarendon Boulevard, Suite 510, Arlington, VA 22209-2783 (E-mail: djpmsmd@aol.com).

[Haworth co-indexing entry note]: "Cannabis in Multiple Sclerosis: Women's Health Concerns." Petro, Denis J. Co-published simultaneously in *Journal of Cannabis Therapeutics* (The Haworth Integrative Healing Press, an imprint of The Haworth Press, Inc.) Vol. 2, No. 3/4, 2002, pp. 161-175; and: *Women and Cannabis: Medicine, Science, and Sociology* (ed: Ethan Russo, Melanie Dreher, and Mary Lynn Mathre) The Haworth Integrative Healing Press, an imprint of The Haworth Press, Inc., 2002, pp. 161-175. Single or multiple copies of this article are available for a fee from The Haworth Document Delivery Service [1-800-HAWORTH, 9:00 a.m. - 5:00 p.m. (EST). E-mail address: getinfo@haworthpressinc.com].

INTRODUCTION

Women's health issues have received attention as gender differences in disease expression and drug action are discovered. A gender-based approach recognizes the fundamental physiologic differences between men and women. The areas of difference between men and women in the nervous system are extensive including anatomy, cell numbers, neurotransmitter systems, response to hormones, sensation threshold and disease frequencies. Gender and multiple sclerosis (MS) has been the subject of several excellent reviews (Olek and Khoury 2000; Coyle 2000). Specific disorders such as migraine headache, depression and motor neuron disease also show clear gender preferences.

Multiple sclerosis is a disorder with important gender-associated differences in expression. Cannabis also interacts with the endocrine and immune systems of males and females with distinctions. As therapeutic cannabis use among MS patients has increased over the past generation, a review of the subject with attention to women's health concerns is warranted.

Multiple sclerosis is the most common cause of chronic neurological disability in young adults (Rusk and Plum 1998), and is more likely seen in women and in those who grew up in northern latitudes. In a summary of 30 incidence/prevalence studies, the cumulative female-to-male ratio was 1.77:1.00 (Irizarry 1997). With 350,000 MS patients in the United States, the number of female MS patients is approximately 225,000. Gender is clearly a determinant of susceptibility to MS. The increased female incidence in MS is similar to other autoimmune diseases with onset of symptoms in adulthood such as myasthenia gravis, Hashimoto's thyroiditis, Sjögren's syndrome and systemic lupus erythematosus. The female preponderance in MS lessens in those in whom presentation occurs later in life. MS attacks are less frequent during pregnancy while the postpartum period is one of higher risk (Whitaker 1998). While the postpartum increase in risk for MS attacks may discourage childbearing, women who have borne a child fare better in the long term than those women who have not (Runmarker and Anderson 1995). Interestingly, the occurrence of a first pregnancy may lead to some permanent change in immune status.

Recognizing that current MS treatment is less than optimal, the use of cannabis offers an opportunity to demonstrate the therapeutic potential of cannabinoids on a number of neurological symptoms. In a survey of health care in 471 people with MS in the United Kingdom, use of cannabis was acknowledged by 8% (Somerset et al. 2001). Extrapolating to the 60,000 MS patients in the UK provides an estimate of 4,800 MS patients who employ cannabis in the UK and 28,000 in the United States. In a publication commenting on the use of cannabis in South Africa, James (1994) reported the experiences of a female MS patient (p. 369):

A few years ago I had started to eat small quantities of marijuana . . . the effects were immediate and remarkable. Control of bladder functioning which was a humiliating problem is restored to normal and has been a liberating influence in my life-style. I can now go out shopping, to the theater, etc., without anticipation of dread and panic. Painful and disturbing attacks of spasticity are relieved and now restful patterns of sleep are ensured where previously sleep was disrupted by urinary frequency or pain and discomfort not least I can laugh and giggle, have marvelous sex and forget that I have this awful, incurable, intractable disease.

The challenge for physicians is to evaluate patient observations using scientific methodology. Many authors have described individual patient experiences of therapeutic use of cannabis to treat symptoms of MS (Grinspoon and Bakalar 1997; Brown 1998; Iversen 2000). Additional support has been provided by single-patient clinical trials (N-of-1) and prospective double-blind placebo-controlled studies.

TREATMENT OPTIONS: ACUTE EPISODES, DISEASE MODIFICATION AND SYMPTOM MANAGEMENT

Management of an acute episode of demyelination in MS is sometimes achieved to a limited extent with corticosteroids. Disease modification is difficult to assess because MS is a chronic, unpredictable disorder in which the burden of white matter involvement is highly variable and the clinical response to drug treatment is modest. Five drugs have been approved by regulatory authorities to modify the clinical course of MS. Avonex® (interferon-beta-1a), Betaseron® (interferon-beta-1b), Copaxone® (glatiramer acetate/copolymer 1), and Rebif® (interferon beta 1a) have demonstrated efficacy in relapsing-remitting MS and may slow the course of secondary progressive MS. Novantrone® (mitoxantrone) is approved for secondary progressive and progressive relapsing MS. Immunosuppressants such as corticosteroids, methotrexate, and cyclophosphamide have been used to alter the natural history of MS with some success.

CANNABIS IN ACUTE TREATMENT AND DISEASE MODIFICATION

While patients may claim that cannabis can alter the natural history of MS, no clinical trials have been conducted in either acute treatment or disease modification. Data from animal research supports cannabinoids as a potential disease modifying treatment for MS. The immune-mediated disease, experimental autoimmune encephalomyelitis (EAE), is considered the laboratory model of MS. In a study in the Lewis rat and guinea pig, Lyman and colleagues (1989) demonstrated that the oral administration of Δ-9-tetrahydrocannabinol (THC) was effective in the prevention and suppression of EAE. The authors suggested that Δ-9-THC might prove to be a new and relatively innocuous agent for the treatment of immune-mediated diseases such as MS. Since Δ-9-THC is the cannabinoid associated with negative psychotropic actions, investigators used other cannabinoids to assess actions in EAE. Wirguin and colleagues (1994) studied the effect of Δ-8-THC on EAE in the rat. Orally administered Δ-8 THC significantly reduced the incidence and severity of neurological deficit while parenteral administration was not effective. The difference can be explained on first-pass metabolism in the liver, which produces the active metabolite. Additional support for beneficial effects of cannabinoids in EAE was reported by Achiron and co-investigators (2000) using a synthetic non-psychotropic cannabinoid, dexanabinol (HU-211). The authors suggested that dexanabinol may provide an alternate treatment of acute exacerbations of MS. Finally, Guzman, Sanchez and Galve-Roperh (2001) reviewed the experimental evidence showing the protective effects of cannabinoids from toxic insults such a glutamatergic over-stimulation, ischemia and oxidative damage. The authors described the potential of cannabinoids to downregulate inflammatory cytokine production.

If cannabinoid drugs are to be used in acute treatment of MS or in disease modification, then studies in female patients will be needed. These studies involve assessment of drug effects on fertility, pregnancy and in nursing mothers. Since inclusion of women in early clinical trials is usually insufficient to identify gender-based differences in response, animal models are used to identify potential pharmacologic and toxicological effects (Christian 2001). Unfortunately, current animal models do not consistently demonstrate gender-based differences seen in humans. The cannabinoid Δ-9-THC is marketed in the United States as Marinol® and information concerning use in women is provided in the Physicians' Desk Reference (2002). Marinol is included in Category C (FDA designation for drugs with animal data showing harm to the fetus with no controlled human studies). The drug labeling states that Marinol should be used only if the potential benefit justifies the potential risk to the fetus. Likewise, its use in nursing mothers is not recommended since Marinol is concentrated in and secreted in human breast milk and is absorbed by the nursing baby.

Drug interaction studies would be needed to investigate the potential for significant interactions with drugs commonly used by women. Because cannabinoids are highly bound to plasma proteins and might displace other protein-bound drugs, dosage adjustment for other highly protein-bound drugs may be needed. In addition, drugs metabolized by hepatic mixed-function oxidase enzymes may be inhibited by cannabinoids (Benowitz and Jones 1977). In the PDR drug interaction section for Marinol, specific precautions are included regarding potential interactions with a number of drugs including sympathomimetic agents, antihistamines, tricyclic antidepressants, muscle relaxants, barbiturates and theophylline. Other drugs which may be important in female patients include birth control drugs, hormones administered to treat symptoms associated with menopause, steroids, and drugs used in the treatment of osteoporosis.

The effects of inhaled cannabis on fetal development have been studied extensively. In a study of six one-year-old infants exposed daily to cannabis prenatally and through breastfeeding, no malformations were found in cannabis-exposed infants (Tennes et al. 1985). A prospective study of the effects of prenatal exposure to cigarettes and cannabis on growth from birth to adolescence found no significant effects on growth measures at birth although a smaller head circumference observed at all ages reached statistical significance among the adolescents born to heavy marijuana users (Fried et al. 1999). Finally, the relationship between maternal use of cannabis and pregnancy outcome was investigated in a study of 12,000 women in the UK (Fergusson et al. 2002). Five percent of mothers reported smoking cannabis before and/or during pregnancy. The use of cannabis during pregnancy was not associated with increased risk of perinatal mortality or morbidity. The babies of women who used cannabis weekly before and during pregnancy were lighter than those of non-users and had shorter birth lengths and smaller head circumferences. The findings of this study are consistent with earlier studies that have found an absence of statistical association between cannabis use and antenatal or perinatal morbidity and mortality. The reduced birth weight seen with regular or heavy cannabis use suggests that to optimize fetal growth and minimize the risk of an adverse pregnancy outcome, pregnant women should limit cannabis use during pregnancy. In female patients during the reproductive years, fertility and pregnancy are usually not affected by MS. While MS activity seems to decrease during pregnancy, exacerbation rates increase in the first 6 months postpartum (Birk and Rudick 1986). Since cannabinoids are secreted in human breast milk and absorbed by the nursing baby, cannabis use while breast-feeding should be avoided.

Special studies of cannabis in menopausal and post-menopausal women have been conducted. Mendelson and colleagues (1985) studied LH levels in menopausal women after marijuana smoking and found no significant difference in LH levels when compared to values for healthy menopausal women. In a study of the acute effects of marijuana smoking in post-menopausal women, Benedikt and colleagues (1986) noted statistically significant increases in pulse rate, intoxication levels and the confusion component of the Profile of Mood States Questionnaire (POMS). The finding of neuropsychological performance impairment in post-menopausal women is not unlike the findings in moderate cannabis users (Pope et al. 2001) and in heavy cannabis users (Solowij et al. 2002). The degree of impairment in memory and attention are not surprising in chronic heavy users. Pope (2002) presents the consensus opinion that some cognitive deficits persist for hours or days after acute intoxication with cannabis has subsided. Since cognitive impairment is associated with MS, the potential for significant adverse effect on memory and attention in MS patients using therapeutic cannabis should be a subject of future clinical research.

CANNABIS IN SYMPTOM MANAGEMENT

Manifestations of MS are protean and depend on the location of persistent central nervous system lesions. Since MS lesions have a predilection for certain anatomic locations, recognizable clinical syndromes are common in MS. Surveys of symptoms in MS have been carried out with the most common symptoms including fatigue, balance impairment, muscle disturbances (weakness, stiffness, pain and spasm), and bowel and bladder impairment (Compston 1997). In chronic MS, signs and symptoms of motor dysfunction are found in at least 75 percent of patients (Miller 2000) with sensory impairment noted in 50 percent. Cerebellar abnormalities (ataxia, tremor, nystagmus or dysarthria) are found in at least a third of MS patients. Autonomic symptoms including bowel, bladder or sexual dysfunction are found in at least 50 percent of patients.

A survey of cannabis-using MS patients in the USA and UK by Consroe and colleagues (1997) reported improvements after cannabis use in spasticity, chronic pain, acute paroxysmal phenomena, tremor, emotional dysfunction, anorexia/weight loss, fatigue, diplopia, sexual dysfunction, bowel and bladder dysfunction, vision dimness, dysfunction of walking and balance, and memory loss (descending rank order). While the authors of this study discuss the potential shortcomings of the survey design, this report suggests that cannabis may significantly relieve signs and symptoms of MS such as spasticity and pain along with a number of other complaints.

IMPAIRED MOBILITY: SPASTICITY

In the 19th century, O'Shaughnessy (1842) used hemp extract in treating muscle spasms associated with tetanus and rabies. Reynolds (1890) reported using cannabis to treat muscle spasms, as well as for epilepsy, migraine, and other indications. While medicinal cannabis use continued in the years after the work of O'Shaughnessy and Reynolds, little was published concerning cannabis and spasticity until the 1970s. A survey of 10 spinal-cord injured males was published in 1974 in which 5 patients reported reduced spasticity, 3 patients noted no effect and 2 patients did not have significant spasticity (Dunn and Davis 1974).

The use of cannabis to treat spasticity associated with MS has been reported by a number of investigators over the subsequent interval. Petro (1980) reported one patient with MS who used cannabis to treat nocturnal leg fatigue and spasms associated with spasticity. Petro and Ellenberger (1981) conducted a double-blind clinical trial that demonstrated statistically significant reduction in spasticity following the oral administration of Δ-9-THC in doses of 5 and 10 mg. Investigators have confirmed the observation using Δ-9-THC (Hanigan et al. 1985; Ungerleider et al. 1988; Maurer et al. 1990), cannabis (Meinck et al. 1989) and nabilone (Martyn et al. 1995). Additional preclinical support for the benefit from cannabis in spasticity was provided by the report of Baker and colleagues (2000). In this study, cannabinoid receptor agonism improved tremor and spasticity in mice with chronic relapsing experimental allergic encephalomyelitis (CREAE) and indicated that the endogenous cannabinoid system may be active in control of spasticity and tremor. Further support for cannabinoid receptor involvement was provided in an animal study in which cannabinoid receptor (CB_1) changes were found in regions of the brain involved in the control of motor symptoms (Berrendero et al. 2001). The role of the endocannabinoid system in spasticity was demonstrated in CREAE mice in a further study, which manipulated tone using cannabinoid receptor agonists and antagonists (Baker et al. 2001).

Since a considerable body of scientific evidence supports the efficacy of cannabinoids in spasticity, review articles (Gracies et al. 1997; Consroe 1999) and medical texts (Compston 1999; Compston 2001) include cannabis as a treatment option in spasticity. In *Brain's Diseases of the Nervous System Eleventh Edition* (Compston 2001), among the treatments for spasticity associated with MS, cannabinoids are listed along with baclofen, dantrium, benzodiazepines and tizanidine.

Gender issues are involved in MS-associated spasticity. Since females are more likely to experience demyelination at an earlier age than males, the burden of white matter disease over time may be greater in females. The earlier appearance of symptoms in females is somewhat counterbalanced by a greater prevalence of spinal MS seen in males and occurring later in life. The late occurring form of MS often involves progressive spinal lesions presenting with spasticity and pain.

TREMOR

Tremor in MS is treated with beta-blockers, anticonvulsants or, in rare cases, stereotactic procedures. Experimental evidence for benefit from cannabis is provided in a preclinical study by Baker and colleagues (2000) in which treatment with a CB_1 antagonist resulted in increased forelimb tremor. Since isolation of tremor from spasticity may be difficult in experimental animals, interpretation of such evidence may be questioned. In the survey of patients with MS by Consroe and associates (1997), 90% of subjects with tremor reported improvement after cannabis. In a study of 8 MS patients with tremor and ataxia, oral THC was effective in 2 of 8 subjects with both subjective and objective improvement (Clifford 1983).

NYSTAGMUS

Nystagmus is an eye movement abnormality often associated with MS. In an N-of-1 clinical trial, a 52-year-old man with MS and pendular nystagmus was studied in the United Kingdom over 3 months before and after cannabis in the form of cigarettes, nabilone and cannabis oil-containing capsules (Schon et al. 1998). The investigators demonstrated improved visual acuity and suppression of the patient's pendular nystagmus after inhaled cannabis and were able to correlate the therapeutic effect with acute changes in serum cannabinoid levels. Nabilone and orally administered cannabis oil capsules had no effect. Because of the anatomical relationships involved in eye movement control, the authors suggest an effect at the level of the dorsal pontine tegmentum. In support of action at the level of the deep brain stem is the benefit seen with cannabis in intractable hiccups (Gilson and Busalacchi 1998) and evidence supporting cannabinoid analgesic actions mediated in the rostral ventromedial medulla (Meng et al. 1998). Responding to the report of benefit in nystagmus associated with MS, Dell'Osso (2000) reported an individual with congenital nystagmus whose oscillations dampened after smoking cannabis. Dell'Osso commented that while he had seen similar reports from patients, cannabis research is discouraged in the United States.

POSTURAL REGULATION

The complex integration of sensory and motor function required for postural regulation is impaired in many patients with MS. Impairment of posture is most disabling for patients, distressing for caregivers, and frustrating for physicians. Lesions of spinal, cerebral and cerebellar pathways result in loss of balance. In a study of 10 MS patients, inhaled cannabis caused increased postural tracking error both in MS patients and in normal control subjects (Greenberg et al. 1994). The authors admitted in their publication that dynamic posturography "is not a measure of spasticity." Some authors have reported incorrectly that this study is a negative study in spasticity. Since cerebellar dysfunction is a common finding in MS seen in a third to 80 percent of patients, one can anticipate that many MS patients with both motor and cerebellar symptoms may find improved spasticity and impaired balance. Cannabinoids should be used with caution in patients with the combination of corticospinal (spasticity) and cerebellar (balance) deficits.

FATIGUE

Fatigue is one of the most frequently reported symptoms in MS and is clearly distinct from fatigue experienced in an otherwise healthy individual. The mechanism for fatigue in MS is unknown. No differences have been found in the level of MS-associated fatigue between men and women. Clinical trials have demonstrated that amantadine may be beneficial; however, the supporting evidence is weak (Branas et al. 2000). In a single-blind trial of modafinil in patients with MS (Rammohan et al. 2002), fatigue scores were improved during treatment (200 mg/day). In the only study addressing the effect of cannabis on fatigue, Consroe (1997) reported survey data which showed from 60 to 70% of subjects reported cannabis reduced fatigue states (tiredness, leg weakness). No controlled clinical trials of cannabinoids have investigated this condition.

PAIN

Because of the nature of MS as a disruption of transmission of nerve impulses, paroxysmal manifestations are commonly seen including tonic brainstem attacks, trigeminal neuralgia, and spasticity. Anticonvulsants and antidepressants are commonly used in MS pain syndromes, with some benefit. Cannabinoids have not been studied extensively in MS-associated pain. In other pain models, cannabinoids have demonstrated efficacy comparable to potent analgesics, such as the opioids (Campbell et al. 2001). Gender differences can affect pain via biological differences in the nociceptive and perceptual systems. In humans, women are, in general, more sensitive to painful stimuli when compared to men (LeResche 2001). The prevalence of pain syndromes in female patients with MS has not been studied.

BLADDER DYSFUNCTION

Bladder impairment in MS is seen in up to 80% of patients at some time during the course of the disease and can vary from slight inconvenience to potentially life-threatening when renal function is compromised. The complex interaction between bladder detrussor and sphincter function is disrupted with spinal cord lesions in MS. Drugs used in the treatment of spasticity such as baclofen and diazepam are effective in treating bladder symptoms in many MS patients by inhibiting the urethral sphincter. MS patients, as the example of the female patient from South Africa described earlier (James, 1994), report improvements in bladder function after cannabinoid use. Based on the observations of improved urinary tract function, an open-label pilot study of cannabis based medicinal extract (CBME) has been reported by Brady and colleagues (2001). In this study sublingual CBME improved lower urinary tract function in 10 patients with advanced MS and refractory urinary tract dysfunction over 8 weeks of treatment.

SEXUAL DYSFUNCTION

Treatment of sexual dysfunction in male MS patients includes a range of options including pharmacological treatments such as sildenafil (Viagra®), papaverine or phentolamine. No treatment other than local administration of artificial lubrication is available for treatment of sexual dysfunction in females. In the Consroe survey of cannabis effects on MS signs and symptoms (1997), 51 subjects reported sexual dysfunction with 62.7% claiming improvement in sexual function after cannabis. No analysis by gender was reported. Based on previously reported survey data, the clinical study of cannabis as a treatment of sexual dysfunction in MS appears warranted.

DISCUSSION

Neurologists in practice in the 1970s noted two distinct patient groups using therapeutic cannabis. Military personnel injured in Vietnam claimed that cannabis was helpful in controlling symptoms associated with traumatic spinal injury. Female patients described beneficial effects from cannabis in treating spasticity, migraine headache or menstrual pain. These observations led to a number of small clinical trials supporting the claims of individual patients. Because of regulatory hurdles in conducting clinical research with cannabis, the total number of patients treated with cannabinoid drugs remains low.

Fortunately, interest in the subject has increased with the initiation of several large-scale cannabis studies in MS in the United Kingdom. The National Institute of Clinical Excellence (NICE), the UK regulatory authority, will assess the results of clinical trials scheduled be completed by the end of 2002.

Over the years, many patients have asked questions concerning the efficacy and safety of cannabis as a therapeutic agent. While cannabis remains as a prohibited drug in the United States, Δ-9-THC is marketed as Marinol® without objection. One can contrast a potential package insert for cannabis with that for the antispastic drug, Lioresal® Intrathecal. With the use of Lioresal via a spinal pump, the drug labeling states that in clinical trials "13 deaths occurring among the 438 patients treated with Lioresal Intrathecal in premarketing studies." Interestingly, two MS patients died suddenly within 2 weeks of drug administration. Imagine the regulatory reaction if a single patient would die after cannabis use. A potential risk associated with cannabis is secondary to the inhalation of cannabis containing smoke. The evidence of significant health risk associated with cigarette smoking is overwhelming. While many patients avoid inhalation risks by using oral cannabis, the rapid action of an inhaled formulation is effective with symptoms such as flexor spasms or tonic brainstem attacks. One study noted an elevated risk of myocardial infarction (4.8 times baseline) in the 60 minutes after cannabis inhalation (Mittleman et al. 2001). While cannabis was considered a rare trigger of acute myocardial infarction, risk elevation was associated with obesity, current cigarette smoking and male gender.

Additional safety concerns associated with cannabis use in MS include the negative effects of cannabis on balance and cognition. While these negative effects may limit the potential usefulness of cannabis as a treatment of chronic symptoms in MS, many MS patients may yet benefit from cannabis.

While the interest in cannabis as a therapeutic agent for MS is high, many unanswered scientific questions remain including:

1. How does cannabis compare with current standard treatments for MS symptoms?
2. Can alternative delivery systems be developed to provide rapid onset of action with greater safety when compared to inhaled cannabis?
3. Can specific cannabinoids be used more effectively to stimulate or block cannabinoid system receptor activity?
4. Can the immune-modulating actions of cannabis be used to alter the natural history of MS?
5. Can the long-term risks and benefits of cannabis be quantified to determine a useful risk/benefit ratio in treating the life-long disability in MS?

CONCLUSIONS

Evidence in support of cannabis treatment for spasticity associated with MS includes animal studies and a small number of clinical trials using cannabinoid drugs. Clinical reports of benefit in tremor and nystagmus have been published in MS patients. Potential other signs and symptoms in MS, which may be improved with cannabis, include fatigue, pain, bladder disturbances and sexual dysfunction. Women are twice as likely as men to develop MS. Gender specific concerns in female patients include use of cannabis during pregnancy, potential effects on the fetus, and risks associated with breast-feeding. Large-scale clinical trials may provide some answers concerning the potential of cannabis in treatment of MS.

REFERENCES

Achiron, A., S. Miron, V. Lavie, R. Margalit, and A. Biegon. 2000. Dexanabinol (HU-211) effect on experimental autoimmune encephalomyelitis: implications for the treatment of acute relapses of multiple sclerosis. *J Neuroimmunol* 102(1):26-31.

Baker, D., G. Pryce, J.L. Croxford, P. Brown, R.G. Pertwee, J.W. Huffman, and L. Layward. 2000. Cannabinoids control spasticity and tremor in a multiple sclerosis model. *Nature* 404:84-7.

Baker, D., G. Pryce, J.L. Croxford, P. Brown, R.G. Pertwee, A. Makriyannis, A. Khanolkar, L. Layward, F. Fezza, T. Bisogno, and V. Di Marzo. 2001. Endocannabinoids control spasticity in a multiple sclerosis model. *FASEB J* 15(2):300-2.

Benedikt, R.A., P. Cristofaro, J.H. Mendelson, and N.K. Mello. 1986. Effects of acute marijuana smoking in post-menopausal women. *Psychopharmacol* 90:14-7.

Benowitz, N.L., and R.T. Jones. 1977. Effect of delta-9-tetrahydrocannabinol on drug distribution and metabolism: antipyrine, pentobarbital and ethanol. *Clin Pharmacol Ther* 22(3):259-68.

Berrendero, F., A. Sanchez, A. Cabranes, C. Puerta, J.A. Ramos, A. Garcia-Merino, and J. Fernandez-Ruiz. 2001. Changes in cannabinoid CB_1 receptors in striatal and cortical regions of rats with experimental allergic encephalomyelitis, an animal model of multiple sclerosis. *Synapse* 41:195-202.

Birk, K., and R. Rudick. 1986. Pregnancy and multiple sclerosis. *Arch Neurol* 43:719-26.

Brady, C.M., R. DasGupta, O.J. Wiseman, K.J. Berkley, and C.J. Fowler. 2001. Acute and chronic effects of cannabis-based medicinal extract on refractory lower urinary tract dysfunction in patients with advanced multiple sclerosis–early results. *Congress of the IACM* Abstracts, p. 9.

Branas, P., R. Jordan, A. Fry-Smith, A. Burls, and C. Hyde. 2000. Treatment for fatigue in multiple sclerosis: A rapid and systematic review. *Health Technol Assess* 4(27):1-61.

Brown, D.T. 1998. The therapeutic potential for cannabis and its derivatives. *Cannabis: The Genus Cannabis*. Amsterdam: Harwood Academic.

Cambell, F.A., M.R. Tramer, D. Carroll, D.J.M. Reynolds, R.A. Moore, and H.J. McQuay. 2001. Are cannabinoids an effective and safe treatment option in the management of pain? A qualitative systematic review. *Brit Med J* 323:13-16.

Christian, M.S. 2001. Introduction/overview: gender-based differences in pharmacologic and toxicologic responses. *Int J Toxicol* 20(3):145-8.

Clifford, D.B. 1983. Tetrahydrocannabinol for tremor in multiple sclerosis. *Ann Neurol* 13:669-71.

Compston, A. 1999. Treatment and management of multiple sclerosis. *McAlpine's Multiple Sclerosis*. New York: Churchill Livingstone.

Compston, A. 2001. Multiple sclerosis and other demyelinating diseases. *Brain's Diseases of the Nervous System.* New York: Oxford University Press.

Consroe, P. 1999. Clinical and experimental reports of marijuana and cannabinoids in spastic disorders. *Marijuana and Medicine.* Totowa, NJ: Humana Press.

Consroe, P., R. Musty, J. Rein, W. Tillery, and R. Pertwee. 1997. The perceived effects of smoked cannabis on patients with multiple sclerosis. *Eur Neurol* 38:44-8.

Coyle, P.K. 2000. Women's Issues *Multiple Sclerosis: Diagnosis, Medical Management, and Rehabilitation* New York: Demos Medical Publishing.

Dell'Osso, L.F. 2000. Suppression of pendular nystagmus by smoking cannabis in a patient with multiple sclerosis. *Neurology* 54(11):2190-1.

Dunn, M., and R. Davis. 1974. The perceived effects of marijuana on spinal cord injured males. *Paraplegia* 12:175.

Fergusson, D.M., L.J. Horwood, and K. Northstone. 2002. Maternal use of cannabis and pregnancy outcome. *Brit J Obstet Gyn* 109(1):21-7.

Fried, P.A., B. Watkinson, and R. Gray. 1999. Growth from birth to early adolescence in offspring prenatally exposed to cigarettes and marijuana. *Neurotoxicol Teratol* 21(5):513-25.

Gilson, I., and M. Busalacchi. 1998. Marijuana for intractable hiccups. *Lancet* 351:267.

Gracies, J.M., P. Nance, E. Elovic, J. McGuire, and D.M. Simpson. 1997. Traditional pharmacological treatments for spasticity. Part II: General and regional treatments. *Muscle & Nerve* 20 Suppl 6:S92-S120.

Greenberg, H.S., S.A.S. Werness, J.E. Pugh, R.O. Andrus, D.J. Anderson, and E.F. Domino. 1994. Short-term effects of smoking marijuana on balance in patients with multiple sclerosis and normal volunteers. *Clin Pharmacol Ther* 55:324-8.

Grinspoon, L., and J.B. Bakalar. 1997. Common medical uses: multiple sclerosis. *Marijuana, the Forbidden Medicine.* Rev. and exp. Ed. New Haven: Yale University Press.

Guzman, M., C. Sanchez, and I. Galve-Roperh. 2001. Control of the cell survival/death decision by cannabinoids. *J Mol Med* 78:613-25.

Hanigan, W.C., R. Destree, and X.T. Truong. 1985. The effect of Δ-9-THC on human spasticity. *Clin Pharmacol Ther* 35:198.

Iversen, L.L. 2000. *The Science of Marijuana.* New York: Oxford University Press.

Irizarry, M.C. 1997. Multiple sclerosis. *Neurologic Disorders in Women.* Boston: Butterworth-Heinemann.

James, T. 1994. The baby and the bathwater. *S Afr Med J* 84(6):369.

LeResche, L. 2001. Gender, cultural, and environmental aspects of pain. *Bonica's Management of Pain 3rd Edition* Philadelphia: Lippincott Williams & Wilkins.

Lyman, W.D., J.R. Sonett, C.F. Brosnan, R. Elkin, and M.B. Bornstein. 1989. Delta-9 tetrahydrocannabinol: a novel treatment for experimental autoimmune encephalomyelitis. *J Neuroimmunol* 23:73-81.

Martyn, C.N., L.S. Illis, and J. Thom. 1995. Nabilone in the treatment of multiple sclerosis. *Lancet* 345:579.

Maurer, M., V. Henn, A. Dittrich, and A. Hoffmann. 1990. Delta-9 tetrahydrocannabinol shows antispastic and analgesic effects in a single case, double-blind trial. *Eur Arch Psych Clin Neurosci* 240(1):1-4.

Meinck, H.M., P.W. Schonle, and B. Conrad. 1990. Effect of cannabinoids on spasticity and ataxia in multiple sclerosis. *J Neurol* 236(2):120-2.

Mendelson, J.H., P. Cristofaro, J. Ellingboe, R. Benedikt and N.K. Mello. 1985. Acute effects of marijuana on luteinizing hormone in menopausal women. *Pharmacol Biochem Behav* 23:765-8.

Meng, I.D., B.H. Manning, W.J. Martin, and H.L. Fields. 1998. An analgesia circuit activated by cannabinoids. *Nature* 395:381-3.

Mittleman, M.A., R.A. Lewis, M. Maclure, J.B. Sherwood, and J.E. Muller. 2001. Triggering myocardial infarction by marijuana. *Circulation* 103(23):2805-9.

Olek, M.J., and S.J. Khoury. 2000. Multiple Sclerosis. *Women and Health*. San Diego: Academic Press.

O'Shaughnessy, W.B. 1842. On the preparation of the Indian hemp or ganjah *(Cannabis indica)*: the effects on the animal system in health, and their utility in the treatment of tetanus and other convulsive diseases. *Trans Med Phys Soc Bombay* 8:421-61.

Petro, D.J. 1980. Marijuana as a therapeutic agent for muscle spasm or spasticity. *Psychosomatics* 21(1):81-5.

Petro, D.J. and C. Ellenberger. 1981. Treatment of human spasticity with Δ-9-tetrahydrocannabinol. *J Clin Pharmacol* 21:413S-416S.

Physicians' Desk Reference 56th Edition. 2002. Montvale, NJ: Medical Economics.

Pope, H.G. 2002. Cannabis, cognition, and residual confounding. *J Amer Med Assoc* 287(9):1172-4.

Pope, H.G., A.J. Gruber, J.I. Hudson, M.A. Huestis, and D. Yurgelun-Todd. 2001. Neuropsychological performance in long-term cannabis users. *Arch Gen Psychiatry* 58:909-15.

Rammohan, K.W., J.H. Rosenberg, D.J. Lynn, A.M. Blumenfeld, C.P. Pollak, and H.N. Nagaraja. 2002. Efficacy and safety of modafinil (Provigil®) for the treatment of fatigue in multiple sclerosis: a two centre phase 2 study. *J Neurol Neurosurg Psychiatry* 72(2):179-83.

Reynolds, J.R. 1890. On the therapeutic uses and toxic effects of *Cannabis indica*. *Lancet* 1:637-8.

Runmarker, B. and O. Anderson. 1995. Pregnancy is associated with a lower risk of onset and a better prognosis in multiple sclerosis. *Brain* 118:253-61.

Rusk, A. and F. Plum. 1998. Neurologic Health and Disorders. In *Textbook of Women's Health* Philadelphia: Lippincott-Raven.

Schon, F., P.E. Hart, T.L. Hodgson, A.L.M. Pambakian, M. Ruprah, E.M. Williamson, and C. Kennard. 1999. Suppression of pendular nystagmus by smoking cannabis in a patient with multiple sclerosis. *Neurology* 53(9):2209-10.

Solowij, N., R.S. Stephens, R.A. Roffman, T. Babor, R. Kadden, M. Miller, K. Christiansen, B. McRee, and J. Vendetti. 2002. Cognitive functioning of long-term heavy cannabis users seeking treatment. *J Amer Med Assoc* 287(9):1123-31.

Somerset, M., R. Campbell, D.J. Sharp and T.J. Peters. 2001. What do people with MS want and expect from health-care services? *Health Expectations* 4:29-37.

Tennes, K., N. Avitable, C. Blackard, C. Boyles, B. Hassoun, L. Holmes and M Kreye. 1985. Marijuana, prenatal and postnatal exposure in the human. In: Pinkert, T.M., ed. Current research on the consequences of maternal drug abuse. *NIDA Res Monogr* 59:48-60.

Ungerleider, J.T., T. Andyrsiak, L. Fairbanks, G.W. Ellison, and L.W. Myers. 1988. Delta-9-THC in the treatment of spasticity associated with multiple sclerosis. *Pharmacological Issues in Alcohol and Substance Abuse* 7(1):39-50.

Whitaker, J., 1998. Effects of pregnancy and delivery on disease activity in multiple sclerosis. *N Engl J Med* 339:339-40.

Wirguin, I., R. Mechoulam, A. Breuer, E. Schezen, J. Weidenfeld, and T. Brenner. 1994. Suppression of experimental autoimmune encephalomyelitis by cannabinoids. *Immunopharmacology* 28:209-14.

Index

2-AG (2-arachidonylglycerol), 51-62

Abortion (spontaneous), AEA
(anandamide) degradation
and, 41-43
Acetylcholine, 150-152
AEA (anandamide) degradation in
pregnancy
AMT (AEA membrane transporter)
and, 39-40
apoptosis induction and, 40-41
CBRs (cannabinoid receptors)
CB$_1$R (brain-type), 38-45
CB$_2$R (spleen-type), 38-45
endocannabinoid degradation and,
41-43
FAAH (fatty acid amide hydrolase)
and
distribution of, 39-40
gestation and, 43-45
importance of, 45-46
lymphocytes and, 43-45
fertility issues and, 41-43
future perspectives of, 45-46
introduction to, 1-3,37-39
LIF (leukemia inhibitory factor)
and, 41-43
Marinol
(delta-9-tetrahydrocannabinol)
and, 41
reference and research literature
about, 46-49
spontaneous abortion and, 41-43
Th1/Th2 cytokines and, 37-46
AEA membrane transporter. See AMT
(AEA membrane transporter)

AMA (American Medical
Association), 107-108
American Medical Association. See
AMA (American Medical
Association)
AMT (AEA membrane transporter),
39-40
Anandamide. See AEA (anandamide)
degradation in pregnancy
Anticonvulsants, 167-168
Anti-emetics, 67-71
Apoptosis induction, 40-41
Avonex (interferon-beta-1a), 163

Bain Commission, 108
Bari, M., 37-49
Battista, N., 37-49
Beta-blockers, 167-168
Betaseron (interferon-beta-1b), 163
Bladder dysfunction, 169-170
Brazleton Neonatal Assessment Scale,
90-91

Cannabidiol. See CBD (cannabidiol)
Cannabis based medicine extract. See
CBME (cannabis based
medicine extract)
Cartoni, A., 37-49
Case studies
of HG (hyperemesis gravidarum)
cannabis treatments, 64-81
of Jamaican women, therapeutic
cannabis use, 121-133
of MS (multiple sclerosis) cannabis
treatments, 155-160

of Jamaican women, therapeutic
cannabis use, 131-133
of MS (multiple sclerosis) cannabis
treatments, 171-172
of nursing-related issues, 118
of obstetric and gynecological
cannabis treatments, 28-29
of prenatal cannabis exposure, 99
of production processes, medical
hashish and herbal cannabis,
142-143
of suckling triggers and responses,
newborns, 59

GABA (gamma-aminobutyric acid),
150-152
Gamma-aminobutyric acid. *See* GABA
(gamma-aminobutyric acid)
GCIS (Global Clinical Impression
Scale), 147
Gestation, FAAH (fatty acid amide
hydrolase) and, 43-45
Glatiramer acetate/copolymer 1
(Copaxone), 163
Global Clinical Impression Scale. *See*
GCIS (Global Clinical
Impression Scale)
Growth stunting effects, 47-59

Harm reduction models
AMA (American Medical
Association) and, 107-108
Bain Commission and, 108
Centre for Economic Policy
Research and, 113
Controlled Substances Act (1970)
and, 108
DEA (Drug Enforcement
Administration) and, 107-108
FAMM (Families Against
Mandatory Minimums) and,
116

FBI (Federal Bureau of
Investigation) and, 116
future perspectives of, 118
historical perspectives of, 106-107
introduction to, 1-3,105-107
IOM (Institute of Medicine) and,
109-115
MAMA (Mothers Against Misuse
and Abuse) and, 110-111
medicinal cannabis
as harm reduction medication,
108-111
historical perspectives of,
107-108
Marinol (delta-9-tetrahydro-
cannabinol), 109-110,117
OTC (over-the-counter)
medications and, 110-111
National Commission on
Marihuana and Drug Abuse
and, 108,114
nursing care issues and, 105-120
ONDCP (Office of National Drug
Control Policy) and, 114-115
prohibition, impact of, 116-118
reference and research literature
about, 118-120
Schaffer Commission and, 108,113
Schneider Institute for Health
Policy and, 114
social/recreational cannabis and,
111-116
Substance Abuse and Mental
Health Services
Administration and, 116
Hazelnuts, endocannabinoid content
of, 55
HG (hyperemesis gravidarum)
cannabis treatments
case studies of, 64-81
Compassionate Use Act (1996,
California) and, 72
drug therapies and
anti-emetics, 67-71
Atavan, 71